PROFESSIONAL DEVELOPMENT SERIES

ETHICS AT WORK
Fire in a Dark World

GEORGE MANNING
Professor of Psychology
Northern Kentucky University

KENT CURTIS
Professor of Industrial Technology and Education
Northern Kentucky University

U254
PUBLISHED BY
SOUTH-WESTERN PUBLISHING CO.
CINCINNATI, OH   WEST CHICAGO, IL   DALLAS, TX   LIVERMORE, CA

Copyright © 1988
by South-Western Publishing Co.
Cincinnati, Ohio

All Rights Reserved

The text of this publication, or any part thereof, may not be reproduced or transmitted in any form or by any means, electronic or mechanical, including photocopying, recording, storage in an information retrieval system, or otherwise, without the prior written permission of the publisher.

ISBN: 0-538-21254-3
Library of Congress Catalog Card Number: 86-62746

3 4 5 6 7 8 E 2 1 0

Printed in the United States of America

About The Authors

Dr. George Manning

Dr. Kent Curtis

George Manning is a professor of psychology and business at Northern Kentucky University. He is a consultant to business, industry, and government; his clients include AT&T, Sun Oil, IBM, Marriott Corporation, United Auto Workers, the Internal Revenue Service, and the National Institutes of Health. He lectures on economic and social issues including quality of work life, work force values, and business ethics. He serves as advisor to such diverse industries and professions as energy, transportation, justice, health, finance, labor, commerce, and the military.

He received graduation honors from George Williams College, the University of Cincinnati, and the University of Vienna. He was selected Professor of the Year at Northern Kentucky University, where his teaching areas include management and organization, organizational psychology, and personal adjustment. He maintains an active program of research and study in organizational psychology. His current studies and interests include the changing meaning of work, leadership development, and coping skills for personal and social change.

Kent Curtis has served as an administrator and faculty member at Northern Kentucky University since its inception in 1970. He is a professor in the departments of industrial technology and education. His teaching areas include supervisory development, human relations in business and industry, techniques of research design, counseling, and group dynamics.

He received a baccalaureate degree in biology from Centre College, a master's in counseling from Xavier University, and a doctorate in adult technical education from the University of Cincinnati. He has designed numerous employee and management training and development programs, which are presented to Fortune 500 companies, small businesses, and federal, state, and local government agencies.

Kent also presents open seminars and on-site programs in the areas of time and stress management, communication skills, and team building. His current studies and interests include developing effective "executive pairs" (secretary/manager teams); the manager as an effective teacher; and improving the quality of work life in organizations using employee involvement groups.

PREFACE

Ethics at Work is the most fundamental book in *The Human Side of Work* series because it deals with the "why" rather than the "how to" in our lives. It raises questions that can be unsettling to individuals accustomed to black-and-white answers. Tests and exercises in moral dilemmas, levels of morality, personal values, and values compatibility help clear the cobwebs and provide self-study too often neglected.

Our goal is for you to understand key concepts and principles in personal and business ethics and to clarify personal values in preparation for dealing with moral issues in real-life situations. The result should be a clearer understanding of your philosopher's pie, a fuller swing in moral dilemmas, a better understanding of what is personally important, greater tolerance of others' values, and more "fire in a dark world."

HOW TO USE THIS BOOK

This is a desk book for ready reference, a handbook for teaching others, and a workbook for personal development in the area of ethics. The material is arranged in a logical sequence for learning.

The best approach is to *interact* with the material. Read the narrative, take the tests and exercises, examine the interpretations, review the principles and techniques—then ask, "How does this apply to me? How can I use this concept or information to improve? Then take action. Also, use the related readings, cases, and applications to improve your knowledge and skills.

To increase your interest and improve overall learning, try the following:

1. Use the learning objectives, discussion questions, and study quizzes included in each part of the book. They will focus your reading, improve your comprehension, and increase your retention of the material.

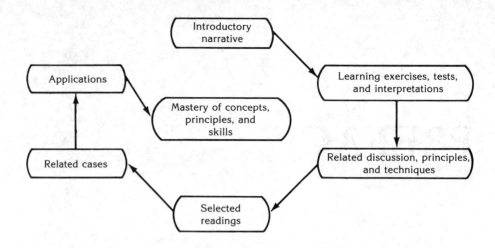

2. Share your tests and exercises with family, friends, and co-workers—those you affect in the area of ethics, and those who affect you. In this way, you can make tangible use of what you learn and may even help others.

3. Use the margins to write your own ideas and personalize the material: underline; make notes; interact with the book.

Good luck in your learning!

HOW TO TEACH FROM THIS BOOK

Personalize *Ethics*—for yourself and for the learner. Use the information, exercises, questions, activities, and tests to complement your own teaching style and resources; use any or all of the materials provided to suit the needs and goals of the group.

Steps

First, scan the material for topics and exercises. Second, outline a curriculum and lesson plan based on time frames and learning goals. Third, arrange learning aids, media, and other resources for smooth instruction. For assistance in this area, refer to the suggested readings, cases, applications, and films that accompany each part of the text. Also, see Appendix A for suggestions on teaching, testing, and grading as well as for information about other books in *The Human Side of Work* series.

Instruction

Multimedia, multimethod instruction usually works best. Each class period ideally would include a lecture to set the stage, learning exercises to personalize the subject, a discussion to interpret results, and use of related activities such as cases and readings to enhance knowledge and skills. A film, followed by group discussion and panel debate, is an ideal learning enhancer. See Appendix C for an annotated list of excellent films.

Final Note

Because this book is easy to read and covers the factual information needed by the learner, class periods should be used primarily for group involvement. Learning activities and group discussion will personalize the subject and promote maximum enjoyment and learning.

Specific topics, questions, and activities include:

- What is real, true, and valuable to you? Find out about your *philosopher's pie* on pages 13–14.

- What are *full-swing morality* and axiological arrest? See pages 29–33.

- What is your *level of morality?* If Hitler asked you to electrocute a stranger, would you? See pages 133–146.

- What values guide you in *moral dilemmas* — on the job and in the home? See pages 98–110.

- What are the *ethical principles* that successful organizations follow? See pages 78–81.

Ethics at Work: Fire in a Dark World is intrinsically interesting. People relate naturally to such topics as moral dilemmas, full-swing morality, business ethics, and personal values. But they won't learn the material unless they get involved with it. As the instructor, the more practical you can make the subject, the better; the more personalized ethics is, the more helpful it will be. In this spirit, we conclude with a favorite proverb:

> I listen and I hear;
> I see and I remember;
> I do and I understand.
>
> *Confucius* (551–479 B.C.)

Good luck in your teaching!

Request: We want your suggestions. If you have questions or see a way to improve this book, please write. Thank you.

George Manning
Kent Curtis
Northern Kentucky University
Highland Heights, Ky. 41076

ACKNOWLEDGMENTS

The Human Side of Work is written by many people. It is the result of countless hours and endless effort from colleagues, students, and others who have helped in some important way. From initial draft to final form, many hands bring these books to life. To each we are grateful.

For this book, recognition is given to the following scientists and authors whose ideas and findings provide theoretical framework and important factual data:

Gordon Allport
Ed Gray
Robert Hay
Morris Keeton
Lawrence Kohlberg
Gardner Lindzey

Bronislaw Malinowski
Stanley Milgram
Joseph Petrick
Jean Piaget
Jerry Richards

Bertrand Russell
Eduard Spranger
Harold Titus
Vauvenargues
Philip Vernon

Appreciation goes to the following colleagues and supporters for substantive help in research, manuscript review, preparation, and advice:

Al Austin
Marianne Bailey
Tim Baker
Sherrie Bayman
Irene Brownfield
Robert Caplon
Ken Carter
Robert Didio
Vicky Earhart
Michael Fightmaster

Charlotte Galloway
Alecia Greis
Rosemary Hutchinson
Erhard Linnes
James McCue
Steve McMillen
Richard Majancsik
Steve Martin
Glen Mazis

Arthur Miller
Ernie Morrissey
Vince Schulte
David Sprouse
Bill Stewart
Cliff Stone
Ralph Tesseneer
Helen Tucker
Susan Wehrmeyer

We want to thank J. Ellen Gerken for many of the figures, illustrations, and photographs.

George Manning
Kent Curtis

CONTENTS

PART ONE   MORAL DILEMMAS   5

    Introduction   6
    No Easy Subject   8
    The Roots of Ethics   9
    Philosopher's Pie   13
    Quo Vadis: "Where Are You Going?"   15
    Exercise: What Is Real? What Is True? What Is Valuable?   15
    Ethics, Humankind, and the Other Animals   17
    Traditional and Contemporary Definitions of Good   17
    Exercise: Personal Definition of Good and Right   27
    Exercise: Values and Practices   28
    Full-Swing Morality and Axiological Arrest   29
    Exercise: Were I to Die Today . . .   33
    Recommended Resources   34
    Reference Notes   34
    Study Quiz   39
    Discussion Questions and Activities   41

PART TWO   LEVELS OF MORALITY   43

    Moral Development—How the Fire Is Lit   44
    Levels of Morality   46
    The Search for Meaning   52
    Virtue—The Nature of Level III, Stage 6 Morality   54
    Recommended Resources   58
    Reference Notes   58
    Study Quiz   61
    Discussion Questions and Activities   63

PART THREE   ETHICS AND WORK   65

    Ethics and Mental Health   66
    Ethics and Society   67
    The Ethical Relationship Between the Individual and Society   72
    Ethics "at Work" Yesterday and Today   73
    Ethical Orientations of Organizations   78

Exercise: Organizational Ethics	79
Social Values	81
Exercise: Social Values Continuum—Who Is Important to You?	81
Ethics and Leadership—Who Lights the Fire?	85
Exercise: Work-Force Values and Leadership Actions	87
Styles of Leadership	88
Recommended Resources	89
Reference Notes	89
Study Quiz	93
Discussion Questions and Activities	95

PART FOUR DYNAMICS OF ETHICAL CHOICE   97

Personal Values	98
Exercise: Personal Values—What Is Important to You?	99
Values in Human Relationships	112
Exercise: Value Compatibility—Do We Think Alike?	112
Recommended Resources	120
Reference Notes	120
Study Quiz	121
Discussion Questions and Activities	123

READINGS   125

How Could the Jonestown Holocaust Have Occurred?	126
If Hitler Asked You to Electrocute a Stranger, Would You?	133
The Parable of the Sadhu	147
The Myth of Sisyphus	155
Wheels	158
Can an Executive Afford a Conscience?	168
Rites of Passage	179

CASES   187

The Superhonest Politician	188
The Teacher in the Middle	194
A Doctor's Case	196
Locks Versus Lives	200
"We Just Don't Do Things That Way Around Here . . ."	202
Government Jobs	204
The 19-Year-Old Bride	206
R.V.'s in the Parking Lot	207
The Honor System	209
The Right to Strike	211

APPLICATIONS   213

Beliefs and Values Questionnaire (BVQ)	215
The Kidney Machine	219

	The Fallout Shelter	223
	Values Flag	225
	Values Auction	229

APPENDIX A	BACKGROUND INFORMATION, TEACHING SUGGESTIONS, AND TESTING AND GRADING	233
	Audience	234
	Content and Style	234
	Testing and Review Process	235
	Teaching Formats	237
APPENDIX B	ADDITIONAL REFERENCES	243
APPENDIX C	SUGGESTED FILMS	247
APPENDIX D	INVENTORY OF PHILOSOPHICAL BELIEFS	251
APPENDIX E	STUDY QUIZ ANSWERS	261
APPENDIX F	THE RELATIONSHIP OF THE QUIZ QUESTIONS AND THE DISCUSSION AND ACTIVITIES TO THE PART OBJECTIVES	263

Ethics

eth•ics (eth'iks), noun pl., [construed as singular or plural], 1. the study of standards of conduct and moral judgment; moral philosophy. 2. the system or code of morals of a particular philosopher, religion, group, profession, etc. 3. the branch of philosophy dealing with values relating to human conduct with respect to the right and wrong of certain actions and to the goodness and badness of the motives and ends of such actions.

> *Always do what is right. It will gratify most of the people, and astound the rest.*
>
> *— Mark Twain*

Source: Mark Twain, from an address to the Young People's Society, Greenpoint Presbyterian Church, Brooklyn, New York, 16 February 1901.

PART ONE
Moral Dilemmas

Learning Objectives

After completing Part One, you will better understand:

1. the definition of ethics;
2. the importance of ethics;
3. the complexity of ethical questions;
4. the religious and secular roots of ethics;
5. why ethics is a concern unique to humankind;
6. historical and contemporary definitions of "good" and "right";
7. the relative strength of ethical beliefs.

INTRODUCTION

Ethics is the branch of philosophy concerned with the intent, means, and consequences of moral behavior. It is the study of moral judgments and right and wrong conduct. Some human judgments are factual (the earth is round); others are aesthetic (she is beautiful); and still others are moral (people should be honest and should not kill). Moral judgments are judgments about what is right and wrong, good and bad.[1] The Spanish writer Cervantes wrote about ethics in *Don Quixote:*

> I know that the path of virtue is straight and narrow, and the road of vice broad and spacious. I know also that their ends and resting places are different; for those of vice, large and open, end in death; and those of virtue, narrow and intricate, end in life; and not in life that has an end, but in that which is eternal.[2]

The word *ethics* is derived from the Greek *ethos*, referring to a person's fundamental orientation toward life. Originally, ethos meant "a dwelling place." For the philosopher Aristotle, ethos came to mean "an inner dwelling place," or what is now called "inner character." The Latin translation of ethos is "mos, moris," from which comes the English word *moral*. In Roman times, the emphasis shifted from internal character to overt behavior—acts, habits, and customs.[3]

In more recent times, ethics has been viewed as an overall human concern:

> One of the chief problems is to determine what the basis of a moral code should be, to find out what one ought to do. Is right that which is the word of God given to man in the Ten Commandments? Is it what is revealed to us by conscience and intuition? Is it whatever will increase the sum of human happiness? Is it that which is the most reasonable thing to do? Is it whatever makes for the fullness and perfection of life? Above all, is there any absolute right, anything embedded, so to speak, in the nature of the universe, which should guide our actions? Or are right and wrong simply relative, dependent on time and place and cultural pattern, and changing with environment and circumstance? What, in short, is the basis of our moral values? These questions are of vital importance in a day when intellectual power threatens to outrun moral control and thus destroy humankind.[4]

Ethical questions are important in all areas of life—work, social, and personal. Put yourself in the shoes of:

- *The manager:* At 1:00 a.m., the security guard informs you that there is a fire in the hotel kitchen. Do you immediately call the fire department and notify all occupants, knowing that doing so may upset guests and that media coverage may harm future business? Or do you postpone these actions until you have personally seen the fire and attempted to extinguish it?

- *The citizen:* You are driving your car when you come upon the scene of an accident. One person will die without immediate medical care. You take the victim and speed to the hospital. The extra speed causes another accident in which another person dies. How should you be judged? Was your act right because your motive was good, or was your act wrong because its consequences were bad?[5]

- *The parent:* You have two daughters. One always complains when you send her on errands. The other doesn't like going either but usually goes without arguing. Typically, you send the daughter who does not complain more often than the one who does. Is this right?[6]

- *The salesman:* You learn that your company is selling faulty equipment that could be dangerous. Your wife needs medical treatment that costs a large percentage of your income. You have reason to believe that if you confront your employer you will lose your job. What would you do?

- *The fireman:* It is World War II, and you are a fireman in a city in Germany that is under constant bombing. One day, after an especially heavy attack, you leave the bomb shelter to go to your fire station. On the way, you decide to see whether your family is safe. Although your home is quite distant, you go there first. Is this right or wrong?[7]

- *The friend:* You promise to keep your best friend's secret; then she tells you that her son is selling drugs and even has sold them at a nearby grade school. Your friend is upset, but plans on taking no action. What would you do?

- *The researcher:* You are working as a researcher on a study begun 40 years ago by the United States Public Health Service. The study's original purpose was to determine the effects of syphilis on the human body. You learn that 25 years ago scientists discovered that penicillin is an almost totally effective cure for the disease. You also learn that there is no intention to use this information to treat the subjects of the study. What would you do?[8]

- *The physician:* You have discovered that your patient has a contagious disease and that he is engaged to be married to a woman who does not know of his condition. Is it your duty to remain silent, or is it your duty to inform the woman, provided the man refuses to tell her?[9]

- *The teacher:* Yani, an art student of yours, shows you a picture he has painted and announces his intention to put it in a public display. He appears very proud of his work, but you know the painting is inferior. Should you reveal your true opinion, or should you keep your thoughts to yourself?[10]

- *The secretary:* You are an executive secretary who has been with the company for 20 years. You provide sole support for your family (boy, 12; girl, 10; mother, ailing). Your new boss, the company president, has made it clear to you that continued employment depends on occasional sexual favors. What would you do?

These moral dilemmas show the range of ethical questions that people face and the consequences moral judgments can have. As a person, you are constantly making decisions about what is the best or right action to take with family, friends, and colleagues. Ethics also apply in social relations, as groups of people attempt to justify attitudes and actions toward one another.

NO EASY SUBJECT

Ethics is a difficult subject. Ethical dilemmas force you to think about moral issues with elusive answers. This is more true today than ever before. Consider the questions that people have been faced with only within the past 15 to 20 years:

- *The conscious creation of new forms of life:* What are the benefits and penalties of creating new forms of life through recombinant genetics? If it could be done, should people be cloned? If so, who should be cloned?

- *The preservation of human life through organ transplants and mechanical means:* Is it ethical to use one person's organs to preserve another person's life? If so, whose organs do you take? When, if ever, is it acceptable to turn off life-supporting machines and allow someone to die?

- *Exploration and the use of space:* Should people be exploring space? Are the huge financial sums spent on space exploration justified in light of human misery on earth?

- *Nuclear energy:* What should be done with our knowledge about atomic energy? Should we build bombs that can destroy life, or should we apply this knowledge to human welfare? What should be done and who is to decide?

Aside from the moral issues created by developments in science and medicine, there are many ethical problems brought on by population and economic growth. An example from agriculture makes this point:

About 150 years ago, there were scattered farms where the city of Chicago now stands. One farmer with a surplus might sell one or two quarts of milk to a neighbor. The farmer's boy usually made the delivery. In this simple transaction, there were few problems and little likelihood of injustice.

Today there are perhaps 18,000 farmers, some of whom have large herds, who supply the Chicago area with milk. The task of the small boy is now handled by more than 100 corporations with 15,000 employees

ILLUS. 1.1

What moral dilemmas have resulted from the use of nuclear energy?

H. ARMSTRONG ROBERTS

in a milk distributor's union. The neighbors, the purchasers of milk, have grown to considerably more than four million people. The possibility of manipulation of control and of injustice is much greater.

Think of this changed condition as applying to a great number of commodities, then magnify this to include national and world trade, and one can see the magnitude of modern ethical problems.[11]

To show how difficult ethical questions can be in daily life, consider the following:

A mother watching her two children at play on the beach notices her little boy hitting his sister with a sand shovel. She shakes her finger at Johnnie and says: "How would you like Mary to hit you with a sand shovel?" The little boy's guilty silence can be interpreted as implicit agreement with the validity of the golden rule — do unto others as you would have them do unto you.

Now imagine another situation. You are sleeping upstairs in your bedroom at night, and you hear someone breaking into your home. You get up, creep downstairs, and find a burglar taking your possessions. You are not detected, so you quietly go back upstairs and pick up the phone to call the police. But then you remember the golden rule and you ask yourself, "If I were the burglar, would I want to be turned in?"[12]

These situations show that even following the golden rule has its limitations and that ethics is no easy subject.

THE ROOTS OF ETHICS

Ethics has both religious and secular roots. Religious ethics are based on a theistic understanding of the world. What is real, true, and good is defined by God. Secular ethics are based on a scientific understanding of the world. Reality, truth, and goodness do not depend on the existence of a God. Both religious and secular ethics share many common values, such as the sanctity of human life and the importance of the golden rule. The primary difference is how values are justified.

The Religious Tradition

All of the world's religions make prescriptions for moral behavior. St. Augustine, for example, who generally is agreed to have had a greater influence on Western religious thought than any other writer outside of Biblical scripture, maintained that the naturally evil inclinations of humanity could be overcome only by divine grace. He believed that if we allow ourselves through faith to be drawn to God, we will overcome our basic immoral nature and eventually be reconciled in the city of God in heaven.[13]

Another Christian philosopher, Thomas Aquinas, taught that all men are endowed with a natural desire to be good. He believed that this inclination could be dormant in an individual and could even be perverted. Nonetheless, he believed it to be present in all people and impossible to destroy. Aquinas taught that to resist God's pull is contrary to human nature and that if we allow ourselves to follow God, we will fulfill our nature and we will be purely good. Further, by acting out this goodness in our day-to-day lives, we will be moral and will experience the greatest meaning of which we are capable.[14]

The majority of people who have ever lived have been influenced by religions such as Christianity and individuals such as St. Augustine and Thomas Aquinas. Consider the words of Ben Franklin: "I believe . . . that the soul of man is immortal and will be treated with justice in another life respecting its conduct in this."

Figure 1.1 presents the percentages of the world's population whose ethics have religious roots. It should be noted that the ethics of the overwhelming majority of people alive today are based on religious teaching.

Consider your own morality and ask what role religion has played in the formation of your ethics. Do you follow the Ten Commandments? Are your morals based on the Bible? Do you turn to religious leaders for advice in moral dilemmas?

The Secular Tradition

Aristotle was one of the first and perhaps most influential of all people to shape the ethics of Western civilization from a secular or nonreligious orientation. He believed that every type of animal has a common essence or nature, and that human beings are essentially, or by nature, rational. He viewed rationality as the central and most significant trait distinguishing humankind from other creatures. Further, Aristotle taught that the good person is the one who lives most rationally and whose moral judgments and social conduct are born of contemplation and reason, in contrast to spontaneity and emotionality.[15] Today, when we address a moral

FIGURE 1.1

The Faithful of Yesterday, Today, and Tomorrow: Adherents in Millions and as a Percentage of World Population*

Religion	1900 Million	%	1980 Million	%	2000 Million	%
Christian	558	34.4	1,433	32.8	2,020	32.3
Roman Catholic	272	16.8	809	18.5	1,169	18.7
Protestant and Anglican	153	9.4	345	7.9	440	7.0
Eastern Orthodox	121	7.5	124	2.8	153	2.4
Other	12	.7	155	3.6	258	4.1
Nonreligious and atheist	3	.2	911	20.8	1,334	21.3
Muslim	200	12.4	723	16.5	1,201	19.2
Hindu	203	12.5	583	13.3	859	13.7
Buddhist	127	7.8	274	6.3	359	5.7
Chinese folk religion	380	23.5	198	4.5	158	2.5
Tribal and shamanist	118	7.3	103	2.4	110	1.8
"New religions"	6	.4	96	2.2	138	2.2
Jewish	12	.8	17	.4	20	.3
Other**	13	.8	36	.8	61	1.0
World population	1,620		4,374		6,260	

*Due to rounding off, percents may not equal 100
**Including Sikh, Confucian, Shinto, Baha'i, Jain, Spiritist, Parsi

Source: Copyright © 1984 Time Inc. All rights reserved. Reprinted by permission from Time.

dilemma by saying, "Let us use reason; let us use logic; let us think rationally about this," we are being ethical in the Aristotelian, secular tradition.

Aristotle taught an ethical doctrine of the "golden mean," or of "moderation." He believed it was good to seek balance between too much and too little, and that the result would be moderation, the ethical ideal. Aristotle viewed courage as the middle ground between rashness and cowardice, and he saw generosity as the ideal between stinginess and prodigality. Aristotle also taught that circumstances helped determine ethical conduct; he believed more physical courage should be expected from a soldier than from an artist.[16] Finally, Aristotle believed that reason must be applied even to the doctrine of the "golden mean":

Part One • Moral Dilemmas 11

> Not every action or every passion admits of a mean; for some have names that already imply badness, such as spite, shamelessness, envy, and in the case of actions, adultery, theft, murder; for all of these and such like things imply by their names that they are themselves bad, and not the excesses or deficiencies of them. It is not possible, then, ever to be right with regard to them; one must be always wrong.[17]

Operating in a secular tradition, many people seek answers to moral questions through personal experience and rational analysis, rather than religious faith. One twentieth-century philosopher who embodied this approach was the French writer Jean-Paul Sartre, an important figure in the existential movement of philosophy. Sartre viewed life as void of meaning other than that which is self-made. He believed that each person must make meaning out of what can be comprehended with his own senses and created with his own faculties. He believed this to be a personal and free act and the key ingredient of authentic character development. Sartre would have all individuals search for the meaning of their own existence, do this freely, and be willing to pay the consequences of what they find. From the void of meaning that he personally faced, Sartre chose existential humanism as a moral philosophy. Using this philosophy, he dedicated himself to improving the human condition as his highest goal.[18]

Another modern philosopher whose moral views were secular, and who also was a humanist, was the Englishman Bertrand Russell. Consider his short essay:

What I Have Lived For

> Three passions, simple but overwhelmingly strong, have governed my life: the longing for love, the search for knowledge, and unbearable pity for the suffering of mankind. These passions, like great winds, have blown me hither and thither, in a wayward course, over a deep ocean of anguish, reaching to the very verge of despair.
>
> I have sought love, first, because it brings ecstasy—ecstasy so great that I would often have sacrificed all the rest of life for a few hours of this joy. I have sought it, next, because it relieves loneliness—that terrible loneliness in which one in shivering consciousness, looks over the rim of the world into the cold, unfathomable, lifeless abyss. I have sought it, finally, because in the union of love I have seen, in a mystic miniature, the prefiguring vision of the heaven that saints and poets have imagined. This is what I sought, and though it might seem too good for human life, this is what—at last—I have found.
>
> With equal passion I have sought knowledge. I have wished to understand the hearts of men. I have wished to know why the stars shine. . . . A little of this, but not much, I have achieved.
>
> Love and knowledge, so far as they were possible, led upward toward the heavens. But always pity brought me back to earth. Echoes of cries of pain reverberate in my heart. Children in famine, victims of torture by oppressors, helpless old people a hated burden to their sons, and the whole world of loneliness, poverty, and pain make a mockery of what human life should be. I long to alleviate the evil, but I cannot, and I too suffer.
>
> This has been my life. I have found it worth living, and would gladly live it again if the chance were offered me.[19]

Think about your own moral behavior and ask to what extent you have been influenced by secular ethics. Are your moral decisions based on concrete experience and rational analysis? Why do you do good deeds for others? Why do you care about what is right and wrong, good and bad?

PHILOSOPHER'S PIE

How does ethics fit with other branches of philosophy? A useful concept is the Philosopher's Pie (see Figure 1.2), which shows the central themes or questions of philosophy.

What is real is the concern of the branch of philosophy called metaphysics. It focuses on fundamental beliefs about the origin and nature of the universe, God, and humanity. A person with a theistic or religious orientation might say what is real is God and creation; a person with a nontheistic or secular orientation may say what is real is nature and evolution. Consider how your own view of reality influences you as you live your life and deal with moral dilemmas.

What is true is the central concern of the branch of philosophy known as epistemology. It focuses on fundamental beliefs about knowledge and truth. The theistic or religious person may believe what is true is the Bible

FIGURE 1.2

Philosopher's Pie

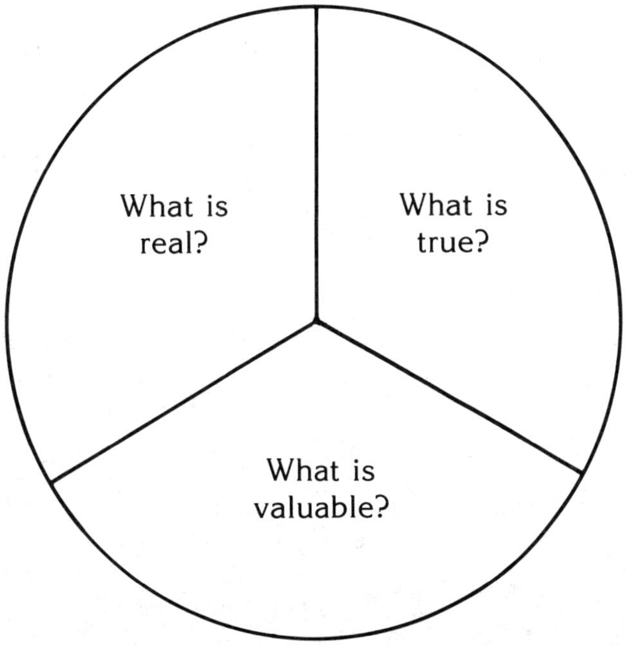

as discovered by revelation; the nontheistic or secular person may believe truth is found in science and is discovered through rational inquiry. Consider your own view about what is true. Is your view based on religious faith or on scientific reason? How does this affect your behavior in moral dilemmas?

Finally, *what is valuable* is the central issue in the branch of philosophy known as axiology, of which ethics is a division. A theistic person may value the Ten Commandments and salvation; a nontheistic person may have essentially secular values—life, liberty, and the pursuit of happiness, truth, beauty, and justice. You can see that the actions of both types of people are guided by different value perspectives. Although people may behave the same in moral dilemmas, they do so for different reasons. Are your own values religious or secular in orientation? For an expanded picture of the Philosopher's Pie showing both theistic and nontheistic world views, see Figure 1.3.

FIGURE 1.3

Philosopher's Pie: Theistic and Nontheistic World Views

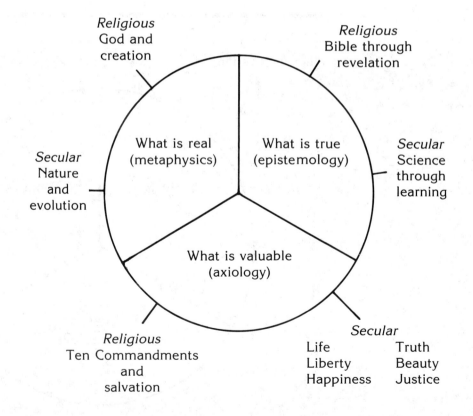

Note that each question in the Philosopher's Pie (what is real, true, and valuable) is influenced by the answer to the other two questions as a general world view evolves—theistic or nontheistic.

QUO VADIS: "WHERE ARE YOU GOING?"

A worthy goal in the study of ethics is to create your own philosopher's pie. Take time to consider what is real, true, and valuable to you; answer, quo vadis, or where are you going? This process has three requirements:

1. *You should be in the mood.* Being in the mood means you feel doubt, curiosity, confusion, or a desire to know the meaning of life. Most people feel in the mood at key crossroads in their lives—when they leave home, when they choose a career, when they choose a mate, when they feel the effects of aging, when they experience personal or emotional loss, when they face sickness and death.

2. *You should choose a good setting.* Many people use a sojourn, a journey in body and mind; many use a retreat, a private place. In either case, your mind and space should be free and uncluttered so that in this vacuum answers can form.

3. *You should write your thoughts.* The process of expressing your views with words that reflect your exact meaning results in clearer thinking and clearer personal direction. Use the following worksheets to respond to the three central questions of philosophy: What is real? What is true? What is valuable to you? (See the Inventory of Philosophical Beliefs in Appendix D to help clarify your beliefs.)

WHAT IS REAL?

To me, what is real is: _____
_____
_____
_____
_____
_____
_____
_____
_____

Date _____

Signed _____

WHAT IS TRUE?

To me, what is true is: _____

_____

_____

_____

_____

_____

_____

_____

_____

Date _____

Signed _____

WHAT IS VALUABLE?

To me, what is valuable is: _____

_____

_____

_____

_____

_____

_____

_____

_____

Date _____

Signed _____

ETHICS, HUMANKIND, AND THE OTHER ANIMALS

Whether based on religious belief or secular thought, ethics is a concern unique to humankind. People are the only creatures who combine emotion (feelings) with knowledge (information) and through abstract reasoning (thought) produce a moral conscience, or a sense of what should be.

Some ideas about right and wrong are of prehuman origin. Indeed, such social virtues as self-sacrifice, sympathy, and cooperation can be seen among many other species, such as elephants, porpoises, and lions. However, more than 40,000 years ago, the human race evolved into beings who could distinguish between what is and what ought to be, and it is this attribute that separates people from all other animals.[20]

Aristotle wrote: "The distinguishing mark between man and the lower animals [is] that he alone is endowed with the power of knowing good and evil, justice and injustice. It is a participation in these that constitutes a family and a city."[21] English essayist William Hazlitt adds, "Man is the only animal that laughs and weeps; for he is the only animal struck by the difference between what things are and what they might have been."[22]

In *The Origin of Species*, biologist and social philosopher Charles Darwin concludes of ethics, humankind, and the other animals:

> I fully subscribe to the judgment of those writers who maintain that, of all the differences between man and the lower animals, the moral sense of conscience is by far the most important . . . it is summed up by that short but impervious word, ought, so full of high significance. It is the most noble of all attributes of man, leading him without a moment's hesitation to risk his life for the life of a fellow creature, or after due deliberation, impelled simply by the deep feeling of right or duty, to sacrifice it in some great cause.[23]*

TRADITIONAL AND CONTEMPORARY DEFINITIONS OF GOOD

Given that human beings are capable of moral reasoning, what has been the result? What have people deemed to be right and good? What ethical principles guide people in moral dilemmas?

The English philosopher Alfred North Whitehead wrote, "We are in the world, not the world in us."[24] He explains that while a concern for right and wrong may be universal to all people, what is considered right

---

*As animals, human beings have been chordates for some 400 million years, placental mammals for about 125 million, primates for 70 million, anthropoids for at least 40 million, and hominids for perhaps 5 million. Only within the past several million years did our human ancestors become terrestrial foragers—and only within the past 100,000 years or so did recognizably modern forms arise. Not until about 12,000 years ago did a few groups of modern humans build permanent settlements, increase in population, practice agriculture, and develop the wondrous diversity of human life known today.

and wrong in human relationships depends on the universe and a person's place in it. We are evolving creatures in an evolving world, and human ethics are changing as well.

In the history of Western civilization, what ought to be has had different meaning in different times and circumstances. Generally, the cultures of the Western world condemn such practices as slavery, witchcraft, and dueling today, even though once these were considered to be acceptable.

There have been many definitions of the ethical person in Western culture. Good and right have been defined in terms of power, personal integrity, natural simplicity, the will of God, pleasure, the greatest good for the greatest number, and duty and right action. Read the following and evaluate your own ideas on these central concepts of good.

Power

If life is a struggle for survival and human beings are fundamentally selfish and greedy, then the best individuals are those who adapt to these market forces and become masters of manipulative relations. So believed Niccolo Machiavelli (1469–1527), an Italian diplomat and political writer. Machiavelli argued for winning and retaining power in a world containing extensive political factionalism and lust for dominion. He maintained that flattery, deceit, and even murder may be necessary if a person is to win and retain power. He stated that a person should never cultivate private virtues that in public life can prove politically suicidal; instead, one should develop vices if these will help perpetuate one's rule. Machiavelli believed that ends justify means and taught the lesson, might makes right.[25]

On a scale of 1 to 10, (1 is low, 10 is high) rate yourself according to how much you agree with Machiavelli's view: _____.

Personal Integrity

The German philosopher Friedrich Nietzsche (1844–1900) believed that human resoluteness, born of independent judgment, was the highest good. Nietzsche was a champion of individualism and encouraged the individual to be independent in thought and strong in conviction, even in the face of group pressure and government authority.[26] Nietzsche believed that if nature is filled with conflict spilling over into society, and human beings are capable of principled, nonconforming conduct, then the best individuals are those who exhibit moral virtue — wisdom, justice, courage, and other ideals — regardless of personal loss or gain.

In this vein, Martin Heidegger (1889–1976), the German existential philosopher, pointed to the Greek ideal of nobility and taught the importance of resolute conviction to personal integrity rather than succumbing to social pressures to conform. Personal integrity, he believed, is intrinsically good, regardless of results. Practicing personal integrity, though, means that one cannot coexist with everyone, so it is incumbent on each person to choose individual lifestyle and commitments carefully.[27]

ILLUS. 1.2

Do ends justify means; does might make right?

On a scale of 1 to 10, how much do you identify with personal integrity as a moral ideal (1 is low, 10 is high): _____.

Natural Simplicity

In the eighteenth century, the Frenchman Jean-Jacques Rousseau (1712–1778) wrote that nature in essence is good; and that because humanity is part of nature, human beings too are naturally good. It followed that to achieve the highest good, one must strive to be most purely natural. Rousseau also held that only with civilization comes corruption, and that children should be raised in a state of simplicity.[28] Writer-philosopher Henry David Thoreau (1817–1862) wrote in a spirit of naturalness and simplicity in *Walden*, "Every morning was a cheerful invitation to make my life of equal simplicity, and I may say innocence, with Nature herself."[29] In this same spirit, many people today resist technological changes, complex lifestyles, and artificial creations.

The French writer Vauvenargues summarizes the importance of naturalness: "Naturalness gets a better hearing than accuracy. It speaks the language of feeling, which is better than that of imagination or of reason, because it is beautiful and appeals to everyone."[30]

ILLUS. 1.3

Is natural simplicity a beauty that appeals to everyone?

Do you relate to the concept of naturalness and simplicity? Evaluate yourself on a scale of 1 to 10 (1 is low, 10 is high): _____.

Will of God

Religious leaders announce visions and make moral judgments, drawing on the authority of a supreme being (or many gods). Saying, "It is the will of Allah," the prophet Muhammad (about 570–632) decreed the "five pillars" of the Islamic faith: (1) repetition of the belief, "There is no god but Allah, and Muhammad is the prophet of Allah," (2) prayer five times daily, (3) the 30-day fast of Ramadan, (4) alms-giving, and (5) the pilgrimage to Mecca. These religious and moral tenets are held most sacred by over 723 million Muslims today. Similarly, nearly 3 billion adherents of many other religions define the ethical good as the "will of God."[31]

No other body of thought has been embraced by so many people, nor has any been so influential in history as has Christianity. At the core of Christian ethics are the life and teachings of Jesus of Nazareth. The ethic Jesus taught was to love God and to love humanity: "Thou shalt love the Lord thy God with all thy heart, and with thy soul, and with thy mind, and with all thy strength: this is the first commandment; and the second is like, namely this, thou shalt love thy neighbor as thyself. There is none other commandment greater than these."[32] Whether based on Christian teaching or not, a belief in love as the highest ethical ideal has guided millions of people since the beginning of the human race.

As you live your life, is the will of God important to you? Evaluate your belief on a scale from 1 to 10 (1 is low, 10 is high): _____.

Pleasure

The idea that pleasure, broadly interpreted as physical enjoyment and avoidance of pain, is the highest state of goodness dates back at least to Aristippus (about 435–366 B.C.). This pupil of the teacher/philosopher Socrates believed that experiencing pleasure and avoiding pain should be the goals of human existence, and that definite pleasure of the moment should not be postponed for uncertain pleasure of the future.[33] To understand the importance of this belief, consider the wars that have been fought because of passion between man and woman, the steps people take to avoid discomfort and pain, and the value people place on self-satisfaction in day-to-day affairs. In *Reflections and Maxims*, Vauvenargues wrote:

> The indifference we display toward moral truth is due to the fact that we determine to indulge our passions in any event, and that is why we do not hesitate when action becomes necessary, notwithstanding the uncertainty of our opinions. It is of little consequence, say men, to know where truth lies, if we know where pleasure lies.[34]

How important is physical pleasure and avoidance of pain to you? Evaluate yourself on a scale of 1 to 10 (1 is low, 10 is high): _____.

Greatest Good for the Greatest Number

Two of the principal architects of the belief that "what is best brings the greatest good for the greatest number" were the nineteenth-century political philosophers Jeremy Bentham (1748–1832) and John Stuart Mill (1806–1873).[35] Their moral philosophy, utilitarianism, reflects the official ethics of both American democracy and Marxist communism. Bentham wrote, "The greatest happiness of all those whose interest is in question is the right and proper, and the only right and proper and universally desirable, end of human action."[36] When you weigh the consequences of moral behavior by considering the best interests of everyone involved, you are being ethical according to utilitarian ideals.

Do you find yourself using a utilitarian approach as you deal with moral dilemmas, striving to do what is best for the greatest number? Evaluate yourself on a scale of 1 to 10 (1 is low; 10 is high): _____.

Duty and Right Action

In *Criticism of Practical Reason* (1788) and *Fundamental Principles of the Metaphysics of Morals* (1785), the German philosopher Immanuel Kant (1724–1804) detailed a view of ethics that has had significant influence on the thinking of Western civilization. Kant believed that people must be their own lawgivers, freely choosing their obligations, and that these, in turn, become their duty. Because people are free to determine

ILLUS. 1.4

Do you believe that what is best brings the greatest good for the greatest number?

ethical beliefs and have free choice in moral dilemmas, all people must be responsible for their own actions.

Kant believed that a moral person will choose duty to conscience, and an immoral person will succumb to base or expedient desires. Further, he believed that if an individual acts from a good motive and a sense of duty, the act is good regardless of the consequences. Thus, if a person seeks to help another, but because of unforseen circumstances, the result is a worsened condition for the other, the helper is nonetheless a good and ethical person. On the other hand, if a person seeks to harm another, but in so doing actually helps the other, this act is nonetheless immoral.[37] The role of Kant's call to duty can be seen in the following incident:

A convoy of 38 merchant ships was crossing the Atlantic during World War II. None of the ships was armed except the "Jervis Bay," which had only six 6-inch guns and no armour plate. One night, an enemy ship suddenly appeared and began firing at the convoy with 11-inch shells. Without a moment's hesitation, the "Jervis Bay" drove toward the enemy, laying down a smoke screen behind which the rest of the convoy could escape.

The "Jervis Bay" fired at the German raider until the last active gun was submerged. Only when the bridge was destroyed and the ship could no longer fight did the wounded captain give the order to abandon ship. Only 68 out of the 250-man crew survived. The rest, along with the captain, went down with the "Jervis Bay." No one protested this act of duty; no one complained; no one suggested another action that should have been taken.[38]

The importance of personal conscience and duty can be seen in the words of Israeli stateswoman Golda Meir: "I can honestly say that I was never affected by the question of the success of an undertaking. If I felt it was the right thing to do, I was for it, regardless of the possible outcome."[39]

As you evaluate your life, how important is duty to you? Do you have a high sense of moral responsibility? Evaluate yourself on a scale of 1 to 10 (1 is low, 10 is high): _____.

Ethics Today

In addition to these central concepts of good, Western ethics today is guided by seven commonly held beliefs:

Life Should Be Preserved. Physician/philosopher Albert Schweitzer said, "The fundamental idea of good is that it consists of preserving life, in favoring it, and wanting to bring it to its highest value, and evil consists in destroying life, doing it injury, hindering its development period." Celebrating peace and life over war and death, psychologist Gordon Allport writes:

> Normal men everywhere reject, in principle and by preference, the path of war and destruction. They like to live in peace and friendship with their neighbors; they prefer to love and be loved rather than to hate and be hated. . . . While wars rage, yet our desire is for peace, and while animosity prevails, the weight of mankind's approval is on the side of affiliation.[40]

How important are peace and life to you? Do you place low, moderate, or high value on the preservation of life? Evaluate yourself on a scale of 1 to 10 (1 is low, 10 is high): _____.

It Is Important to Know the Nature and Meaning of Life. In *The Apology*, the Greek philosopher Plato describes Socrates as saying, "The unexamined life is not worth living."[41] In this spirit, over 23 centuries later, Albert Schweitzer wrote:

> Late on the third day, at the very moment when, at sunset, we were making our way through a herd of hippopotamus, there flashed upon my mind, unforeseen and unsought, the phrase, "Reverence for Life." The iron door had yielded; the path in the thicket had become visible. Now I had found my way to the idea in which affirmation of the world and ethics are contained side by side; now I know that the ethical acceptance of the world and of life, together with the ideals of civilization contained in this concept, has a foundation in thought.[42]

How important is it to you to know the meaning of life? Do you care a great deal about this question? Or do you assign it relatively low status in your value system? Evaluate yourself on a scale from 1 to 10 (1 is low, 10 is high): _____.

The Welfare of Others Should Be the Concern of Each Individual. The golden rule exists in some form in at least eight major religions. The Hindus teach, "Do not to others which, if done to thee, would cause thee pain; this is the sum of duty." Confucius said, "What you would not want done to yourself, do not do unto others." Jesus taught, "As ye would that men should do to you, do ye also to them likewise." When we make moral judgments in consideration of another person's welfare, we are using the golden rule.

Some people are primarily concerned with personal welfare; some are more altruistic and concerned with the welfare of others. Where do you stand? Evaluate yourself on a scale of 1 to 10 (1 is concern for self, 10 is concern for others): _____.

Happiness Is a Worthy Goal That Flows Naturally. The following story makes this point:

> A big cat saw a little cat chasing its tail and asked, "Why are you chasing your tail?" Said the kitten, "I have learned that the best thing for a cat is happiness and that happiness is in my tail. Therefore, I am chasing it. And when I catch it, I shall have happiness."
> Said the old cat, "My son, I too have paid attention to the problems of the universe. I too have judged that happiness is in my tail. But I have noticed that whenever I chase after it, it keeps running from me, and when I go about my business, it just seems to follow after me wherever I go."[43]

Mrs. Wiggs of the Cabbage Patch describes happiness as a worthy goal that comes naturally.

> I believe in gittin' as much good outen life as you kin—not that I ever set out to look for happiness; seems like the folks that does never finds it. I jes' do the best I kin where the good Lord puts me at, an' it looks like I got a happy feelin' in me most all the time.[44]

Finally, think of the happiness and goodness of the following natural experiences: a craftsman whistling while he works, a child building sand castles, a mother nursing her baby, and a physician saving a life.

Can you relate to the pursuit of happiness as a high value? To what degree? Evaluate yourself on a scale of 1 to 10 (1 is low, 10 is high): _____.

Love Is Good. The Lebanese poet, Kahlil Gibran, speaks of love:

> But let there be spaces in your togetherness,
> And let the winds of the heavens dance between you.
> Love one another, but make not a bond of love:
> Let it rather be a moving sea between the shores of your souls.
> Fill each other's cup, but drink not from one cup.
> Give one another of your bread, but eat not from the same loaf.
> Sing and dance together and be joyous, but let each one of you be alone,
> Even as the strings of a lute are alone though they quiver with the same music.
> Give your hearts, but not unto each other's keeping.
> For only the hand of Life can contain your hearts.
> And stand together, yet not too near together:
> For the pillars of the temple stand apart,
> And the oak tree and the cypress grow not in each other's shadow.[45]

In *The Art of Loving,* psychologist Erich Fromm writes:

> Beyond the element of giving, the active character of love becomes evident in the fact that it always implies certain basic elements. . . . These are care, responsibility, respect, and knowledge. . . . [And] love is union with somebody, or something, outside oneself, under the condition of retaining the separateness and integrity of one's own self. It is an experience of sharing, of communion, that permits the full unfolding of one's inner activity. . . .[Finally,] love is one aspect of what I have called the productive orientation: the active and creative relatedness of man to his fellow man, to himself, and to nature.[46]

How important is love to you? Is this a low, medium, or high value in your life? Evaluate yourself on a scale of 1 to 10 (1 is low, 10 is high): _____.

Knowledge Is Good. The ethical ideal is born both of the desire to be good and of the knowledge of what is good. One without the other is insufficient. In moral dilemmas, good intentions alone are not enough to guarantee good results. Also necessary is knowledge in its various forms: information, reason, imagination, wisdom, and truth. Knowledge must also be applied, as Rebecca McCann's poem, "Inconsistency," implies:

> I'm sure I have a noble mind,
> And honesty and tact;
> And no one's more surprised than I,
> To see the way I act![47]

ILLUS. 1.5

Knowledge is important in its various forms.

Printed with permission of Safeway Stores, Inc., 1987

How important is knowledge to you? Do you place high value on discovering and applying truth in moral dilemmas? Evaluate yourself on a scale of 1 to 10 (1 is low, 10 is high):

Individual Rights Should Be Protected. In 1776, a historic revolution was launched with the following declaration:

> We hold these truths to be self-evident, that all men are created Equal, that they are endowed by their Creator with certain inalienable Rights, that among these are Life, Liberty, and The Pursuit of Happiness—that to secure these rights, Governments are instituted among men, deriving their just powers from the consent of the Governed—that whenever any form of Government becomes destructive of these ends, it is the Right of the People to alter and abolish it and institute a new Government, laying its foundation and organizing its powers in such form, as to them should seem most likely to effect their safety and happiness.[48]

In 1789, the United States Constitution and the Bill of Rights elaborated on the rights of individuals in American society. Note, however, that as late as 1947 Harry Truman said, "I want our Bill of Rights implemented in fact. We have been trying to do this for 150 years." From this, you can see that moral goals do not ensure moral practices. Still, the idea is powerful and well entrenched in Western culture that the good of each individual, so long as it does not harm the good of other individuals, is the ethical ideal.

Do you place primary value on the individual or on the group? Do you believe society should meet the needs of individuals, or that individuals should meet the needs of society? Evaluate yourself on a scale of 1 to 10 (1 emphasizes society, 10 emphasizes the individual): _____.

In the face of ethical questions, the moral person tries to sort out right from wrong. In this effort, traditional and contemporary definitions of

ILLUS. 1.6

Should primary value be placed on the individual or on the group?

National Urban League

good guide Western culture. Although one value may conflict with another, and although not all values are held to the same degree by all people, a sense of having done the right thing usually results when one behaves with strength, with personal conviction, in a state of naturalness, with religious authority, for personal satisfaction, for the welfare of all, out of personal conscience, to preserve life, to understand life, with love, with knowledge, and with respect for the individual. As you consider these values, which are most important to you? What is your moral ideal?

To gain a picture of your personal definition of good and right, complete the following exercise.

PERSONAL DEFINITION OF GOOD AND RIGHT

Directions

Transpose your scores from pages 18–26 to the scales below by circling the appropriate number for each. High scores show the concepts and beliefs that are important to you in moral dilemmas; low scores indicate values that are relatively less important.

Central Concepts of Good and Right

Power	1	2	3	4	5	6	7	8	9	10
Personal integrity	1	2	3	4	5	6	7	8	9	10
Natural simplicity	1	2	3	4	5	6	7	8	9	10
Will of God	1	2	3	4	5	6	7	8	9	10
Pleasure	1	2	3	4	5	6	7	8	9	10
Greatest good for greatest number	1	2	3	4	5	6	7	8	9	10
Duty and right action	1	2	3	4	5	6	7	8	9	10

Commonly Held Beliefs

Preservation of life	1	2	3	4	5	6	7	8	9	10
Meaning of life	1	2	3	4	5	6	7	8	9	10
Welfare of others	1	2	3	4	5	6	7	8	9	10
Happiness	1	2	3	4	5	6	7	8	9	10
Loving relationships	1	2	3	4	5	6	7	8	9	10

Knowledge   1 2 3 4 5 6 7 8 9 10

Individual rights   1 2 3 4 5 6 7 8 9 10

The following exercise measures guiding values and practices in your life. It is an excellent vehicle for clarifying what is important to you and the means you use to achieve your goals.

VALUES AND PRACTICES

Directions

What values and practices guide you as you live your life? Look at the two lists below. Rank the 16 values in the first list according to which is most *important* to you (1 is most, 2 is next, 16 is least). Then, rank the 16 practices in the second list according to which is most *characteristic* of you (1 is most, 2 is next, 16 is least).

Important Values	Characteristic Practices
_7_ Pleasure	_3_ Creative
_13_ Survival	_4_ Enthusiastic
_1_ Responsibility	_5_ Practical
_8_ Order	_1_ Honest
_12_ Security	_9_ Fun loving
_9_ Achievement	_6_ Goal directed
_2_ Love	_14_ Structured
_11_ Wealth	_10_ Dependable
_10_ Growth	_7_ Decisive
_3_ Truth	_8_ Variety loving
_14_ Recognition	_11_ Helpful
_16_ Beauty	_13_ Independent
_15_ Power	_15_ Influential
_6_ Peace	_12_ Benevolent
_4_ Justice	_16_ Controlled
_5_ Freedom	_2_ Intellectual

Choose the four most important values and the four most characteristic practices (those with the lowest numbers). These can be termed your *critical quarters* (1/4 of 16).

Important Values	Characteristic Practices
RESPONSIBILITY	HONEST
LOVE	INTELLECTUAL
TRUTH	CREATIVE
JUSTICE	ENTHUSIATIC

DISCUSSION

Evaluate yourself. Are you living your life in line with the four values most important to you? Do your practices support your values? Are your values and practices reflected in both your personal and work life?

FULL-SWING MORALITY AND AXIOLOGICAL ARREST

Although people are the only animals capable of moral reason (whether religious or secular), and although as a human being you may subscribe to many ethical ideals, how strong is your morality? What ethical beliefs do you uphold in life-and-death situations? Of course, each person is different in this regard. Figure 1.4 summarizes a study on moral convictions. The results show that almost no one would kill another person in order to obtain food in noncannibalistic societies. On the other hand, the majority of people would be willing to forsake less important religious and conventional customs to prevent starvation.

There is a concept in ethics that can be used to assess the strength of one's moral beliefs. This concept is called full-swing morality and axiological arrest. Think for a moment about the sport of baseball, in which a full swing is needed to hit a home run. An arrested swing will result in less success — a triple, double, single, or a foul ball. The same is true for questions of right and wrong and good and bad: in moral dilemmas, a home run results only when one completes a full swing and does not suffer axiological arrest, falling short in one's moral follow-through.

A full swing is comprised of six points, beginning through completion:[49]

- Point 1 is to *know* what one believes.
- Point 2 is to *choose freely* what one believes.
- Point 3 is to *cherish* what one believes.
- Point 4 is to *declare* what one believes.

FIGURE 1.4

The Strength of Moral Convictions—Approximate Percentage of the Population Showing Various Behaviors Under Starvation Conditions

Activities Induced by Starvation	Percentage of Population Succumbing to Pressure of Starvation
1. Cannibalism (in noncannibalistic societies)	Less than 1/3 of 1 percent
2. Murder of family members and friends	Less than 1 percent
3. Murder of other members of one's group	Not more than 1 percent
4. Murder of strangers who are not enemies	Not more than 2 to 5 percent
5. Infliction of various bodily and other injuries on members of one's social group	Not more than 5 to 10 percent
6. Theft, larceny, robbery, forgery, and other crimes against property that have a clear-cut criminal character	Hardly more than 7 to 10 percent
7. Prostitution and other dishonorable sexual activities	Hardly more than 10 percent
8. Violation of fundamental religious and moral principles	Hardly more than 10 to 29 percent
9. Violation of various rules of honesty and fairness in pursuit of food, such as misuse of rationing cards, hoarding, and taking unfair advantage of others	From 20 to 99 percent, depending on the nature of the violation
10. Violation of less important religious, moral, conventional, and similar norms	From 50 to 99 percent
11. Surrender or weakening of aesthetic activities irreconcilable with food-seeking activities	From 50 to 99 percent

FIGURE 1.4—*continued*

12. Weakening of sexual activities, especially coitus	From 70 to 90 percent during prolonged and intense starvation

Source: Adapted from Pitirim A. Sorokin, Man and Society in Calamity (New York: Dutton, Inc., 1942), 81; renewal © 1970 by Helene P. Sorokin, published by E. P. Dutton & Co., Inc. Reprinted with permission from Sergei P. Sorokin, M.D.

- Point 5 is to *act* on one's beliefs.
- Point 6 is to *habitually act* on one's beliefs.

Axiological arrest occurs when a person fails to complete all six points in the morality swing and, in effect, fails to hit an ethical home run.

Consider the case of Jackie, Jane, Jill, Judy, Jodie, and JoAnn, each facing a moral dilemma (what to do about Grandpa; what to do about sexual relations; what to do about income tax):

- Jackie knows what she believes but has not examined other alternatives. Hers is an unthinking stance, with little or no personal commitment.
- Jane knows what she believes, chooses it freely, but does not particularly cherish her belief. Hers is an intellectual choice, with little or no emotion.
- Jill knows what she believes, chooses it freely, and values it personally. She experiences self-satisfaction in her belief.
- Judy knows what she believes, chooses it freely, cherishes it personally, and declares her belief. She publicly states her values.
- Jodie knows what she believes, chooses it freely, cherishes it personally, declares it publicly, and acts on her belief. She takes action and accepts the consequences.
- JoAnn knows what she believes, chooses it freely, cherishes it personally, declares it publicly, acts on it, and does this habitually. JoAnn exhibits full-swing morality, no axiological arrest, and hits an ethical home run. JoAnn shows maximum strength of moral conviction.

See Figure 1.5 for a picture description of full-swing morality and axiological arrest.

To personalize the subject of moral strength, evaluate your own values—love, responsibility, freedom, equality, and so forth. Consider a moral dilemma in which your values play a part. Ask yourself, is your moral strength full swing, or do you experience axiological arrest? See Figure 1.6.

FIGURE 1.5

Full-Swing Morality and Axiological Arrest

Moral Dilemma: what to do about grandpa; what to do about sexual relations; what to do about income tax.

Points on the Swing	Jackie	Jane	Jill	Judy	Jodie	JoAnn
Knows beliefs	✓	✓	✓	✓	✓	✓
Chooses beliefs		✓	✓	✓	✓	✓
Cherishes beliefs			✓	✓	✓	✓
Declares beliefs				✓	✓	✓
Acts on beliefs					✓	✓
Acts habitually on beliefs						✓

Each person experiences axiological arrest at some point on the morality swing, except JoAnn, who hits an ethical home run.

FIGURE 1.6

Personal Moral Strength

Sample moral dilemma: what to do about discrimination (sex, race, religion).

Points on the Swing	Check (✓) if appropriate
Do you *know* what you believe?	____
Do you *freely choose* what you believe?	____
Do you *cherish* your belief privately?	____
Do you *declare* your belief publicly?	____
Do you *act* on your belief and accept the consequences?	____
Do you *habitually act* on your belief and accept the consequences?	____

One way to know what values are important to you and to evaluate the strength of conviction you have shown toward these values is to complete the following exercise.

WERE I TO DIE TODAY . . .

Directions

If you were the editor of a newspaper and were asked to compose your own obituary notice, what would you have to say?

Name _____,

age _____, died today from _____.

_____ is survived

by _____.

At the time of death, principal endeavor was _____

_____

_____.

_____ will be honored for

_____

_____;

will be remembered by _____ because

of _____;

will be missed by _____ because

of _____;

will be loved by _____.

Made contributions in the areas of _____

_____;

always hoped to _____

_____;

wanted most to _____

_____;

was proud of _____

_____.

Services will be _____.

Ethics, Part One Exercise • Were I to Die   33

Flowers may be sent _____.
In lieu of flowers, _____.

R.I.P.
━━━━━━━━━━━

DISCUSSION

How do you feel about your obituary? Could you R.I.P. (rest in peace) because you have L.W.I. (lived with integrity)? If you have completed your philosopher's pie to the best of your ability and have pursued full-swing morality in all of your dealings, your answer is probably yes.

RECOMMENDED RESOURCES

The following reading case, application, and film are suggested for greater insight into the material in Part One:

Reading	— How Could the Jonestown Holocaust Have Occurred?
Case	— The Superhonest Politician
Application	— Beliefs and Values Questionnaire (BVQ)
Film	— Young Goodman Brown

REFERENCE NOTES

1 Harold Titus and Morton Keeton, *Ethics for Today*, 5th ed. (New York: D. Van Nostrand Company, 1975), 25.

2 Cervantes, *Don Quixote*, vol. 6.

3 Titus and Keeton, *Ethics for Today*, chap. 2.

4 Edmund W. Sinnott, *The Biology of the Human Spirit* (New York: The Viking Press, 1955), 47.

5 Jean Piaget, *The Moral Judgement of the Child*, trans. Marjorie Gabain (New York: Free Press, 1966); and Marcus Lieberman, "Estimation of a Moral Judgment Level Using Items Whose Alternatives form a Graded Scale" (Paper presented at the annual meeting of the

American Educational Research Association, New York, February 1971).

6. Piaget, *The Moral Judgement of the Child*, and Lieberman, "Estimation of Moral Judgment Level."

7. Piaget, *The Moral Judgement of the Child*, and Lieberman, "Estimation of Moral Judgment Level."

8. Jane E. Brody, "Morality: All in the Name of Science," *New York Times*, 30 July 1972, E2.

9. Titus and Keeton, *Ethics for Today*, 369.

10. Titus and Keeton, *Ethics for Today*, 101.

11. Titus and Keeton, *Ethics for Today*, 241.

12. Joseph Petrick, University of Cincinnati, 1986.

13. Vernon J. Bourke, ed., *The Essential Augustine* (Indianapolis: Hackett Publishing, 1964); and David Knowles, *The Evolution of Medieval Thought* (New York: Vintage Press, 1962).

14. Titus and Keeton, *Ethics for Today*, 194–95.

15. Titus and Keeton, *Ethics for Today*, 192–93; and Aristotle, *The Nicomachean Ethics*, trans. Hippocrates G. Apostle (Dordrecht/Boston: D. Reidel Publishing Company, 1975), book 10, chap. 5.

16. Titus and Keeton, *Ethics for Today*; and Aristotle, *The Nicomachean Ethics*.

17. Aristotle, *The Nicomachean Ethics*, book B, chap. 6, 29.

18. Based on the work of Jean-Paul Sartre, *Being and Nothingness*, trans. Hazel E. Barnes (Secaucus, N.J.: The Citadel Press, 1974).

19. Bertrand Russell, *The Autobiography of Bertrand Russell: 1872–1914* (Boston: Little, Brown & Company, 1967), 3–4.

20. Titus and Keeton, *Ethics for Today*, 39.

21. Aristotle, *Politics*, i, 3.

22. William Hazlitt, *Lectures on the English Comic Writers*, lecture no. 1.

23. Charles Darwin, *The Origin of Species by Means of Natural Selection* (New York: The Modern Library, 1936), 471.

24. Alfred North Whitehead, *Science and the Modern World*, Lowell Lectures, 1925 (New York: The Macmillan Company, 1925), 124–25.

25. Niccolo Machiavelli, *The Prince* (Chicago: University of Chicago Press, 1952); and Antony Jay, *Management and Machiavelli* (New York: Bantam Books Inc., 1967).

26. Friedrich Nietzsche, *Thus Spake Zarathustra*, trans. Thomas Common (New York: Modern Library, 1917), prologue, no. 3, as found in Titus and Keeton, *Ethics for Today*, 178.

27 Martin Heidigger, *Being and Time*, trans. John Macquarrie and Edward Robinson (New York: Harper & Row Publishers, Inc., 1962).

28 Titus and Keeton, *Ethics for Today*, 67.

29 Henry David Thoreau, *Walden* (New York: C. N. Potter/Crown Publishers, 1970).

30 *The Reflections and Maxims of Vauvenargues*, trans. S. G. Stevens (London: Humphrey Milford, 1940), 121.

31 Titus and Keeton, *Ethics for Today*, 327.

32 Luke 10:27.

33 Radoslav A. Tsanoff, *The Great Philosophers*, 2nd ed. (New York: Harper & Row, Publishers, Inc., 1953), 102–103.

34 *The Reflections and Maxims of Vauvenargues*, 115.

35 Titus and Keeton, *Ethics for Today*, 153–57; and Jeremy Bentham, *An Introduction to the Principles of Morals and Legislation*, chap. 10 (London: Oxford University Press, 1879); and John Stuart Mill, *Utilitarianism* (New York: E. P. Dutton and Company, 1910), 6.

36 Titus and Keeton, *Ethics for Today*, 153–57; and Bentham, *Principles of Morals and Legislation*, Chap. 10; and Mill, *Utilitarianism*, 6; and Anthony Quinton, *Utilitarian Ethics* (New York: St. Martin's Press, 1973), 28.

37 Titus and Keeton, *Ethics for Today*, 142.

38 "World War—Epic of the Jervis Bay," *Time* (25 November 1940): 22–23.

39 Marie Syrkin, *Golda Meir: Woman with a Cause* (London: V. Gollancze, 1964).

40 Gordon Allport, *The Nature of Prejudice* (Boston: Beacon Press, 1954), XIV.

41 Plato, *Apology*, 24.

42 Albert Schweitzer, *Out of My Life and Thought* (New York: Holt, 1949), 124.

43 C. L. James, "On Happiness," in Caesar Johnson, *To See a World in a Grain of Sand* (Norwalk, Conn.: The C. R. Gibson Company, 1972).

44 Alice Caldwell Hegan, *Mrs. Wiggs of the Cabbage Patch* (New York: The Century Company, 1901), 125.

45 Kahlil Gibran, *The Prophet* (New York: Alfred A. Knopf, Inc., 1977).

46 Erich Fromm, *The Art of Loving* (New York: Bantam Books, Inc., 1963), 20–21, 26–27, 30–31.

47 Rebecca McCann, "Inconsistency," in *Complete Cheerful Cherub* (New York: Covici, Friede, Inc./Crown Publishers, 1932), 224.

48 *The Declaration of Independence*, 4 July 1776.

49 Louis E. Raths, Merrill Harmin, and Sidney Simon, *Values and Teaching* (Columbus, Ohio: Charles E. Merrill Publishing, 1966), 27–36.

STUDY QUIZ

As a test of your understanding and the extent to which you have achieved the objectives in Part I, complete the following questions. See Appendix E for the answer key.

1. Each of the following statements is an ethical judgment, except:
    a. It is wrong to steal
    b. Democracy is a good system of government
    c. The discovery of truth should be the scientist's goal
    d. Man is an animal

2. The Greek word for ethics, *ethos*, originally stood for:
    a. physical beauty
    b. social justice
    c. inner character
    d. religious faith

3. Ethics has both _____ and _____ roots.
    a. scientific, poetic
    b. religious, secular
    c. statutory, common
    d. male, female

4. St. Augustine taught an ethical view that was essentially:
    a. religious
    b. nonreligious
    c. political
    d. none of the above

5. The percentage of the world's population having a religious orientation toward ethics is approximately:
    a. 20 percent
    b. 40 percent
    c. 60 percent
    d. 80 percent

6. Aristotle had a(n) _____ orientation toward ethics.
    a. secular
    b. mystical
    c. economic
    d. none of the above

7. The three key questions of the philosopher's pie are:

   a. What is pure, what is good, what is necessary?
   b. What is real, what is true, what is valuable?
   c. Who is important, what is important, why is it important?
   d. What is physical, what is mental, what is spiritual?

8. Quo vadis means:

   a. Where are you going?
   b. Where have you been?
   c. Where are you now?
   d. Who are you?

9. More than _____ years ago, the human race evolved into beings who could distinguish right from wrong.

   a. 100,000
   b. 80,000
   c. 60,000
   d. 40,000

10. In order, the following individuals are associated with: power, personal integrity, natural simplicity, will of God, pleasure, utilitarianism, and duty as central concepts of good:

    a. Nietzsche, Kant, Jesus, Aristippus, Muhammad, Rousseau, Mill
    b. Rousseau, Aristippus, Muhammad, Nietzsche, Mill, Jesus, Kant
    c. Kant, Nietzsche, Jesus, Mill, Muhammad, Aristippus, Rousseau
    d. Machiavelli, Nietzsche, Rousseau, Muhammad, Aristippus, Mill, Kant

11. The statement "The unexamined life is not worth living" is attributed to:

    a. Plato
    b. Socrates
    c. Aristotle
    d. none of the above

12. Axiological arrest refers to:

    a. rules of moral behavior
    b. civil law and order
    c. falling short in one's values
    d. none of the above

DISCUSSION QUESTIONS AND ACTIVITIES

The following questions and activities help personalize the subject. They are appropriate for classroom exercises and homework assignments.

1. What values are important to you? Are your values theistic or nontheistic in orientation? How do your views on what is real and what is true influence your views on what is important?

   _____
   _____
   _____

2. How strong is your value system? Do you exhibit full-swing morality or suffer from axiological arrest? Explain.

   _____
   _____
   _____

3. Use small-group discussion to consider ethics in America today. What are the dominant definitions of good and right? What people and events have had primary influence on America's values?

4. Share a true-life moral dilemma — school, work, or home. Discuss the role of values, the role of religion, the strength of moral conviction.

PART TWO

Levels of Morality

Learning Objectives

After completing Part Two, you will better understand:

1. how morality is developed;
2. the levels and stages of moral development—preconventional, conventional, and postconventional;
3. the relationship between virtue (level III, stage 6 morality) and the search for meaning.

MORAL DEVELOPMENT — HOW THE FIRE IS LIT

The English philosopher John Locke viewed the newborn child as a *tabula rasa*, or blank tablet, on which a life script would be written. He believed that experience and learning would shape the content, structure, and direction of each person's life. In this sense, the ethics of the infant are amoral — that is, no concept of good and bad or right and wrong is inborn.

After birth, babies soon discover that they are rewarded for certain things and punished for others. As a result of this early programming, they develop an understanding of what the adult world considers good and bad. Thus, a social conscience is begun, and this becomes the foundation for future moral development.[1]

Through modeling and socialization, the older community passes on ethics to young people. The words and actions of parents, teachers, and older companions teach and reinforce morality before children develop their own critical faculties.

In all societies, a definition of good exists that dictates the appropriateness of moral behavior and serves as the basis for the development of young people. Consider the moral programming in the Girl Scout Promise and Law and the Boy Scout Laws:

The Girl Scout Promise

On my honor, I will try:
   To serve God and my country,
   To help people at all times,
   And to live by the Girl Scout Law.

The Girl Scout Law

I will do my best:
   to be honest
   to be fair
   to help where I am needed
   to be cheerful
   to be friendly and considerate
   to be a sister to every Girl Scout
   to respect authority
   to use resources wisely
   to protect and improve the world around me
   to show respect for myself and others through my words and actions.[2]

ILLUS. 2.1, 2.2

Moral development results from early training.

Girl Scouts of the U.S.A.

BOY SCOUTS OF AMERICA

The Boy Scout Laws

A Boy Scout is:

1. Trustworthy—A Scout's honor is to be trusted. If he were to violate his honor by telling a lie, or by cheating, or by not doing exactly a given task when trusted on his honor, he may be directed to hand over his Scout Badge.

2. Loyal—He is loyal to all to whom loyalty is due: his Scout leader, his home and parents, and country.

3. Helpful—He must be prepared at any time to save a life, help injured persons, and share the home duties. He must do at least one "Good Turn" for somebody every day.

4. Friendly—He is a friend to all and a brother to every other Scout.

5. Courteous—He is polite to all, especially to women, children, older people, and the weak and helpless. He must not take pay for being helpful or courteous.

6. Kind—He is a friend to animals. He will not kill or hurt any living creature needlessly, but will strive to save and protect all harmless life.

7. Obedient—He obeys his parents, Scoutmaster, Patrol Leader, and all other duly constituted authorities.

8. Cheerful—He smiles whenever he can. His obedience to orders is prompt and cheery. He never shirks nor grumbles at hardships.

9. Thrifty—He does not wantonly destroy property. He works faithfully, wastes nothing, and makes the best use of his opportunities. He saves his money so that he may pay his own way, be generous to those in need, and helpful to worthy projects. He may work for pay, but must not receive tips for courtesies or "Good Turns."

10. Brave—He has the courage to face danger in spite of fear, and to stand up for the right against the coaxings of friends or the jeers or threats of enemies, and defeat does not down him.

11. Clean—He keeps clean in body and thought, stands for clean speech, clean sport, clean habits, and travels with a clean crowd.

12. Reverent—He is reverent toward God. He is faithful in his religious duties, and respects the convictions of others in matters of custom and religion.[3]

Ben Franklin's advice to "teach children obedience first so that all other lessons will follow the easier" captures the spirit in which moral values are taught.[4]

On a societywide scale, the ethics of adults are similarly programmed. Swiss psychologist Jean Piaget writes that heteronomy (rules as sacred external laws laid down by authorities) is the unifying factor in adult societies, and that in every society there are individuals and groups (governmental, religious, and educational) who believe in certain moral ideals, and who see their task to be one of imprinting these ideals on succeeding generations.[5]

LEVELS OF MORALITY

Regardless of the code of ethics a society teaches, on what basis does the individual make ethical decisions? What motive, goal, or frame of reference does the person bring to moral dilemmas? There are many ideas on this question, but the work of social psychologist Lawrence Kohlberg occupies center stage.

Kohlberg explains that each person makes ethical decisions according to three levels of moral development.[6] The chart in Figure 2.1 describes these levels, defines two stages within each level, and presents examples of reasoning at each stage. As you read the chart, evaluate your own ethics. At which level do you usually operate?

Different people go through the six stages of moral development at different rates, and some people never reach the principled morality of stages 5 and 6. The egocentric orientation of stages 1 and 2 is most characteristic of preadolescent children, whereas the community-oriented morality of stages 3 and 4 is common in teenagers and most adults. The self-direction and high principles of stages 5 and 6 are characteristic of only 20 percent of the adult population, with only 5 to 10 percent of the population operating consistently at level 6.[7]

The case and analysis that follow show how levels of morality influence human conduct in the face of moral dilemmas:

The Stolen Drug

In Europe, a woman was near death from a rare kind of cancer. There was one drug that the doctors thought might save her. It was a form of radium that a druggist in the same town had recently discovered. The

FIGURE 2.1

Levels, Stages, and Examples of Moral Development

Levels of Moral Development	Stages of Moral Development	Examples of Moral Reasoning at Each Stage
Level I *Preconventional morality:* the individual is aware of cultural prescriptions of right and wrong behavior. Response is based on two concerns: will I be harmed (punishment)? will I be helped (pleasure)?	*Stage 1:* at this stage, physical consequences determine moral behavior. Avoidance of punishment and deference to power are characteristic of this stage.	"I won't hit him because he may hit me back."
	Stage 2: individual needs are the primary concern of the person operating at this stage, and personal pleasure dictates the rightness or wrongness of behavior.	"I will help him because he may help me in return."
Level II *Conventional morality:* morality is characterized by group conformity and allegiance to authority. The individual acts in order to meet the expectations of others and to please those in charge.	*Stage 3:* the approval of others is the major determinant of behavior at this stage, and the good person is viewed as the one who satisfies family, friends, and associates.	"I will go along with you because I want you to like me."
	Stage 4: compliance with authority and upholding social order are primary ethical concerns at this stage. Right conduct is "doing one's duty," as defined by those in leadership positions.	"I will comply with the order because it is wrong to disobey."
Level III *Postconventional morality:* this is the most advanced level of moral development. At this level, the individual is	*Stage 5:* social ethics are based on rational analysis, community discussion, and mutual consent. There is	"Although I disagree with his views, I will uphold his right to have them."

FIGURE 2.1–continued

Levels of Moral Development	Stages of Moral Development	Examples of Moral Reasoning at Each Stage
concerned with right and wrong conduct over and above self-interest, apart from the views of others, and without regard to authority figures. Ethical judgments are based on self-defined moral principles.	tolerance for individual views, but when there is conflict between individual and group interests, the majority rules. This stage represents the "official" morality of the American Constitution.	
	Stage 6: at this stage, what is right and good is viewed as a matter of individual conscience, free choice, and personal responsibility for the consequences. Morality is seen as superseding the majority view or the prescriptions of authority; rather, it is based on personal conviction.	"There is no external force that can compel me to do an act that I consider morally wrong."

[Handwritten note: MOTIVES, MEANS, & CONSEQUENCES ARE NECESSARY INGREDIENTS OF VIRTUOUS — LEVEL III STAGE 6 MORALITY.]

Source: Lawrence Kohlberg, "Cognitive-Development Approach to Moral Education," *The Humanist* (November-December, 1972): 13–16; and Lawrence Kohlberg, "Stages of Moral Development as a Basis for Moral Education," in Moral Education: Interdisciplinary Approaches, ed. C. M. Beck, B. S. Crittenden, and E. V. Sullivan (Toronto: University of Toronto Press, 1971), 86–88; and Lawrence Kohlberg, "The Cognitive-Developmental Approach to Socialization," in Handbook of Socialization Theory and Research, ed. D. A. Goslin (Chicago: Rand McNally & Company, 1969).

---

drug was expensive to make, but the druggist was charging ten times what the drug cost him. He paid $200 for the radium and charged $2,000 for a small dose of the drug.

The sick woman's husband, Heinz, went to everyone he knew to borrow the money, but he could only get together about $1,000, which was half of what it cost. He told the druggist that his wife was dying and asked him to sell it cheaper, or let him pay later. But the druggist said, "No, I discovered the drug and I'm going to make money from it." Heinz became desperate and broke into the man's store to steal the drug for his wife.[8]

When confronted with the moral dilemma of either letting his wife die or stealing the drug, Heinz stole the drug. Was he right or wrong?

Figure 2.2 presents examples of moral reasoning Heinz may have used at each stage of moral development.

FIGURE 2.2

Heinz Reasons: Should I Steal the Drug?

Moral Stages	Arguments For	Arguments Against
Stage 1: orientation to punishment	It isn't wrong to take the drug. It is really only worth $200, and I probably won't get caught anyway.	It is wrong to take the drug. After all, it is worth $2,000. Besides, I would probably get caught and be punished.
Stage 2: orientation to pleasure	If I don't want to lose my wife, I should take the drug. It is the only thing that will work.	I should not risk myself for my wife. If she dies, I can marry somebody else. It would be wrong for me to give up my own well-being for her well-being.
Stage 3: orientation to social approval	I have no choice. Stealing the drug is the only thing for a good husband to do. What would my family and friends say if I didn't try to save my wife?	I must not steal the drug. People won't blame me for not stealing the drug; it is not the kind of thing people would approve of.
Stage 4: orientation to social order	When I got married, I vowed to protect my wife. I must steal the drug to live up to that promise. If husbands do not protect their wives, the family structure will disintegrate, and with it, our society.	Stealing is illegal. I have to obey the law, no matter what the circumstances. Imagine what society would be like if everybody broke the law.
Stage 5: orientation to social rights and responsibilities	I should steal the drug. The law is unjust because it does not protect my wife's right to life. Therefore, I have no obligation to obey the law. I should steal the drug.	As a member of society, I have an obligation to respect the druggist's right to property. Therefore, it would be wrong for me to steal the drug.
Stage 6: orientation to ethical principles	The principle of the sanctity of life demands that I steal the drug, no matter what the consequences.	The principle of justice and the greatest good for the greatest number prevents me from stealing the drug, even for the good of my wife.

Source: Adapted from Zick Rubin and Elton B. McNeil, *The Psychology of Being Human,* 3d ed. (New York: Harper & Row, Publishers, Inc., 1981), *321–324.*

The following cases show the importance of levels of morality in history.

Nazi Death Camps

In April 1961, Adolf Eichmann, accused executioner of 5 million Jews in Nazi Germany during World War II, testified at his trial in Jerusalem:

> In actual fact, I was merely a little cog in the machinery that carried out the directives of the German Reich. It was really none of my business. Yet what is there to "admit"? I carried out my orders.[9]

Level II, stage 4 moral reasoning is reflected in Eichmann's statement.

Civil Disobedience

In March 1922, Mohandas Gandhi, the Indian spiritual and political leader, addressed a British court with these words:

> Nonviolence is the first article of my faith. It is also the last article of my creed. But I had to make a choice. I had to either submit to a system that I considered had done irreparable harm to my country, or incur the risk. . . . I am here, therefore, to invite and cheerfully submit to the highest penalty that can be inflicted upon me for what in law is a deliberate crime and what appears to me to be the highest duty of a citizen.[10]

Level III, stage 6 morality is seen in the life and teaching of Gandhi. With similar moral reasoning, Socrates refused to admit social wrong in his farewell address to the Athenian people. Instead, he drank the lethal hemlock, setting an example of moral heroism that has inspired Western civilization for over 2,000 years.

ILLUS. 2.3

Gandhi taught through moral convictions.

Watergate

Think of the importance of the three levels and six stages of morality in the American political fiasco called the Watergate affair.

Morality and Watergate

Late in the summer of 1972, as the presidential campaign swung into high gear, six men were arrested after breaking into the headquarters of the Democratic National Committee. Those headquarters were located in Washington, D.C., in a building complex called the Watergate. The break-in, subsequent coverup, and eventual investigation became known as "the Watergate affair."

The six burglars were soon convicted, but the true scope of the criminal conspiracy remained hidden for some time. It was ultimately discovered that the burglars were acting not on their own initiative, but under the direction of members of the Committee to Re-elect the President (CREEP). This was revealed only after an elaborate attempt to cover up the link, including extensive perjury on the part of highly placed officials in CREEP and in the White House. These events caused an entire nation to stop and wonder why intelligent, respected, and apparently "moral" men would condone and commit such crimes.

There is no single, satisfying answer to this question. Different individuals had different reasons for participating in the crimes of Watergate. But it may help to recognize that these men were confronted with difficult moral dilemmas and to analyze the decisions they made in terms of levels of morality.

Some of the men involved may have rationalized their participation in terms typical of stages 1 and 2: they may have burglarized for the sake of money, and lied in order to avoid punishment. Other participants in the Watergate affair may have exhibited moral reasoning typical of stages 3 or 4. For instance, a CREEP official named Herbert Porter testified at the Congressional Watergate hearings (1973) that he had committed perjury because of group pressure.

The following is an excerpt of an exchange between Porter and Senator Howard Baker:

Baker: At any time, did you ever think of saying, I do not think this is quite right?
Porter: Yes I did.
Baker: What did you do about it?
Porter: I did not do anything about it.
Baker: Why didn't you?
Porter: In all honesty, probably because of the fear of group pressure that would ensue from not being a team player.

Porter's reasoning is typical for individuals at stage 3, where right and wrong are determined by group norms.

Other participants, like Jeb Stuart Magruder, the deputy director of CREEP, justified their involvement in the Watergate crimes as being essential to "national security" and the preservation of the social order. This sort of moral reasoning is typical of individuals at stage 4. At this stage, if the system is seen as more basic than the rights of its individual members, it is being viewed from a stage 4 perspective.

Finally, consider the moral arguments of Archibald Cox, the Harvard Law School professor who served as Special Watergate Prosecutor until his dismissal by President Nixon. Cox argued that "the rights of speech, privacy, dignity, and other fundamental liberties . . . must be respected by both government and private persons." This emphasis on constitutional rights and responsibilities is typical of individuals at stage 5.[11]

In a survey of 370 college students conducted during the winter of 1973–1974, Candee found support for the conclusion that attitudes about Watergate depend on a person's stage of moral reasoning. As a first step, Candee determined each subject's stage by examining answers to questions about moral dilemmas. Most of the subjects were at stage 3, 4, or 5. Next, he examined the relationship between those stages and attitudes toward Watergate. In general, he found that subjects at stages 3 and 4 were more likely to approve of the acts of the Watergate participants, than subjects at stage 5. For example, approximately 48 percent of the subjects at stage 3 and 23 percent of the subjects at stage 4 thought that Magruder was right to perjure himself in order to cover up the break-ins; in contrast, only 5 percent of the subjects at stage 5 thought so.[12]

Answer the following questions to help personalize the subject of levels of morality: at what level of moral reasoning do you operate? Are you stage 1–2 (egocentric), 3–4 (community-oriented), or 5–6 (principled) in your response to ethical dilemmas at work, in your community, and with your family?

THE SEARCH FOR MEANING

In the search for ethical ideals, people inevitably face the meaning of their own existence. The path their reasoning follows is: "How can I know what is the right thing to do unless I know why I am here?" This concern for meaning, so basic with humankind, is unique among all animal species. This is because human beings are the only animals who try to discover what sort of creatures they are. They are the only beings who consciously wonder, "Who am I, and what is important to me?"

Aristotle began his *Metaphysics* with the statement, "All men by nature desire to know." In contrast, the behavior of other animals is determined primarily by the struggle for survival. Lacking the ability to think in abstractions and to reason, they do not face the problem of choosing real from false values, and they have no concern about the moral consequences of their behavior.[13] As social philosopher Erich Fromm states, "Man is the only animal who finds his own existence a problem that he has to solve and from which he cannot escape."[14]

The search for meaning in life is common to all people, but what each person finds is unique to that person. One person may define meaning in a social sense—having children and raising a family. Another may define meaning in religious terms—to do one's part in God's divine plan. Still another may view meaning in a personal sense—to know oneself and one's place in the universe.

The following letter, written in 1933, shows how the search for meaning is unique to each person. It was prompted by a request from the historian Will Durant, who asked the famous author H. L. Mencken to explain what meaning life held for him.

A Letter from H. L. Mencken to Will Durant

You ask me, in brief, what satisfaction I get out of life, and why I go on working. I go on working for the same reason that a hen goes on laying eggs. There is in every living creature an obscure but powerful impulse to active functioning. Life demands to be lived. Inaction, save as a measure of recuperation between bursts of activity, is painful and dangerous to the healthy organism — in fact, it is almost impossible. Only the dying can be really idle.

The precise form of an individual's activity is determined, of course, by the equipment with which he came into the world. In other words, it is determined by his heredity. I do not lay eggs, as a hen does, because I was born without any equipment for it. For the same reason I do not get myself elected to Congress, or play the violin, or teach metaphysics in a college, or work in a steel mill. What I do is simply what lies easiest to my hand. It happens that I was born with an intense and insatiable interest in ideas, and thus like to play with them. It happens also that I was born with rather more than the average facility for putting them into words. In consequence, I am a writer and editor, which is to say, a dealer in them and concocter of them.

There is very little conscious volition in all this. What I do was ordained by the inscrutable fates, not chosen by me. In my boyhood, yielding to a powerful but still subordinate interest in exact facts, I wanted to be a chemist, and at the same time my poor father tried to make me a businessman. At other times, like any other relatively poor man, I have longed to make a lot of money by some easy swindle. But I became a writer all the same, and shall remain one until the end of the chapter, just as a cow goes on giving milk all her life, even though what appears to be her self-interest urges her to give gin.

I am far luckier than most men, for I have been able since boyhood to make a good living doing precisely what I have wanted to do — what I would have done for nothing, and very gladly, if there had been no reward for it. Not many men, I believe, are so fortunate. Millions of them have to make their livings at tasks that really do not interest them. As for me, I have had an extraordinarily pleasant life, despite the fact that I have had the usual share of woes. For in the midst of those woes I still enjoyed the immense satisfaction that goes with free activity. I have done, in the main, exactly what I wanted to do. Its possible effects upon other people have interested me very little. I have not written and published to please other people, but to satisfy myself, just as a cow gives milk, not to profit the dairyman, but to satisfy herself. I like to think that most of my ideas have been sound ones, but I really don't care. The world may take them or leave them. I have had my fun hatching them.

Next to agreeable work as a means of attaining happiness I put what Huxley called the domestic affections — the day to day intercourse with family and friends. My home has seen bitter sorrow, but it has never seen any serious disputes, and it has never seen poverty. I was completely happy with my mother and sister, and I am completely happy with my wife. Most of the men I commonly associate with are friends of very old standing. I have known some of them for more than thirty years. I seldom see anyone, intimately, whom I have known for less than ten years. These friends delight me. I turn to them when work is done with unfailing eagerness. We have the same general tastes, and see the world much alike. Most of them are interested in music, as I am. It has given me more pleasure in this life than any other external thing. I love it more every year.

As for religion, I am quite devoid of it. Never in my adult life have I experienced anything that could be plausibly called a religious impulse. My father and grandfather were agnostics before me, and though I was sent to Sunday-school as a boy and exposed to the Christian theology I was never taught to believe it. My father thought that I should learn what it was, but it apparently never occurred to him that I would accept it. He was a good psychologist. What I got in Sunday school — beside a wide acquaintance with Christian hymnology — was simply a firm conviction that the Christian faith was full of palpable absurdities, and the Christian God preposterous. Since that time I have read a great deal in theology — perhaps much more than the average clergyman — but I have never discovered any reason to change my mind.

The act of worship, as carried on by Christians, seems to me to be debasing rather than ennobling. It involves grovelling before a Being who, if He really exists, deserves to be denounced instead of respected. I see little evidence in this world of the so-called goodness of God. On the contrary, it seems to me that, on the strength of His daily acts, He must be set down a most stupid, cruel and villainous fellow. I can say this with a clear conscience, for He has treated me very well — in fact, with vast politeness. But I can't help thinking of his barbaric torture of most of the rest of humanity. I simply can't imagine revering the God of war and politics, theology and cancer.

I do not believe in immortality, and have no desire for it. The belief in it issues from the puerile egos of inferior men. In its Christian form it is little more than a device for getting revenge upon those who are having a better time on this earth. What the meaning of human life may be I don't know: I incline to suspect that it has none. All I know about it is that, to me at least, it is very amusing while it lasts. Even its troubles, indeed, can be amusing. Moreover, they tend to foster the human qualities that I admire most — courage and its analogues. The noblest man, I think, is that one who fights God, and triumphs over Him. I have had little of this to do. When I die I shall be content to vanish into nothingness. No show, however good, could conceivably be good forever.[15]

Mencken's life was nontheistic, to say the least. In contrast, most people have a large religious component in their world view. Whether you are religious or nonreligious, what you should keep in mind is the central importance of the meaning of life as it touches on moral questions. How a person exists depends on why the person exists.

VIRTUE — THE NATURE OF LEVEL III, STAGE 6 MORALITY

Moral evolution has followed a path from preconventional to postconventional ethics (level III, stage 6). Increasingly, people as individuals versus people as society have become the basis of moral judgments. The sentiment that "just because the majority of a group or society judge an act to be right or wrong does not make it so" reflects this orientation toward individual conscience (personal principles), as opposed to collective thought (community standards) or self-service (egocentric morality).[16]

At level III, stage 6 morality, a person's view of right and wrong depends on the meaning one attaches to personal existence, and this meaning is based on self-discovered and self-accepted values. This moral orientation is represented in the words of the American philosopher, Ram Dass:

> Everything must be seen through one's own microscope, and one has to reach one's own conclusions in one's own way. Until we do that, there is no Savior, no Guru, no blessings, and no guidance that could be of any help.[17]

This view is also the orientation of German writer Hermann Hesse's young Siddhartha, even after he had listened to the teachings of Buddha Gautama:

> Do not be angry with me, O Illustrious One," said the young man. "I have not spoken to you thus to quarrel with you about words. You are right when you say that opinions mean little, but may I say one thing more? I did not doubt you for one moment. Not for one moment did I doubt that you were the Buddha, that you have reached the highest goal that so many thousands of Brahmins and Brahmins' sons are striving to reach.
>
> You have done so by your own seeking, in your own way, through thought, through meditation, through knowledge, through enlightenment. You have learned nothing through teachings, and so I think, O Illustrious One, that nobody finds salvation through teachings. To nobody, O Illustrious One, can you communicate in words and teachings what happened to you in the hour of your enlightenment.
>
> The teachings of the enlightened Buddha embrace much, they teach much—how to live righteously, how to avoid evil. But there is one thing that this clear, worthy instruction does not contain; it does not contain the secret of what the Illustrious One himself experienced—he alone among hundreds of thousands.
>
> That is what I thought and realized when I heard your teachings. That is why I am going on my way—not to seek another and better doctrine, for I know there is none, but to leave all doctrines and all teachers and to reach my goal alone—or die. But I will often remember this day, O Illustrious One, and this hour when my eyes beheld a holy man."[18]

The following example depicts level III, stage 6 morality. It shows the importance for all people to determine their own moral principles, whether religious or secular, and to decide on ethical conduct in light of the meaning they attach to their own life. It also shows that an individual's actions are most virtuous when they proceed from the highest motives, utilize the best means, and achieve the best consequences. The absence of any one of these qualities will result in less than level III, stage 6 morality—and less than one's potential for moral virtue.

Statement of the Problem

Susan is an art student about to graduate from college. She is offered a position with a daily newspaper. The position pays well and she is interested in that type of employment, but in order to work on the newspaper staff, she must draw cartoons that express the sentiments of the paper's owners and managers, not her own sentiments or convictions. The paper is jingoistic and isolationist, whereas Susan wishes to promote international machinery for the peaceful settlement of disputes. The paper also stresses property rights, while Susan wishes to emphasize human rights. Should she accept the position?

How the Problem Is Handled

Susan is very pleased with the job offer. She feels that it is an honor and a compliment. But she does not accept at once. There are some questions in her mind that she wishes to think over. She begins to weigh the pros and cons. During this process, she talks with friends and consults a number of older people whose judgment she respects.

In favor of accepting the position, Susan reasons that it is a good position, it pays well, and she may not get another offer as good—in fact, no other position of this nature may be open in the near future. Furthermore, the position will give her experience and contacts, and she would like to take up this type of work as a profession.

When her friend, Donna, hears about the offer, she says, "Heck, Susan, you're in luck. Grab it while you can. Why in the world would you even hesitate?" Another friend adds, "What if you don't accept the position? Someone else will, so what's the difference?"

The older people with whom Susan talks are less simplistic in their advice. They suggest that she think the issues through carefully. While they are not all in agreement in the advice they offer, they do bring to light some aspects that Susan has not considered. Susan asks for an interview with the manager of the newspaper to gain more information about the position and what would be expected of her.

By this time, some of the arguments against accepting the offer are beginning to take shape in Susan's mind; most important is the fact that when working for the newspaper she must express and promote sentiments opposite to her own. This means that she will be promoting social attitudes and movements in which she does not believe. She asks, "What will this position do to me? Can I be successful in work that is promoting a cause in which I do not believe? Do I want my reputation and my influence to count on behalf of the issues I will be asked to promote?"

As Susan weighs the relative merits of the two courses of action, certain convictions emerge. First, if she accepts the position, she may not be able to throw all of her mind and heart into the work. Consequently, she is not likely to be as creative as she would be if she were promoting causes in which she believed. Second, if she does manage to throw her whole energy into the work, she will soon become a different type of person, with different sentiments and convictions. As her name becomes identified with causes, and as she forms friendships in these circles, the possibility of breaking away will be increasingly difficult. Wouldn't it be better, she reasons, to accept another position with a lower salary if need be and retain her personal integrity?

After a few days of uncertainty, Susan declines the offer and asks the placement bureau to keep her name on the active list for new openings.

Analysis

Motives. Susan's motives undoubtedly are good. She wants to do the right thing if she can discover it. This is evident in her approach to the problem and in the questions she asks as she considers the alternatives. Also, her desire to get a good position so that she may be able to earn a living and practice her profession is commendable. The problem centers around the means to be chosen and the general consequences to her and to society of the use of these means.

Means. The problem is handled by Susan in a highly moral way: (1) She thinks about the problem before making a decision. She makes a genuine and intelligent attempt to discover all of the relevant factors in the situation. As a result, her decision is made with more facts in mind than would have been the case otherwise. (2) She weighs the relative merits of the alternative possibilities. She judges the case on the basis of long-term considerations, not merely on the basis of immediate interests. (3) She takes into account the social effects of her decisions, not merely her personal interests. (4) She seeks advice from the people who she thinks may throw additional light on the problem. (5) The final decision is her own. It is made on the basis of principle and on the basis of her personal value system.

Consequences. The essence of level III, stage 6 morality is the ability and willingness to weigh all relevant facts in moral dilemmas and to base actions on the results of such reflection at the point of decision making. In Susan's case, time will tell the moral consequences of her decision. With the passage of time, the knowledge of the results of her actions may lead to new moral dilemmas and the necessity for new moral decisions.[19]

In summary, level III, stage 6 morality begins with good motives, is effected by good means, and results in good consequences. At this level and stage of morality, the saying that the ends justify the means is no more acceptable than to say the means justify the ends, or that good intentions are all one needs to assure good results. This is because any one of these qualities without the other two will result in inferior morality.

ILLUS. 2.4

Moral virtue is based on good motives, good means, and good consequences.

Photo courtesy of Good Samaritan Hospital in Cincinnati/Don Denney, Photographer

All three — motives, means, and consequences — are necessary ingredients of virtuous, level III, stage 6 morality.

To personalize this discussion, think about your own life and the moral dilemmas you face. Are your motives high-minded; are your means high-principled; are the consequences of your behavior ideal; does your moral behavior reflect the meaning you attach to your existence?

RECOMMENDED RESOURCES

The following readings, cases, and films are suggested for greater insight into the material in Part Two:

Readings — If Hitler Asked You to Electrocute a Stranger, Would You?
The Parable of the Sadhu
The Myth of Sisyphus

Cases — The Teacher in the Middle
A Doctor's Case

Films — Moral Development
Conformity and Independence
The Abilene Paradox

REFERENCE NOTES

1 John Locke, *An Essay Concerning Human Understanding*, 1690.

2 Media Services Department, Girl Scouts of the U.S.A., November, 1985.

3 *Boy Scouts of America: Handbook for Boys*, rev. (New York: 1931), 34–37.

4 Benjamin Franklin, *Poor Richard* (New York: Ballantine Books, 1977).

5 Ronald Duska and Mariellen Whelan, *Moral Development: A Guide to Piaget and Kohlberg* (New York: Paulist Press, 1975), 13.

6 Duska and Whelan, *Moral Development*, 42–79.

7 Duska and Whelan, *Moral Development*, 42–49; and Lawrence Kohlberg, "Cognitive-Development Approach to Moral Education," *The Humanist* (November-December 1972): 13–16; and Lawrence Kohlberg, "Stages of Moral Development as a Basis for Moral Education," in *Moral Education: Interdisciplinary Approaches*, eds. C. M. Beck, B. S. Crittenden, and E. V. Sullivan, Toronto: University of Toronto Press, 1971), 86–88; and Lawrence Kohlberg, "The Cognitive-Developmental Approach to Socialization," in *Handbook*

of Socialization Theory and Research, ed. D. A. Goslin (Chicago: Rand McNally & Company, 1969).

8 Lawrence Kohlberg, "The Development of Children's Orientations Toward a Moral Order: I. Sequence in the Development of Moral Thought," *Vita Humana* 6 (1963): 18–19.

9 Testimony of Adolph Eichmann (April 1961) at the Nuremberg War Trials, in Kohlberg, "The Cognitive-Developmental Approach to Socialization."

10 Mohandas Gandhi in his defense against a change of sedition, 23 March 1922, in Bartlett, *Famous Quotations*, 727.

11 Zick Rubin and Elton B. McNeil, *The Psychology of Being Human*, 3d ed. (New York: Harper & Row, Publishers, Inc., 1981), 324–25.

12 Dan Candee, "The Moral Psychology of Watergate, *Journal of Social Issues* 31, no. 2 (1975), 183–192.

13 Aristotle, *Metaphysics*, book 1, chap. 1.

14 Erich Fromm, *The Art of Loving* (New York: Bantam Books, Inc., 1963).

15 M. Lincoln Schuster (ed.), *The World's Great Letters* (New York: Simon and Schuster, 1940), 506–510.

16 Harold Titus and Morton Keeton, *Ethics for Today*, 5th ed. (New York: D. Van Nostrand Company, 1975), 42.

17 Ram Dass, "The Only Dance There Is," as found in Will Forpe and John C. McCollister, *The Sunshine Book: Expressions of Love, Hope and Inspiration* (Middle Village, N.Y.: Jonathan David Publishers, Inc., 1979), 48.

18 Hermann Hesse, *Siddhartha* (New York: Macmillan, Inc., 1962), 33–34.

19 Titus and Keeton, *Ethics for Today*, 102–104.

STUDY QUIZ

As a test of your understanding and the extent to which you have achieved the objectives in Part Two, complete the following questions. See Appendix E for the answer key.

1. The English philosopher John Locke believed the fate of each person is written at birth and that environmental experiences have little importance in the outcome of a person's life.

    a. true
    b. false

2. There are _____ Boy Scout Laws.

    a. 4
    b. 8
    c. 12
    d. none of the above

3. The concept of rules as sacred laws laid down by authorities is called:

    a. ontology
    b. heteronomy
    c. absolutism
    d. none of the above

4. Psychologist Lawrence Kohlberg has identified _____ levels and _____ stages of moral development.

    a. two, four
    b. four, eight
    c. three, six
    d. none of the above

5. Kohlberg believes that only _____ percent of the adult population operates consistently at the highest level and stage of moral development.

    a. 1 to 2
    b. 5 to 10
    c. 15 to 20
    d. 25 to 30

6. The statement "I will help you if you help me" is a reflection of level _____, stage _____ moral development.

    a. III, 5
    b. II, 4
    c. I, 2

7. The sentiment "Mine is not to question why; mine is just to do or die" reflects level _____, stage _____ moral development.

   a. III, 6
   b. I, 1
   c. II, 4

8. Human beings are the only creatures who:

   a. protect personal territory
   b. use signs and sounds to communicate
   c. question "Who am I and what is important?"
   d. sacrifice personal life to save another

9. In evaluating the morality of any act, the three critical factors are:

   a. time, place, person
   b. honesty, liberty, love
   c. motives, means, consequences
   d. none of the above

DISCUSSION QUESTIONS AND ACTIVITIES

The following questions and activities help personalize the subject. They are appropriate for classroom exercises and homework assignments.

1. What individuals and experiences have been important in your moral development? Who lit the fire? What was taught?

   _____
   _____
   _____

2. As you evaluate yourself, identify the level of morality at which you currently operate — I, II, or III. Give examples.

   _____
   _____
   _____

3. Have you experienced a need to find meaning in your life? Discuss.

   _____
   _____
   _____

4. Gather in small groups to discuss the individuals and forces affecting moral development in the world today. What level of morality is being taught? What values are being learned?

5. Consider an actual moral dilemma faced by one of the members of your discussion group. Analyze the dilemma according to motives, means, and consequences. Are the motives high-minded, the means high-principled, and the consequences positive? Does moral behavior reflect the meaning attached to personal existence?

PART THREE

Ethics and Work

Learning Objectives

After completing Part Three, you will better understand:

1. the influence of ethics on the individual and society;
2. the ethical orientations of organizations;
3. how social values influence moral behavior;
4. the role of leadership in shaping ethical behavior.

ETHICS AND MENTAL HEALTH

Whether based on religious belief or secular reason, a sense of right and wrong has long been recognized as an important element for the psychological health of the individual.

In the religious tradition, Swiss psychologist Carl Jung states that religion serves as a foundation for moral behavior, and that this foundation can be critical for mental health. According to Jung, people need to know what is right and that they themselves are good. Many discover the answers to these questions in the context of religious faith:

> Among all of my patients in the second half of life . . . every one of them fell ill because he had lost what the living religions of every age have given their followers, and none of them have been really healed who did not regain his religious outlook.

In the secular tradition, over 2,000 years before Sigmund Freud described the roles and relationships between the id, ego, and superego of the human personality, Plato recognized the importance of a three-way ethical struggle within the individual.

In *Dialogues,* Plato describes Reason as driving a chariot, the Soul, with arms straining to control two steeds, Spirit and Appetite, who often pull in opposite directions. The goal of Reason is to achieve balance between these two powerful internal forces in all human beings. Plato believed that only through Reason could one achieve the ethical ideal and become a good person.

Poet and philosopher Kahlil Gibran joins secular reason with religious faith, suggesting that human reason, given by God, is the best moral guide.

> When Reason speaks to you, hearken to what she says, and you shall be saved. Make good use of her utterances, and you shall be as one armed. For the Lord has given you no better guide than Reason, no stronger arm than Reason. When Reason speaks to your inmost self, you are proof against Desire. For Reason is a prudent minister, a loyal guide, and a wise counsellor. Reason is light in darkness, as anger is darkness amidst light. Be wise—let Reason, not Impulse, be your guide.

The insecurity and hesitancy that typically is a part of the anxious personality can have its roots in moral behavior. If people fail to freely choose and publicly act on their values, thereby suffering axiological arrest, they tend toward guilt and feelings of inferiority. Gradually, they isolate themselves from social involvement, and ultimately, they lose their emotional health. Ethics plays a central role in mental health.

ETHICS AND SOCIETY

All societies develop ethics based on social custom. Such group morality helps preserve shared values. Almost universal among societies are the customary negative values or taboos—neglect and cruelty toward children, treachery toward family and community, and murder (especially of one's family or community members). Other behaviors almost universally valued include parental care, respect for other people, and some control of sexuality (among all societies, there are customs regarding relations between the sexes, marriage, and family).[1] Physical circumstances also influence a society's values.

To better understand these concepts, consider the ancient Eskimo culture in which lasting economic partnerships between males result in mutual support and sharing, even of mates. The higher need for economic survival over marital fidelity in a scarce environment helps explain the practice of lending one's wife to one's partner whose own wife has died or is ill.[2] Thus, an act considered right in one society may be considered wrong in another; the conventional morality of an act is determined by how closely it reflects social custom; social customs are based on shared values; and the values of a society may depend on physical circumstances.

Describing the importance of social custom and group morality, anthropologist Bronislaw Malinowski writes of the Trobriand Islanders:

> The savages have a class of obligatory rules not endowed with any mystical character, not set forth "in the name of God," not enforced by any supernatural sanction, but provided with a purely social binding force.

ILLUS. 3.1

Accepted customs in one society may not be acceptable in another.

THE BETTMANN ARCHIVE, INC.

The inert and uncritical way in which these rules are obeyed may be due to the general "conformism of savages" as we might call it. But in the mean, these rules are followed because their practical utility is recognized by reason and testified by experience.

Also, injunctions of how to behave in associating with friends, relatives, superiors, equals, and so on, are obeyed, because any deviation from them makes a man feel and look, in the eyes of others, ridiculous, clumsy, and socially uncouth.

There are precepts of good manners, very developed in Melanesia and most strictly adhered to. There are further rules laying down the proceedings at games, sports, entertainments, and festivities, rules that are the soul and substance of the amusement or pursuit, and are kept because it is felt and recognized that any failure to "play the game" spoils it.[3]

As further illustration of the role of social custom in moral behavior, consider what the chiefs of Tahiti told the English explorer Captain James Cook when he asked why the men ate apart from the women. They looked at him in wonder and disbelief at such a foolish question. They thought and thought, and then they announced, "Because it is right."[4]

The following list of recommended etiquette shows how social customs can influence business practices today.

Guide to Foreign Gifts

- Don't rely on your own taste.

- Don't bring a gift to an Arab man's wife; in fact, don't ask about her at all. Bringing gifts for the children is, however, acceptable.

- In Arab countries, don't admire an object openly; the owner may feel obligated to give it to you.

- Do not bring liquor to an Arab home.

- Don't try to outgive the Japanese. It causes great embarrassment and obligates them to reciprocate even if they cannot afford to do so.

- Do not insist that your Japanese counterpart open the gift in your presence. This is not their custom and can easily cause the recipient embarrassment.

- Hold your gift with two hands when presenting it to a Japanese business person, but don't make a big thing of the presentation.

- Be careful when selecting colors or deciding on the number of items. The color purple, for example, is inappropriate in Latin America because it is associated with Lent.

- Avoid giving knives or handkerchiefs in Latin America. Knives suggest the cutting off of the relationship, and handkerchiefs imply that you wish the recipient hardship. To offset the bad luck, the recipient must offer you money.

- In West Germany, red roses imply that you are in love with the recipient. Also, perfume is too personal a gift for business relationships.

- In the People's Republic of China, expensive presents are not acceptable and cause great embarrassment. Give a collective gift from your company to theirs.

- In China, a banquet is acceptable, but you will insult your hosts if you give a more lavish banquet than the one they have given you.[5]

Whether ethics are based on secular reason or religious beliefs, they are important to the health and survival of society. Through ethics, people reconcile the rights and goals of the individual with the rights and goals of the group.

As long ago as the 12th century B.C., King Hammurabi wrote a secular code of ethics for the people of Babylon. His legislation dealt with matters such as accusations, witnesses and judges, military laws, injuries, rents, and slaves.[6]

Similarly, the secular ethics of Confucianism, founded on "right relationships," have guided Chinese culture for over 2,400 years. Right relationships include:

- kindness in a father, filial piety in a son;

- gentleness in an elder brother, obedience in a younger;

- righteousness in a husband, submission in a wife;

- kindness in elders, deference in juniors;

- benevolence in a ruler, loyalty in a minister.[7]

In *Analects,* Confucius wrote, "The way of the superior man is threefold . . . virtuous, he is free from anxieties; wise, he is free from perplexities; bold, he is free from fear."[8]

As recently as 1961, the Communist Party of the Soviet Union authorized and published a secular code of ethics. This code has 12 principles by which all citizens should live:

Moral Code of the Builder of Communism

The party holds that the moral code of the builder of communism should comprise the following principles:

Devotion to the communist cause; love of the socialist motherland and of other socialist countries.

Conscientious labor for the good of society — he who does not work, neither shall he eat.

Concern on the part of everyone for the preservation and growth of public wealth.

A high degree of public duty; intolerance of actions harmful to the public interest.

Collectivism and comradeship with mutual assistance; one for all and all for one.

(continued)

Moral Code of the Builder of
Communism — continued

> Human relations and mutual respect between individuals — man is to man a friend, comrade, and brother.
>
> Honesty and truthfulness, moral purity, modesty, and unpretentiousness in social and private life.
>
> Mutual respect in the family and concern for the upbringing of children.
>
> An uncompromising attitude to injustice, parasitism, dishonesty, careerism, and money-grubbing.
>
> Friendship and brotherhood among all peoples of the USSR; intolerance of national and racial hatred.
>
> An uncompromising attitude to the enemies of communism, peace, and the freedom of nations.
>
> Fraternal solidarity with the working people of all countries, and with all peoples.[9]

Ethics in the religious tradition have also been important in the societies of both the Eastern and Western world. A major influence in Eastern culture has been the teaching of Siddhartha Gautama of the Sakyas (Buddha), born 563 B.C. Buddha prescribed an ethical ideal that would free people from suffering, sorrow, pain, disease, loneliness, and death. In his sermon, the "Dharmacakrapravartanasutra" (Discourse on the Turning of the Wheel of the Law), Buddha taught "Four Noble Truths" and a "Noble Eight-Fold Path." These teachings, discovered through "Enlightenment," form the spiritual and ethical beliefs of over 295 million people today.[10] The Four Noble Truths are:

- All individual existence leads to misery;
- The cause of this misery is Desire;
- Freedom is only possible through Passionlessness;
- The way to freedom is found through the Noble Eight-Fold Path.

The Noble Eight-Fold Path includes the following principles:

- Right views — knowing that the destruction of suffering comes from the elimination of capital desire:

- Right goals — aspiring to love and service and the attainment of pure spirituality;

- Right speech — to be truthful, kind and humble, never harsh, gossiping, or slanderous;

- Right actions — to avoid killing, stealing, unchastity, lying, intoxication, envy, anger, the love of money, and laziness;

- Right livelihood — one must never harm another living creature in order for oneself to live;

- Right character — to be in control of oneself;

- Right meditation — to think purely;

- Right contemplation—leading to Nirvana, the highest possible state of being.[11]

Another example of religious ethics is Hinduism. This religion teaches that a good person lives according to "Ten Great Virtues"—contentment, truthfulness, purity, self-control, suppression of sensual appetite, respect for the property of others, wisdom, knowledge of the supreme soul, avoidance of anger, and forgiveness.[12]

One of the most important influences on the ethics of the Western world was the Hebrew prophet Moses, who presented the Ten Commandments as well as the Pentateuch (the biblical books of Genesis, Exodus, Leviticus, Numbers, and Deuteronomy) to the Israelites approximately 1446 B.C.[13] This religious code of ethics serves as the primary basis of Judeo-Christian morality even to this day:

1. I am your God, who brought you out of the land of Egypt, out of the house of slaves.

2. You shall have no other gods besides me. You shall not make unto you a graven image of God nor any manner of likeness, that is in heaven above and the earth beneath and that is in the water under the earth. You shall not bow down unto them, nor serve them. For I, your God, am a jealous God, visiting the iniquity of the fathers upon the children, even to the third and fourth

ILLUS. 3.2

Ethics in religion is important in both the Eastern and Western worlds.

UN Photo

generation of them who hate me; but showing love to the thousandth of them who love me and keep my commandments.

3. You shall not take the name of your God for an unworthy purpose; for I will not leave unpunished one who takes my name for an unworthy purpose.

4. Remember the Sabbath day to keep it holy. Six days shall you labor and do all your work. But the seventh day is a Sabbath for your God. You shall not do any manner of work, nor your son, nor your daughter, nor your manservant, nor your maidservant, nor any of your cattle, nor your sojourner, who is within your gates. For in six days, I made heaven and earth, the sea, and all that in them is, and I rested on the seventh day. Therefore, I have blessed the Sabbath day and hallowed it.

5. Honor your father and your mother, that your days may be long upon the land which your God gives to you.

6. You shall not murder.

7. You shall not commit adultery.

8. You shall not steal.

9. You shall not bear false witness against your neighbor.

10. You shall not covet your neighbor's house. You shall not covet your neighbor's wife, nor his manservant, nor his maidservant, nor his ox, nor his ass, nor anything that belongs to your neighbor.[14]

THE ETHICAL RELATIONSHIP BETWEEN THE INDIVIDUAL AND SOCIETY

Are ethics important to society today? Rocket and space scientist Wernher von Braun best answers this question:

> Today, more than ever before, our survival—yours, mine, and our childrens'—depends upon our adherence to ethical principles. Ethics alone will decide whether atomic energy will be an earthly blessing or the source of mankind's utter destruction.

Are ethics important to individuals today? Erich Fromm states:

> People can adapt themselves to slavery, but they react to it by lowering their intellectual and moral qualities. They can adapt themselves to a culture permeated by mutual distrust and hostility, but they react to this adaptation by becoming weak and sterile. People can adapt themselves to cultural conditions that demand the repression of sexual strivings, but in achieving this adaptation they develop, as Freud has shown, neurotic systems. They can adapt themselves to almost any cultural pattern, but insofar as they are contradictory to human nature, they develop mental and emotional disturbances that force them eventually to change these conditions, since they cannot change their nature.[15]

Winston Churchill's words during World War II show the ethical relationship between the individual and society:

> The destiny of mankind is not decided by material computation. When great causes are on the move in the world . . . we learn that we are spirits, not animals, and that something is going on in space and time, and beyond space and time, which, whether we like it or not, spells duty.

The extent to which the citizens of England responded to duty during World War II was the measure to which they felt a moral obligation toward the greater good of society, and this was an expression of individual ethics.

ETHICS "AT WORK" YESTERDAY AND TODAY

History has witnessed a changing definition of the meaning of work. To the ancient Greeks who had slaves to do it, work was a curse. The Hebrews saw work as punishment. The early Christians found work for profit offensive, but by the time of St. Thomas Aquinas, work was being praised as a natural right and a duty — a source of grace along with learning and contemplation. During the Reformation, work became the only way of serving God. Luther pronounced that conscientious performance of one's labor was man's highest duty. Later interpretations of Calvinistic doctrine gave religious sanction to worldly wealth and achievement. This belief, when wedded to Social Darwinism and laissez-faire liberalism, became the foundation for what we call the Protestant ethic. Marx, however, took the concept of work and put it in an even more central position in life: freed from capitalist exploitation, work would become a joy as workers improved the material around them.[16] Today, in the now-classic study, *Work in America*, work is defined as any activity that produces something of value for other people.[17]

Ethics at work depend on work perspectives. If work is viewed as a punishment or duty, moral rules may only minimize the burden. If work is viewed as a human right and joyous opportunity, moral rules may accentuate avenues of reward.

Ethics have been important in the work setting since at least 2700–2200 B.C. During that period, Egyptian labor was called forth by devotion to the Pharaoh. The people believed their king was a god and thus deserving of a supreme offering of energies; to do right was to work in service to the Pharaoh.[18] The following is testimony to the early Egyptian's concern for right conduct at work:

> On a rough tablet of chalk in the British Museum, a chief workman has written down the names of his forty-three workmen and, by each name, the days of the month on which the man failed to appear. Many were of exemplary industry, and rarely missed a day throughout the year;

less confidence could be placed in others, who failed more than a fortnight. Numberless are the excuses for the missing days, which the chief workman has written down in red ink: the commonest is of course illness; in a few instances we find lazy noted down; a few workmen are pious and "are sacrificing to the god"; sometimes a slight indisposition of wife or daughter is considered a valid reason for neglect of work.[19]

In more recent history, Amasa Whitney's factory rules, published in 1830, reflect the work ethics of nineteenth-century America. Figure 3.1 contains these rules.

Today, the U.S. government has numerous laws that reflect moral values and govern the actions of organizations. Examples of major federal laws concerning employee relations are presented in Figure 3.2.

Social philosopher and management consultant Peter Drucker suggests that once an organization reaches the size of 1,000 employees, internal work rules should be developed to maximize efficiency and serve as a guide for employee conduct.[20] Such a code of conduct can be an important determinant of the nature, reputation, and success of the organization.

The best work rules meet the following criteria: they reflect the ethical ideals of the ownership, or, in the case of public organizations, the public trust; they are reviewed periodically for needed revisions; they are few

ILLUS. 3.3, 3.4

The most effective work rules apply to all employees regardless of position.

USDA photo by Earl Otis

FIGURE 3.1
Ethics at Work

RULES & REGULATIONS
To Be Observed By All Persons Employed In The Factory Of
AMASA WHITNEY

FIRST: The Mill will be put into operation 10 minutes before sunrise at all seasons of the year. The gate will be shut 10 minutes past sunset from the 20th of March to the 20th of September, at 30 minutes past 8 from the 20th of September to the 20th of March, Saturdays at sunset.

SECOND: It will be required of every person employed, that they be in the room in which they are employed, at the time mentioned above for the mill to be in operation.

THIRD: Hands are not allowed to leave the factory in working hours without the consent of their Overseer. If they do, they will be liable to have their time set off.

FOURTH: Anyone who by negligence or misconduct causes damage to the machinery, or impedes the progress of the work, will be liable to make good the damage for the same.

FIFTH: Anyone employed for a certain length of time, will be expected to make up their lost time, if required, before they will be entitled to their pay.

SIXTH: Any person employed for no certain length of time, will be required to give at least 4 weeks notice of their intention to leave (sickness excepted) or forfeit 4 weeks pay, unless by particular agreement.

SEVENTH: Anyone wishing to be absent any length of time, must get permission of the Overseer.

EIGHTH: All who have leave of absence for any length of time will be expected to return in that time; and, in case they do not return in that time and do not give satisfactory reason, they will be liable to forfeit one week's work or less, if they commence work again. If they do not, they will be considered as one who leaves without giving any notice.

NINTH: Anything tending to impede the progress of manufacturing in working hours, such as unnecessary conversation, reading, eating fruit, &c.&c., must be avoided.

TENTH: While I shall endeavor to employ a judicious Overseer, the help will follow his direction in all cases.

ELEVENTH: No smoking will be allowed in the factory, as it is considered very unsafe, and particularly specified in the Insurance.

TWELFTH: In order to forward the work, job hands will follow the above regulations as well as those otherwise employed.

THIRTEENTH: It is intended that the bell be rung 5 minutes before the gate is hoisted, so that all persons may be ready to start their machines precisely at the time mentioned.

FOURTEENTH: All persons who cause damage to the machinery, break glass out of the windows, &c., will immediately inform the Overseer of the same.

FIFTEENTH: The hands will take breakfast, from the 1st of November to the last of March, before going to work — they will take supper from the 1st of May to the last of August, 30 minutes past 5 o'clock P.M. — from the 20th of September to the 20th of March between sundown and dark — 25 minutes will be allowed for breakfast, 30 minutes for dinner, and 25 minutes for supper, and no more from the time the gate is shut till started again.

SIXTEENTH: The hands will leave the Factory so that the doors may be fastened within 10 minutes from the time of leaving off work.

Source: Amasa Whitney, "Rules and Regulations," Winchendon, Mass., 5 July 1830.

FIGURE 3.2

U.S. Work Laws Concerning Employee Relations

Federal Law	Description
1. U.S. Constitution: 1st, 5th, and 14th Amendments	Prohibits deprivation of employment rights without due process of law—federal, state, and local governments.
2. Civil Rights Act of 1866 and 1870	Prohibits race discrimination in hiring, placement, and continuation of employment for private employers, unions, and employment agencies.
3. Title VI, 1964 Civil Rights Act	Prohibits discrimination based on race, color, or national origin—employers receiving federal financial assistance.
4. Title VII, 1964 Civil Rights Act	Prohibits discrimination based on race, color, religion, sex, or national origin—private employers; federal, state, and local governments; unions; employment agencies.
5. Executive Orders 11246 and 11375 (1965)	Prohibits discrimination based on race, color, religion, sex, or national origin (affirmative action)—federal contractors and subcontractors.
6. Title I, 1968 Civil Rights Act	Prohibits interference with a person's exercise of rights with respect to race, religion, color, or national origin.
7. National Labor Relations Act	Prohibits unfair representation by unions that discriminate on the basis of race, color, religion, sex, or national origin.
8. Equal Pay Act of 1963	Prohibits sex differences in pay for equal work—private employers.
9. Age Discrimination in Employment Act of 1967 and 1975	Prohibits age discrimination against those between the ages of 40 and 65 years—all employers.
10. Rehabilitation Act of 1973	Prohibits discrimination based on physical or mental handicap (affirmative action).

FIGURE 3.2—*continued*

11.	Vietnam Era Veterans Readjustment Act of 1974	Prohibits discrimination against disabled veterans and Vietnam era veterans (affirmative action).
12.	Occupational Safety and Health Act (OSHA—1970)	Established mandatory safety and health standards in organizations.
13.	Revised Guidelines on Employee Selection (1976)	Established specific rules on employment selection practices.
14.	Mandatory Retirement Act	Employee cannot be forced to retire before age 70.
15.	Privacy Act of 1974	Employees have legal right to examine letters of reference concerning them unless they waive the right.

Source: Andrew D. Szilagyi, Management and Performance *(Santa Monica, Calif.: Goodyear Publishing, 1981), 335.*

in number; they are stated clearly; they are communicated to all employees; they apply equally to all employees, regardless of level of authority or nature of duties.

By using these criteria as guidelines, an organization can achieve five important business and social goals: (1) obtain high standards of performance at all levels of the work force; (2) reduce anxiety and confusion over what is acceptable employee conduct; (3) meet the needs of employees to operate as freely as possible yet remain within a prescribed range of ethical behavior; (4) avoid double standards that undermine employee morale and productivity; and (5) develop an image that is consistent with the organization's ideals.

A comprehensive code of ethics for an organization includes guidelines in each of the following areas:

- Government relations — how does the organization pay its taxes and obey national and international law?

- Employee relations — how does the organization deal with employee welfare and grievances?

- Community and environmental relations — what are the effects of the organization on its social and physical environment?

- Business relations — how does the organization deal with suppliers and competitors?

- Production — what are the standards of quality for the organization's products and services?

- Consumer relations—how does the organization price and advertise its products and services?

In his influential book *Vanguard Management*, James O'Toole identifies the key characteristics of ethical and successful organizations.

- They try to satisfy all of their constituencies—customers, employees, owners, suppliers, dealers, special interest groups, communities, and governments. They subscribe to the utilitarian ideal, the greatest good for the greatest number.
- They are dedicated to high and broad purposes. Profit is viewed as an essential means to a higher end—human service and quality of life.
- They are committed to learning, investing enormous resources and effort to remaining current and responsive to change. They view employee growth and development as a critical foundation of business success.
- They try to be the best at whatever they do. Their performance standards rise continually. Excellence in product and service is an organization-wide commitment and source of pride.[21]

O'Toole goes on to identify the basic rules all excellent organizations seem to have in one form or another.

- Obey the law
- Tell the truth
- Show respect for people
- Follow the Golden Rule
- Primum non nocere ("above all, do no harm," the first rule of medical ethics)
- Practice participation, not paternalism (democracy at work)
- Always act when you have the responsibility to do so[22]

ETHICAL ORIENTATIONS OF ORGANIZATIONS

In dealing with moral dilemmas such as people, products, prices, and profits, organizations typically reflect one of three ethical orientations: (1) profit maximizing; (2) trusteeship; or (3) quality of life management. The following exercise presents a description of each orientation on 14 ethical dimensions. As you complete the exercise, you will see how different ethical orientations influence moral judgments and result in different experiences for employees, customers, and citizens. As you read the descriptions, ask yourself, "What type of organization do you respect; what type of organization do you have; and what can you do to influence the ethics of your organization?"[23]

Ethics at Work: Fire in a Dark World

ORGANIZATIONAL ETHICS

Directions

Evaluate your organization by circling the most descriptive response for each of the fourteen ethical dimensions.

Ethical Dimension	Profit Maximizing	Trusteeship	Quality of Life Management
1. Social definition of good:	What is good for me is what counts.	What is good for my organization is what counts.	What is good for humankind is good for my organization, and ultimately is best for me.
2. Democracy at work:	I am a rugged individualist and will do as I please.	I am an individualist, but I recognize the value of employee participation in the decision-making process.	Democratic management is fundamental to a successful organization.
3. Attitudes toward profit:	I seek as much profit as the market will bear.	I want a substantial profit.	Profit is necessary, but not to the exclusion of other considerations that influence human welfare.
4. Attitude toward wealth:	My wealth is more important than other people's feelings.	Money is important, but so are people.	Other people's needs are more important than my wealth.
5. Labor relations:	Labor is a commodity to be bought and sold.	Labor has certain rights that must be recognized.	It is essential to preserve employee dignity, even if profit is reduced.
6. Consumer protection:	Let the buyer beware.	Let us not cheat the customer.	Customer welfare comes first; satisfaction guaranteed.
7. Self-interest versus altruism:	My interest comes first.	Self-interest and the interest of others are considered.	I will always do what is in the best interest of all concerned.
8. Employee relations:	Employee personal problems must be left at home.	I recognize that employees have needs and goals beyond economics.	I employ the whole person and am concerned with achieving maximum employee welfare.
9. Management accountability:	Management is accountable solely to the owners.	Accountability of management is to the owners, customers, employees, and suppliers.	Accountability of management is to owners, customers, employees, suppliers, and society in general.

Ethical Dimension	Profit Maximizing	Trusteeship	Quality of Life Management
10. Attitude toward technology:	Progress is more important than people's feelings.	Technology is important, but so are people.	Human needs are more important than technology advances.
11. Minority relations:	Minorities have their place in society, but not with me.	Some people are more important than others, and they should be treated accordingly.	Everyone—regardless of age, color, creed, or sex—should be treated equally.
12. Attitude toward government:	Government is best when it stays out of my way.	Government is a necessary evil.	Business and government should work together to solve society's problems.
13. Human/environment interface:	The environment exists for economic ends.	People should control and manipulate the environment.	People must preserve the environment for the highest quality of life.
14. Aesthetic values:	Aesthetic values? What are they?	Aesthetic values are okay, but not to the exclusion of economic needs.	Aesthetic values must be preserved, even if economic costs are increased.

Source: Robert Hay and Ed Gray, "Social Responsibilities of Business Managers," *Academy of Management Journal* 18, no. 1 (March 1974): 142.

SCORING

Assign a score of 1 to each *profit maximizing* response, a 2 to each *trusteeship* response, and a 3 to each *quality of life management* response. Add the total and enter here: _____.

INTERPRETATION

The terms *profit maximizing, trusteeship,* and *quality of life management* roughly correlate with Kohlberg's levels of morality—I, II, III. Profit maximizing reflects preconventional morality. In this case, the organization's focus is on individual gain and avoiding punishment. Trusteeship reflects conventional morality, wherein the organization behaves to conform to the expectations of others and to satisfy higher authorities. Quality of life management reflects postconventional morality. Here, the orientation of the organization is to do what is right over and above self-interest and apart from the views of others. With this orientation, ethical conduct is based on the highest moral principles.

Scores	Level of Morality
14–23	Profit maximizing—level I, preconventional

✓ 24–32   Trusteeship—level II, conventional
✓ 33–42   Quality of life management—level III, postconventional

The question may be asked, "Is the price an organization pays too high when it operates under a quality-of-life-management philosophy? Won't such an organization fail in competition with rough-riding, profit-maximizing organizations?" Research does not bear this out. Data show a positive and significant relationship between the ethical orientation of organizations and the level of profit. The higher the orientation, the higher the level of profit when computed over a period of years.[24]

Why? Perhaps the answer is in the character of the work force. Most people are attracted to what they consider good and right and are repulsed by what they see as bad and wrong. In a free society, people are allowed to work where they wish and employers are allowed to employ whom they wish. Individuals and organizations with high ethical orientations attract each other and then, as one, focus on the achievement of a common business mission. Important parties outside of the organization take note of this and elect such principled organizations over unprincipled organizations because they genuinely respect, trust, and like them. Employees want to work for them, other businesses want to deal with them, government officials want to support them, and customers want to buy from them. In one word, they have a positive reputation.

SOCIAL VALUES

Ethical judgments in business are based in part on social values, and social values differ among individuals. The following questionnaire is designed to help you evaluate your own social values on a continuum between self-concern and concern for others. This exercise is especially helpful for clarifying values in the workplace.

SOCIAL VALUES CONTINUUM— WHO IS IMPORTANT TO YOU?

Directions

Read through the following situations and check the response you most prefer. Assume that no other alternatives are available.

1. You are a young business consultant who has recently completed an expensive study for a company, and you know you can offer no more service of value to your client. However, your superiors feel the company can afford more research. You would:

   ____ A. plan as many studies as the company can afford

   ____ B. plan a few more projects

    ____ C. plan one more small project to satisfy your superiors

    ____ D. plan another project, but stall so the company will reject it

    ____ E. tell your superiors that a new study is not warranted

2. You are a financial officer of a manufacturing firm. You learn that the company's representatives are routinely bribing distributors to push the firm's products. You tell the chief executive officer that unless the payoffs cease you will quit. The chief executive knows all about it and says the bribes will continue. You would:

    ____ A. forget about it

    ____ B. seek the opinion of other employees before deciding your course of action

    ____ C. start looking for another job quietly

    ____ D. attempt to convince the chief executive, but not offer to quit

    ____ E. quit

3. You are asked to help find a replacement for an employee, a personal friend of yours, who is to be demoted. Your boss has requested the action be kept secret, but your friend wants to know what is happening. In this personal struggle, you would:

    ____ A. say nothing and find the replacement

    ____ B. say nothing, but stall on finding a replacement

    ____ C. arrange for your friend to discover the truth without your saying anything and stall on finding a replacement

    ____ D. tell your friend the truth

    ____ E. refuse to participate

4. As an employee of a company, you would occasionally take home:

    ____ A. items worth $25 or less

    ____ B. items worth $10 or less

    ____ C. items worth a dollar or so

    ____ D. items worth less than a dollar

    ____ E. nothing

5. You are a purchasing agent for a large firm. One day during a conversation with a product representative, you are asked if you will purchase a needed product from the agent's company with the implication that it will be well worth your while. In this situation, you would:

    ____ A. ask, "How worthwhile?"

    ____ B. say you will think about it

_____ C. imply that you are interested and leave the conversation open

_____ D. frown and ignore the comment

_____ E. say no and explain your position

6. You are a traveling salesperson with an expense account of $100 per day, but you seldom spend that much. The company does not require proof of all expenses, so hedging is possible. You would:

_____ A. report expenses for each day that total $100 whether factual or not

_____ B. report expenses for most days that total $100 whether factual or not

_____ C. add expenses to your account on occasion

_____ D. report only your actual expenses

_____ E. report only those expenses you can prove

7. You are a butcher and you suspect your company is selling horse meat to some companies as ingredients in canned goods for human consumption. As the butcher, you would:

_____ A. not get involved

_____ B. discuss the matter with other employees

_____ C. learn who your company sells horse meat to, but you are not sure what you will do about it

_____ D. confront and encourage your boss to correct the problem

_____ E. if your company does not stop the practice, inform regulating agencies and the general public

8. A large shipment of typewriters was sent to the warehouse where you are employed as receiving clerk. You discover the inventory is three short. You are almost certain they have been taken by company employees or by your boss. No one else has access to the warehouse. You would:

_____ A. do nothing

_____ B. be concerned, but if nothing happens after a week, forget it

_____ C. report the loss to your boss and let him handle it

_____ D. tell your boss and watch everyone very closely

_____ E. get actively involved (send a memo to all company personnel and see if anyone "suddenly" locates the missing typewriters)

9. As the personnel officer, you have been told that the company you work for will be closing in three months, but the company's management

does not want to make it public. Several members of the Chamber of Commerce have asked about the rumor. They do not want to spend thousands of dollars remodeling the shopping center if your company is moving. You would:

___ A. tell them nothing

___ B. suggest they contact you in a few weeks

___ C. suggest they see the company president

___ D. hint that there may be a move

___ E. answer their questions honestly, and then inform management

10. A co-worker, Beth, has revealed to you that she has been taking $5 to $10 now and then from the cash register. She has been doing this for over a year and has never been caught or suspected. You would:

___ A. do the same

___ B. tell her you do not want to know about it

___ C. ask her if she feels that it is right

___ D. tell her it is dishonest and you believe she should tell the supervisor

___ E. pressure her to tell the supervisor and replace the stolen money

Source: Marianne Bailey and Naomi Miller, Northern Kentucky University, 1983–1984.

SCORING AND INTERPRETATION

Record your answers to each of the ten situations on the following scale. If you answered "A" for the first one, put a check mark in the "A" area. If you answered "C" for the second one, put a check mark in the "C" area, and so on, until you have recorded ten check marks on the line. Your marks reveal how you rate on a continuum of social values between self-concern and concern for others. The more check marks you have in A and B, the more inclined you are to act in self-interest in moral situations; the more check marks you have in D and E, the more inclined you are to act in the interest of others. Consider whether this rating is satisfactory to you, and whether you are reflecting this in your dealings with others — at work and at home.

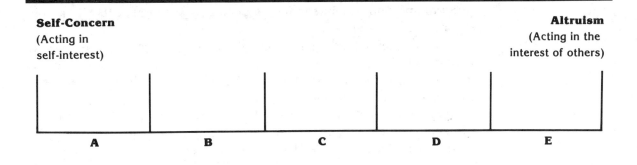

Self-Concern					Altruism
(Acting in self-interest)					(Acting in the interest of others)
A	B	C	D	E	

ETHICS AND LEADERSHIP— WHO LIGHTS THE FIRE?

Many people look toward leaders for moral guidance. This tendency is universal in young people and common among adults. It also reflects the importance of ethics for those in leadership positions, whether in organizations—such as supervisors, managers, and owners—or in society—such as parents, teachers, and government officials.

<u>Subordinates will forgive the leader who fails to manage by objectives, or is inefficient in the use of time, or fails to achieve the smoothest human relations; but subordinates will not forgive the leader who is</u>

ILLUS. 3.5

What the leader says and does sets the standard of conduct for the employees.

immoral and nonprincipled. Such a person lacks moral authority and is not trusted or respected.

Every leader should have a code of conduct that serves as a compass to guide and judge behavior. By having such a code, the leader can ask of any act, "Is it right and to what extent?" Concern over ethical questions is a mark of leadership.

What a leader says and does in the sphere of morality has enormous influence on those who follow. More than any memo, directive, or brass band, the actions of the leader communicate.

> Within any group, a sequence is set in motion by the behavior of the group's supervisor. The leader's actions toward subordinates set the tone for their behavior toward one another and for their performance on the job. An effective supervisor accomplishes, through personal behavior, the building of a group oriented toward cooperative accomplishment of the task or mission.[25]

Because of the ability to influence moral behavior, the leader in the work setting should continually address two questions: (1) What standards of conduct do I wish to promote? (2) Are my actions helping to accomplish this? The chart in Figure 3.3 shows the relationship between what the leader says, what the subordinate hears, and the behavior this promotes.

FIGURE 3.3

What You Do . . . Is What You Get

When the leader says . . .	the subordinate hears . . .	and the value or behavior that is promoted is . . .
"Get back to me if you run into any problems."	"I don't expect you to handle trouble alone."	Helpfulness
"How can we fit this order into the schedule?"	"I value your opinion."	Respect
"You look like you need a break."	"I care about your welfare."	Concern
"I'm sorry you were ill."	"You were missed."	Self-worth
"If that machine keeps breaking down, we'll order a new one."	"You can count on me to get what you need to do your job."	Dependability
"I really made a mistake on that one."	"I admit it when I am wrong."	Honesty
"How can you prevent that from happening again?"	"You are mature enough to correct your own errors."	Growth
"Although your proposal was seen as too costly by top management, they were impressed. Keep up the good work."	"I thought highly enough of the suggestion to send it upstairs."	Creativity

FIGURE 3.3—*continued*

When the leader says...	the subordinate hears...	and the value or behavior that is promoted is...
"I like the way you took time to help Alice finish that project."	"I value teamwork."	Cooperation
"How would you compare the new procedure with the old one?"	"If the change is giving you problems, tell me."	Communications
"I just heard sales topped last year by 20 percent."	"I think you want to know what's going on."	Productivity
"I have a personal problem I would like to share with you."	"I know you won't use what I tell you to harm me."	Trust
"You look upset."	"I'm available to listen if you want to talk."	Morale
"Thanks to your unit's work, we've improved efficiency by one and one-fourth hours."	"I know you want to hear how well you are doing."	Pride

Source: Marianne Bailey and Doreen Winters, Northern Kentucky University, 1982.

WORK-FORCE VALUES AND LEADERSHIP ACTIONS

Directions

If you were a work-group supervisor, what strong central values would you promote? What behaviors would you demonstrate to teach and reinforce these values? List work-force values you support in column 1; list leadership behaviors that reinforce these values in column 2.

Work-Force Values	Leadership Actions
_____	_____
_____	_____
_____	_____
_____	_____
_____	_____
_____	_____
_____	_____

DISCUSSION

What are the implications of your values and actions? Consider their expected impact on the quality of work and the quality of work life in your organization.

STYLES OF LEADERSHIP

The type of leadership an organization has determines its moral culture. Harold Leavitt of the graduate school of business at Stanford University describes three leadership styles: implementer, problem solver, and pathfinder. See Figure 3.4.

FIGURE 3.4

<u>Leadership Styles</u>

	Implementer	Problem Solver	Pathfinder
Key word	Action	Analysis	Mission
Profile	Highly social, emotional, fast moving.	Logical, rational, casts an intellectually reserved shadow.	Impractical, stubborn, ignores the rules, acts impulsively.
Managerial objective	To persuade, command, manipulate.	To determine the right answers.	To determine the right questions.
Archetypal professions	Direct sales, lobbying, law.	Engineering, accounting, systems analysis.	The arts, theoretical science, entrepreneurship.
Archetypal personalities	Dale Carnegie, Mary Kay Ash, George Patton.	Harold Geneen, Roy Ash, Cardinal Richelieu.	Steven Jobs, Golda Meir, Florence Nightingale, Napoleon.
Archetypal quotes	"I'd rather have him inside the tent pissing out than outside pissing in." Lyndon Baines Johnson.	"Stop! Slide number 105 contradicts slide number 6." Robert McNamara.	"I have a dream." Martin Luther King, Jr.

Source: Harold Leavitt, Corporate Pathfinders (Homewood, Ill.: Dow Jones-Irvin, 1986).

According to Leavitt, the implementer focuses on direct action and manipulation; the problem solver concentrates on analysis and strategy; and the pathfinder is concerned with purpose and vision. Many organizations, says Leavitt, are combinations of the first and second styles; the pathfinding style is urgently needed yet often avoided.

While implementers and problem solvers have different styles, they share a common interest in keeping pathfinders out. Implementers, who are oriented toward getting the job done through direct orders and team effort, react negatively to the determined individualism of pathfinders. Problem solvers, who deal with hard evidence, rules, and details, don't want impractical or abstract visionaries around. For this reason, pathfinders who provide unconventional ideas often are prematurely turned out of an organization, or they simply burn out for lack of support and tolerance.

Leavitt believes all three leadership styles have a role to play in an individual's repertoire and an organization's success. The task of developing a balanced leadership style in a nourishing, nonpredatory culture is a major concern for organizational leadership today.

RECOMMENDED RESOURCES

The following readings, cases, application, and films are suggested for greater insight into the material in Part Three.

Readings — Wheels
Can an Executive Afford a Conscience?

Cases — Locks Versus Lives
"We Just Can't Do Things That Way Around Here . . ."
Government Jobs
R.V.'s in the Parking Lot
The Honor System
The Right to Strike

Application — The Kidney Machine

Films — Coping with Technology: Beyond Bureaucracy, Toward a New Democracy
Social Needs as Business Opportunities
Pollution Control—The Hard Decisions
The Power Pinch

REFERENCE NOTES

1 Harold Titus and Morton Keeton, *Ethics for Today*, 5th ed. (New York: D. Van Nostrand Company, 1975), 423–448.

2 Titus and Keeton, *Ethics for Today*, 423–448.

3 Bronislaw Malinowski, *Crime and Custom in Savage Society* (Paterson, N.J.: Littlefield, Adams, 1959), 51–53.

4 Peter Farb, *Humankind* (New York: Bantam Books, Inc. 1980), 331

5 Kathleen K. Reardon, "It's the Thought That Counts," *Harvard Business Review* (September/October, 1984): 136–141.

6 Walter Kaufmann, "Code of Hammurabi," *Encyclopedia of Morals*, ed. Vergilius Ferm (New York: Philosophical Library, 1956), 195–99.

7 *Sacred Books of the East* (New York: John Wiley & Sons, Inc.), vol. 28, book 7, sec. 2.

8 Confucius, *Analects*, book 14.

9 "The Road to Communism," Documents of the 22nd Congress of the CPSU (Moscow: 1961), 566–67, in Titus and Keeton, *Ethics for Today*, 212.

10 "Global Adherents of All Religions, A.D. 1900–2000," *World Christian Encyclopedia* (New York: Oxford University Press, 1982), 6.

11 T. Walter Wallbank, Arnold Schrier, Donna Maier, and Patricia Gutierrez-Smith, *History and Life: The World and Its People*, 2nd ed. (Homewood, Ill.: Scott, Foresman & Company, 1984), 61; and Charles S. Prebish, "Doctrines of Early Buddhists," in Charles S. Prebish, ed., *Buddhism: A Modern Perspective* (University Park, Penn.: The Pennsylvania State University Press, 1975), 29–31.

12 Kenneth W. Morgan, ed., *The Religion of the Hindus* (New York: Ronald Press, 1953), 12–13.

13 James I. Packer, Merrill C. Tenny, and William White, Jr., eds., *The Bible Almanac* (Nashville: Thomas Nelson Publishers, 1980), 31; and Peter Farb, *Humankind* (Boston: Houghton Mifflin Company, 1978), 150.

14 Exodus 20:1–17.

15 Erich Fromm, *Man for Himself* (New York: Holt, Rinehart and Winston, 1947), 22–23.

16 Report of a special task force to the Secretary of Health, Education, and Welfare, *Work in America* (Cambridge: MIT Press, 1973), 1–2.

17 Report of a special task force, *Work in America*, 1–2.

18 John A. Wilson, *The Culture of Ancient Egypt* (Chicago: The University of Chicago Press, 1951), 70.

19 Adolph Erman, *Life in Ancient Egypt*, trans. H. M. Tirard (New York: Dover Publications, Inc., 1971), 124.

20 Peter Drucker, *Management: Tasks, Responsibilities, Practices* (New York: Harper & Row, Publishers, Inc., 1973), 645.

21 James O'Toole, *Vanguard Management: Redesigning the Corporate Future* (New York: Doubleday & Company, Inc., 1985).

22 O'Toole, *Vanguard Management.*

23 Robert Hay and Ed Gray, "Social Responsibilities of Business Managers," *Academy of Management Journal* 18, no. 1 (March 1974): 135–143.

24 Craig Hickman and Michael A. Silva, *Creating Excellence* (New York: New American Library, 1984); and O'Toole, *Vanguard Management.*

25 David G. Bowers, *Systems of Organizations: Management of the Human Resource* (Ann Arbor: The University of Michigan Press, 1976), 3.

STUDY QUIZ

As a test of your understanding and the extent to which you have achieved the objectives in Part Three, complete the following questions. See Appendix E for the answer key.

1. Freud's id, ego, and superego parallel Plato's three-way struggle between _____, _____, and _____.
    a. love, hate, death
    b. man, woman, child
    c. appetite, reason, spirit
    d. life, death, nature

2. Carl Jung saw _____ as the foundation of moral behavior.
    a. religion
    b. beauty
    c. justice
    d. power

3. Almost universal taboos in all societies are:
    a. cruelty toward children, treachery toward family, murder
    b. dishonesty, infidelity, theft
    c. murder, abandonment, theft
    d. all of the above

4. The practice of lending one's wife to one's friend in Eskimo society shows the influence of _____ on moral behavior.
    a. generosity
    b. trust
    c. environment
    d. religion

5. The secular ethics of Confucianism are founded on _____ _____.
    a. right relationships
    b. ancient legends
    c. divine truth
    d. all of the above

6. Buddha taught _____ noble truths and the _____ path as discovered through _____.
    a. two, fourfold, discourse
    b. four, eightfold, enlightenment
    c. six, twelvefold, science
    d. none of the above

7. The religious ethics of Hinduism teach _____ Great Virtues, including _____, _____, _____.

   a. ten; purity, wisdom, forgiveness
   b. four; love, work, trust
   c. eight; freedom, life, prayer
   d. none of the above

8. All of the following are U.S. work laws concerning employee relations, except:

   a. National Labor Relations Act
   b. Occupational Safety and Health Act
   c. Maritime Act
   d. U.S. Constitution: first, fifth, and fourteenth amendments

9. Dealing with moral dilemmas, organizations typically reflect one of three ethical orientations:

   a. autocratic, democratic, free-rein
   b. profit maximizing, trusteeship, quality of life management
   c. x, y, z
   d. none of the above

10. Social values influence ethics along a continuum from:

    a. old religion to Christianity
    b. self-interest to altruism
    c. folkways to law
    d. none of the above

11. People in leadership positions influence ethical behavior primarily by:

    a. discussion
    b. study
    c. actions
    d. books

DISCUSSION QUESTIONS AND ACTIVITIES

The following questions and activities help personalize the subject. They are appropriate for classroom exercises and homework assignments.

1. Describe a social custom in our society that you support; identify the shared values this custom represents. Describe a social custom you oppose; identify the shared values this custom reflects.

2. Cite examples of the influence of ethics on the behavior of an individual and the behavior of a society. Use personal or historical examples.

3. Describe a moral dilemma you have experienced at work. What was your response: Were your motives high, means principled, and consequences favorable?

4. If you were the president of a company, what values would you promote? What values would guide you as you considered people, products, prices, and profits?

5. Identify leaders who are implementers, problem solvers, and pathfinders. How would you prevent turnout or burnout of pathfinders in an organization?

6. Discuss actual experiences in organizations with different ethical orientations. What is it like to work in profit-maximizing, trusteeship, and quality-of-life-management organizations?

7. Join in a small group to develop a code of ethics for an organization. The length should be between two and ten pages. Present and defend this code of ethics before an audience of interested people

8. Discuss how social values (self-interest and altruism) influence moral behavior. Use examples.

9. Discuss the role of leadership in shaping ethical behavior. Give true-life cases.

PART FOUR

Dynamics of Ethical Choice

Learning Objectives

After completing Part Four, you will better understand:

1. the role of personal values in making moral judgments;
2. the role of ethics in human relationships;
3. your level of compatibility with another person;
4. the importance of open-mindedness, or tolerance, in human relationships.

PERSONAL VALUES

Besides levels of morality, a person's ethics are determined by personal values. The following exercise will help you clarify your personal values and will help explain the dynamics of your own ethical behavior. It is offered to address the following concern:

> I am a human being, whatever that may be. I speak for all of us who move and think and feel and whom time consumes. I am like a man journeying through a forest, aware of occasional glints of light overhead, with recollections of the long trail I have already traveled, and conscious of wider spaces ahead. I want to see more clearly where I have been and where I am going, and above all, I want to know why I am where I am, and why I am traveling at all.[1]

In a sense, personal values are the glasses through which we view the world. People are always making ethical decisions as they see things personally and the way they believe things should be.

The Foxhole

A sergeant said of a soldier in a foxhole: "Never mind him, as long as we can save the squad."

The lieutenant said of the squad: "Never mind them, as long as we can save the platoon."

The captain said of the platoon: "The platoon doesn't matter, as long as we can save the company."

The colonel said of the company: "Never mind the company, as long as we can save the regiment."

The brigadier was interested only in saving the brigade, while the general wanted only to save the army.

"The army doesn't matter," said the leader of the nation, "as long as we can save the country."

"The country doesn't matter," said the mother of the soldier in the foxhole, "as long as my son comes home safely."[2]

What are your personal values? The following questionnaire will help you discover the values you consider most important and those that influence you in moral dilemmas. This learning exercise is particularly helpful for personal counseling and career guidance.

PERSONAL VALUES—
WHAT IS IMPORTANT TO YOU?

Directions

Each of the following questions has six possible responses. Rank these responses by assigning a 6 to the one you prefer the most, a 5 to the next, and so on, to 1, the least preferred of the alternatives. Sometimes you may have trouble making choices, but there should be no ties; you should make a choice.

1. Which of the following branches of study do you consider to be most important for the human race?

    ✓ A. philosophy

    ___ B. political science

    ___ C. psychology

    ___ D. theology

    ___ E. business

    ___ F. art

2. Which of the following qualities is most descriptive of you?

    ___ A. religious

    ___ B. unselfish

    ___ C. artistic

    ___ D. persuasive

    ✓ E. practical

    ___ F. intelligent

3. Of the following famous people, who is most interesting to you?

    ✓ A. Albert Einstein—discoverer of the theory of relativity

    ___ B. Henry Ford—automobile entrepreneur

    ___ C. Napoleon Bonaparte—political leader and military strategist

    ___ D. Martin Luther—leader of the Protestant Reformation

    ___ E. Michelangelo—sculptor and painter

    ___ F. Albert Schweitzer—missionary and humanitarian

4. What kind of person do you prefer to be? One who:

    ___ A. is industrious and economically self-sufficient

    ✓ B. has leadership qualities and organizing ability

Ethics, Part Four Exercise • Personal Values

_____ C. has spiritual or religious values
_____ D. is philosophical and interested in knowledge
_____ E. is compassionate and understanding toward others
_____ F. has artistic sensitivity and skill

5. Which of the following is most interesting to you?
   _____ A. artistic experiences
   _____ B. thinking about life
   __✓__ C. accumulation of wealth
   _____ D. religious faith
   _____ E. leading others
   _____ F. helping others

6. In which of the following would you prefer to participate?
   __✓__ A. business venture
   _____ B. artistic performance
   _____ C. religious activity
   _____ D. project to help the poor
   _____ E. scientific study
   _____ F. political campaign

7. Which publication would you prefer to read?
   _____ A. *History of the Arts*
   _____ B. *Psychology Today*
   _____ C. *Power Politics*
   _____ D. *Scientific American*
   _____ E. *Religions Today*
   __✓__ F. *Wall Street Journal*

8. In choosing a spouse, who would you prefer? One who:
   _____ A. likes to help people
   _____ B. is a leader in his or her field
   _____ C. is practical and enterprising
   __✓__ D. is artistically gifted
   _____ E. has a deep spiritual belief
   _____ F. is interested in philosophy and learning

9. Which activity do you consider to be more important for children?
   - ____ A. scouting
   - ____ B. junior achievement
   - ____ C. religious training
   - ____ D. creative art
   - ✓ E. student government
   - ____ F. science club

10. What should government leaders be concerned with?
    - ____ A. promoting creative and aesthetic interests
    - ____ B. establishing a position of power and respect in the world
    - ____ C. developing commerce and industry
    - ✓ D. supporting education and learning
    - ____ E. providing a supportive climate for spiritual growth and development
    - ____ F. promoting the social welfare of citizens

11. Which of the following courses would you prefer to teach?
    - ____ A. anthropology
    - ____ B. religions of the world
    - ____ C. philosophy
    - ____ D. political science
    - ____ E. poetry
    - ✓ F. business administration

12. What would you do if you had sufficient time and money?
    - ____ A. go on a retreat for spiritual renewal
    - ____ B. increase your money-making ability
    - ____ C. develop leadership skills
    - ____ D. help those who are disadvantaged
    - ✓ E. study the fine arts such as theater, music, and painting
    - ____ F. write an original essay, article, or book

13. Which courses would you promote if you were able to influence educational policies?
    - ____ A. political and governmental studies
    - ✓ B. philosophy and science

____ C. economics and occupational skills

____ D. social problems and issues

____ E. spiritual and religious studies

____ F. music and art

14. Which of the following news items would be most interesting to you?

    ____ A. "Business Conditions Favorable"

    ____ B. "Relief Arrives for Poor"

    ____ C. "Religious Leaders Meet"

    ____ D. "President Addresses the Nation"

    ____ E. "What's New in the Arts"

    __✓__ F. "Scientific Breakthrough Revealed"

15. Which subject would you prefer to discuss?

    ____ A. music, film, and theater

    ____ B. the meaning of human existence

    ____ C. spiritual experiences

    ____ D. wars in history

    __✓__ E. business opportunities

    ____ F. social conditions

16. What do you think the purpose should be for space exploration and manned space flight?

    ____ A. to unify people around the world

    __✓__ B. to gain knowledge of our universe

    ____ C. to reveal the beauty of our world

    ____ D. to discover answers to spiritual questions

    ____ E. to control world affairs

    ____ F. to develop trade and business opportunities

17. Which profession would you enter if all salaries were equal and you felt you had equal aptitude to succeed in any one of the six?

    ____ A. counseling

    ____ B. fine arts

    __✓__ C. science

    ____ D. politics

    ____ E. business

____ F. ministry

18. Whose life and works are most interesting to you?
    ____ A. Madame Curie — discoverer of radium
    ____ B. Gloria Vanderbilt — business woman
    ____ C. Elizabeth I — British monarch
    ____ D. Mother Teresa — religious leader
    ✓ E. Martha Graham — ballerina and choreographer
    ____ F. Harriet Beecher Stowe — author of *Uncle Tom's Cabin*

19. Which television program would you prefer to watch?
    ✓ A. "Art Appreciation"
    ____ B. "Spiritual Values"
    ____ C. "Investment Opportunities"
    ____ D. "Marriage and the Family"
    ____ E. "Political Power and Social Persuasion"
    ____ F. "The Origins of Intelligence"

20. Which of the following positions would you like to have?
    ____ A. political leader
    ____ B. artist
    ____ C. teacher
    ____ D. theologian
    ____ E. writer
    ✓ F. business entrepreneur

Source: Jim McCue and Marianne Bailey, Northern Kentucky University, 1979–1983; based on Gordon Allport, Phillip E. Vernon, and Gardner Lindzey, *The Study of Values: Grade 10-Adult*, 3d ed. (New York: Houghton Mifflin, 1970).

SCORING

Step 1

For each question, insert your score in the appropriate space in Figure 4.1. Note that the letters are not always in the same column.

Example   A 2   B 6   C 4   D 5   E 3   F 1

FIGURE 4.1
Scoring

Question	I	II	III	IV	V	VI
1.	A ___	E ___	F ___	C ___	B ___	D ___
2.	F ___	E ___	C ___	B ___	D ___	A ___
3.	A ___	B ___	E ___	F ___	C ___	D ___
4.	D ___	A ___	F ___	E ___	B ___	C ___
5.	B ___	C ___	A ___	F ___	E ___	D ___
6.	E ___	A ___	B ___	D ___	F ___	C ___
7.	D ___	F ___	A ___	B ___	C ___	E ___
8.	F ___	C ___	D ___	A ___	B ___	E ___
9.	F ___	B ___	D ___	A ___	E ___	C ___
10.	D ___	C ___	A ___	F ___	B ___	E ___
11.	C ___	F ___	E ___	A ___	D ___	B ___
12.	F ___	B ___	E ___	D ___	C ___	A ___
13.	B ___	C ___	F ___	D ___	A ___	E ___
14.	F ___	A ___	E ___	B ___	D ___	C ___
15.	B ___	E ___	A ___	F ___	D ___	C ___
16.	B ___	F ___	C ___	A ___	E ___	D ___
17.	C ___	E ___	B ___	A ___	D ___	F ___
18.	A ___	B ___	E ___	F ___	C ___	D ___
19.	F ___	C ___	A ___	D ___	E ___	B ___
20.	E ___	F ___	B ___	C ___	A ___	D ___
Totals	___	___	___	___	___	___

Step 2

Total the six columns.

Step 3

Place the total for each personal value in the appropriate place in Figure 4.3. Connect the scores with a straight line to form a picture of your overall value orientation. See the example in Figure 4.2.

FIGURE 4.2

Example: Personal Value Orientation

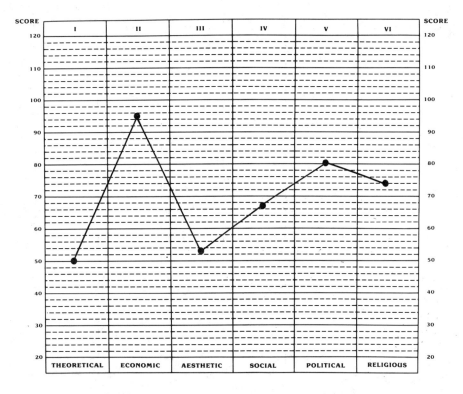

INTERPRETATION

A description of each personal value is as follows:

Theoretical

The primary interest of the theoretical person is the discovery of truth. In the lab, field, and library, and in personal affairs, the purpose of the theoretical person is to know the truth above all other goals. In the pursuit of truth, the theoretical person prefers a cognitive approach, one that looks for identities and differences, as opposed to the beauty or utility of objects. This person's needs are to observe, reason, and understand. Because the theoretical person's values are empirical, critical, and rational, this person is an intellectual and frequently is a scientist or philosopher. Major concerns of such a person are to order and systematize knowledge and to discover the meaning of existence.

FIGURE 4.3

Your Personal Value Orientation

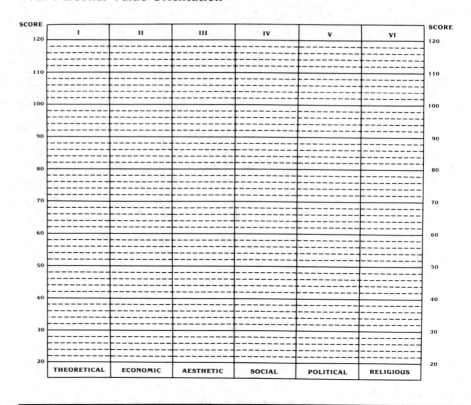

ILLUS. 4.1

The theoretical person is involved in the discovery of truth.

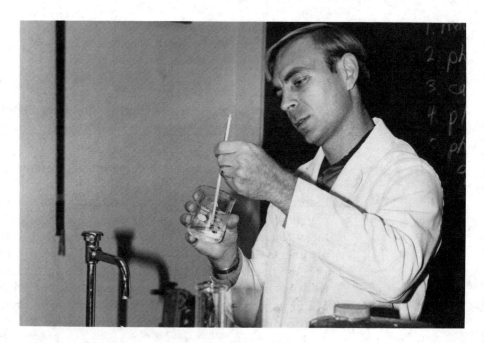

Economic

The economic person is interested in what is useful. Based originally on the satisfaction of bodily needs and self-preservation, the interest in utilities extends to the practical affairs of the business world — the production and marketing of goods, and the accumulation of wealth. This type of person is enterprising and efficient, reflecting the stereotype of the average businessperson. Economic values sometimes come into conflict with other values. The economic person wants education to be practical and regards unapplied knowledge as wasteful. Great feats of engineering and application result from the demands economic people make on people in science. Economic values may conflict with aesthetic values, such as in the advertising and promotion of products and services, except when art meets commercial ends. In relationships with people, the economic person is more likely to be interested in surpassing others in wealth than in dominating them politically or in serving them socially.

ILLUS. 4.2

The economic person often likes the image of wealth.

H. ARMSTRONG ROBERTS

Part Four • Dynamics of Ethical Choice   107

Aesthetic

The aesthetic person finds highest satisfaction in form, harmony, and beauty. The value of each single experience is judged from the standpoint of grace, symmetry, and fitness. The aesthetic person regards life as a procession of events, with each impression to be enjoyed for its own sake. An aesthetic person may not be a creative artist; the aesthetic person finds chief interest in the artistic episodes of life. Unlike the theoretical person, the aesthetic person usually chooses, with the poet John Keats, to consider truth as equivalent to beauty, or agrees with H. L. Mencken, "To make a thing charming is a million times more important than to make it true." In the economic sphere, the aesthetic often sees the process of manufacturing, advertising, and trade as a destruction of important aesthetic values. In social affairs, the aesthetic may be said to be interested in people, but not necessarily in their welfare. The aesthetic person tends toward individualism, self-sufficiency, and idealism in personal relations.

Social

The highest value for this type of person is love. The altruistic or philanthropic aspect of love is the interest of the social person. A humanist by nature, the social person prizes other people as ends in and of themselves, and not as tools or means to other goals. Therefore, the social person is kind, sympathetic, and helpful toward others. Such a person may find the economic and political values to be cold and inhuman. In contrast

ILLUS. 4.3

The aesthetic person finds the greatest satisfaction in harmony and beauty.

TEXAS STATE DEPARTMENT OF HIGHWAYS AND PUBLIC TRANSPORTATION

to the political type, the social person regards love instead of power as the most suitable form of human relationship. In purest form, social values are totally unselfish.

Political

The political person is interested in power and influence, although the person's activities may not fall within the narrow field of politics. Whatever the vocation, the political person seeks to be a "Machtmensch," an individual who is powerful. Leaders in any field usually will have a high interest in power and status. Because competition and struggle play a large part in all of life—between the sexes, between groups, between nations, and between individuals—many philosophers have viewed power as the most universal and most fundamental of human motives. In certain people, however, the desire for direct expression of power is uppermost, and their primary values are social influence and the exercise of authority.

Religious

The highest value of this type of person is spiritual peace. A religious person may or may not belong to an organized religion; people are religious if they but seek to comprehend the cosmos as a whole and to relate themselves to its embracing totality. Religious people have as their goal the creation of the highest and most satisfying value experience. Some people who are religious focus on events, people, and experiences in this world; that is, they experience meaning in the affirmation of life and active participation therein. With zest and enthusiasm, they see something divine in every event. On the other hand, some religious people are transcendental mystics, seeking to unite themselves with a higher reality by withdrawing from life. This type is ascetic and, like the holy men of India, finds inner peace and unity through self-denial and meditation. In many individuals, the affirmation and negation of human existence alternate to yield the greatest value satisfaction.

In evaluating your personal values, you should remember the following points:

- All six values on the questionnaire are positive. The questions do not measure negative values, such as greed or violence.
- Culture influences personal values. Through the processes of imprinting, modeling, and socialization, you learn to place higher importance on some values over others. Thus, the prestige afforded the monarch, priest, businessman, scientist, artist, and teacher depends on the values of each society. In the Pygmy culture, the male with the greatest social esteem usually is not the strongest, wealthiest, most spiritual, most artistic, or most intelligent; rather, he is the one who shares most generously. Consider American society: What

are the primary values for males in the United States today? Are they the same for females? Are they your personal values?

- By forcing choices among six personal values, the questionnaire gives an overall value orientation. This means that your lowest personal value may be more important to you than the highest personal value another individual holds. Similarly, your highest may be less important to you than the lowest of another individual. The questionnaire measures the relative strength of six personal values, so that you obtain a picture of *your* overall value orientation, or an understanding of what is most important to you.

- Ideally, a person's work will allow maximum expression of personal values. This helps explain the achievement and satisfaction of "theoretical" Albert Einstein, "economic" John D. Rockefeller, "aesthetic" Leonardo da Vinci, "social" Martin Luther King, "political" Winston Churchill, and "religious" Martin Luther.

Figure 4.4 shows the value orientations of sample groups of American males and females with different interests and occupations, presented in rank order. How do your values compare with these groups? Does your work allow maximum expression of your personal values?

Different organizations reflect different values, and each organization's success depends on having people in it, especially leaders, who promote its mission. Some people may be ideally suited for theoretical organizations such as universities, economic organizations such as corporations, aesthetic organizations such as performing groups, social organizations such as social service agencies, political organizations such as political parties, or religious organizations such as churches, synagogues, and mosques. Obvious mismatches would be the social person who gives away the store and the person who uses religious position for personal power. Consider your own personal values. Ask yourself what type of organization, if any, would be most appropriate for you.

FIGURE 4.4

Different Personal Values of Different People, in Rank Order

Engineering Students (Male)	Nursing Students (Female)
1. Theoretical	1. Religious
2. Economic	2. Aesthetic
3. Political	3. Social
4. Religious	4. Theoretical
5. Social	5. Political
6. Aesthetic	6. Economic

FIGURE 4.4—*continued*

Business Students (Male)
1. Economic
2. Political
3. Theoretical
4. Social
5. Religious
6. Aesthetic

Business Students (Female)
1. Aesthetic
2. Political
3. Economic
4. Religious
5. Theoretical
6. Social

Personnel and Guidance Workers (Male)
1. Theoretical
2. Social
3. Religious
4. Political
5. Economic
6. Aesthetic

Personnel and Guidance Workers (Female)
1. Social
2. Aesthetic
3. Religious
4. Theoretical
5. Economic
6. Political

Art and Design Students (Male)
1. Aesthetic
2. Theoretical
3. Economic
4. Religious
5. Political
6. Social

Art and Design Students (Female)
1. Aesthetic
2. Religious
3. Social
4. Theoretical
5. Political
6. Economic

Clergymen (Male)
1. Religious
2. Social
3. Political
4. Theoretical
5. Aesthetic
6. Economic

Social Workers (Female)
1. Aesthetic
2. Social
3. Theoretical
4. Political
5. Economic
6. Religious

College Students—All Majors (Male)
1. Political
2. Theoretical
3. Economic
4. Religious
5. Social
6. Aesthetic

College Students—All Majors (Female)
1. Aesthetic
2. Religious
3. Social
4. Political
5. Economic
6. Theoretical

Source: Gordon Allport, Phillip E. Vernon, and Gardner Lindzey, The Study of Values: Grade 10–Adult, *3d ed. (New York: Houghton Mifflin, 1970), 14–15.*

VALUES IN HUMAN RELATIONSHIPS

The following questionnaire allows you to compare your values with those of another person. As a result, you will learn the role of ethics in human relationships. This exercise is particularly helpful for team building, both on the job and in the home.

VALUE COMPATIBILITY—
DO WE THINK ALIKE?

Directions

Presented below are 21 groups of five personal values. In each grouping, rank the importance of the five values to you. See Figure 4.5 for a description of each value. Rank the values according to how you actually feel, not how you think you should feel. In front of each value, place a number from 1 (the value that is least important) to 5 (the most important value). Give a different rating to each value. There are no right or wrong answers. Note that each partner should complete the questionnaire independently.

Your personal values

1. ___ Power
   ___ Order
   ___ Achievement
   ___ Privacy
   ___ Helpfulness

2. ___ Order
   ___ Self-expression
   ___ Independence
   ___ Physical health
   ___ Aesthetic values

3. ___ Self-expression
   ___ Security
   ___ Privacy
   ___ Physical pleasure
   ___ Love

4. ___ Security
   ___ Recognition
   ___ Leadership
   ___ Power
   ___ Physical health

5. ___ Recognition
   ___ Naturalness
   ___ Physical pleasure
   ___ Truth
   ___ Order

6. ___ Naturalness
   ___ Achievement
   ___ Self-expression
   ___ Leadership
   ___ Leisure

7. ___ Achievement
   ___ Independence
   ___ Truth
   ___ Human relationships
   ___ Security

8. ___ Independence
   ___ Privacy
   ___ Leisure
   ___ Religious faith
   ___ Recognition

9. ___ Privacy
   ___ Physical health
   ___ Human relationships
   ___ Material wealth
   ___ Naturalness

10. ____ Physical health
    ____ Physical pleasure
    ____ Religious faith
    ____ Responsibility
    ____ Achievement

11. ____ Physical pleasure
    ____ Leadership
    ____ Helpfulness
    ____ Independence
    ____ Material wealth

12. ____ Leadership
    ____ Truth
    ____ Responsibility
    ____ Aesthetic values
    ____ Privacy

13. ____ Truth
    ____ Leisure
    ____ Physical health
    ____ Helpfulness
    ____ Love

14. ____ Leisure
    ____ Human relationships
    ____ Aesthetic values
    ____ Power
    ____ Physical pleasure

15. ____ Human relationships
    ____ Religious faith
    ____ Love
    ____ Order
    ____ Leadership

16. ____ Religious faith
    ____ Material wealth
    ____ Power
    ____ Self-expression
    ____ Truth

17. ____ Material wealth
    ____ Responsibility
    ____ Order
    ____ Security
    ____ Leisure

18. ____ Responsibility
    ____ Helpfulness
    ____ Recognition
    ____ Human relationships
    ____ Self-expression

19. ____ Helpfulness
    ____ Aesthetic values
    ____ Security
    ____ Naturalness
    ____ Religious faith

20. ____ Aesthetic values
    ____ Love
    ____ Material wealth
    ____ Recognition
    ____ Achievement

21. ____ Love
    ____ Power
    ____ Naturalness
    ____ Independence
    ____ Responsibility

Your partner's personal values

1. ____ Power
   ____ Order
   ____ Achievement
   ____ Privacy
   ____ Helpfulness

2. ____ Order
   ____ Self-expression
   ____ Independence
   ____ Physical health
   ____ Aesthetic values

3. ____ Self-expression
   ____ Security
   ____ Privacy
   ____ Physical pleasure
   ____ Love

4. ____ Security
   ____ Recognition
   ____ Leadership
   ____ Power
   ____ Physical health

5. ____ Recognition
   ____ Naturalness
   ____ Physical pleasure
   ____ Truth
   ____ Order

6. ____ Naturalness
   ____ Achievement
   ____ Self-expression
   ____ Leadership
   ____ Leisure

7. ___ Achievement
   ___ Independence
   ___ Truth
   ___ Human relationships
   ___ Security

8. ___ Independence
   ___ Privacy
   ___ Leisure
   ___ Religious faith
   ___ Recognition

9. ___ Privacy
   ___ Physical health
   ___ Human relationships
   ___ Material wealth
   ___ Naturalness

10. ___ Physical health
    ___ Physical pleasure
    ___ Religious faith
    ___ Responsibility
    ___ Achievement

11. ___ Physical pleasure
    ___ Leadership
    ___ Helpfulness
    ___ Independence
    ___ Material wealth

12. ___ Leadership
    ___ Truth
    ___ Responsibility
    ___ Aesthetic values
    ___ Privacy

13. ___ Truth
    ___ Leisure
    ___ Physical health
    ___ Helpfulness
    ___ Love

14. ___ Leisure
    ___ Human relationships
    ___ Aesthetic values
    ___ Power
    ___ Physical pleasure

15. ___ Human relationships
    ___ Religious faith
    ___ Love
    ___ Order
    ___ Leadership

16. ___ Religious faith
    ___ Material wealth
    ___ Power
    ___ Self-expression
    ___ Truth

17. ___ Material wealth
    ___ Responsibility
    ___ Order
    ___ Security
    ___ Leisure

18. ___ Responsibility
    ___ Helpfulness
    ___ Recognition
    ___ Human relationships
    ___ Self-expression

19. ___ Helpfulness
    ___ Aesthetic values
    ___ Security
    ___ Naturalness
    ___ Religious faith

20. ___ Aesthetic values
    ___ Love
    ___ Material wealth
    ___ Recognition
    ___ Achievement

21. ___ Love
    ___ Power
    ___ Naturalness
    ___ Independence
    ___ Responsibility

Source: Rosemary Hutchinson and Naomi Miller, *Northern Kentucky University, 1980–1984.*

FIGURE 4.5
Value Descriptions

Aesthetic values—pertaining to the appreciation of beauty and the beautiful.

Achievement—gains accomplished or fulfilled by work or effort.

Helpfulness—the desire to aid another; making it easier for a person to do something.

Human relationships—the state of being mutually interested or involved with other people.

Independence—the state of not relying on something else or someone else; not easily influenced.

Leadership—the ability to guide or direct an operation, activity, or performance in a specified manner or direction; to guide or direct others with ease.

Leisure—freedom from work or duties; relaxation; free time to do what one chooses to do.

Love—strong affection; feelings of passion, devotion, or tenderness for another.

Material wealth—large amount of possessions or resources having economic value.

Naturalness—having to do with nature, innocence, and basic simplicity.

Order—the desire for every part or unit to be in its right place in a normal or efficient state.

Physical health—a state of physical well being and freedom from illness; functioning well.

Physical pleasure—a state of physical gratification; bodily enjoyment or satisfaction.

Power—the ability to act or produce an effect; to have control or authority over others.

Privacy—the quality or state of being content when alone; enjoying seclusion.

Recognition—gaining special notice or attention; receiving social respect, honor, or reward.

Religious faith—beliefs related to divinity and spiritual experience.

Responsibility—the ability to answer for one's acts or decisions; the ability to fulfill one's obligations; meeting one's duties.

Security—freedom from worry, especially in matters dealing with physical and economic needs.

FIGURE 4.5—*continued*

Self-expression—the ability to make known, show, or state one's personal feelings, ideas, or beliefs.

Truth—honesty; the real state of things; actuality; the quality of being in accordance with facts.

Source: Oxford American Dictionary *(New York: Oxford University Press, 1980) and* Random House Dictionary of the English Language *(New York: Random House, 1968).*

SCORING

Step 1

Each value appeared in different groupings five times on the questionnaire. On the chart, Figure 4.6, enter the number you assigned to each value each time that value appeared. Then add the total numbers across.

FIGURE 4.6

Your Scoring Chart

Value	Number of groupings listing this value	Your ratings for the value each time it appeared					Total
Aesthetic Values	2, 12, 14, 19, 20						
Power	1, 4, 14, 16, 21						
Physical Pleasure	3, 5, 10, 11, 14						
Order	1, 2, 5, 15, 17						
Achievement	1, 6, 7, 10, 20						
Self-expression	2, 3, 6, 16, 18						
Human Relationships	7, 9, 14, 15, 18						
Material Wealth	9, 11, 16, 17, 20						
Responsibility	10, 12, 17, 18, 21						
Helpfulness	1, 11, 13, 18, 19						
Naturalness	5, 6, 9, 19, 21						
Truth	5, 7, 12, 13, 16						
Leadership	4, 6, 11, 12, 15						
Leisure	6, 8, 13, 14, 17						
Love	3, 13, 15, 20, 21						
Physical Health	2, 4, 9, 10, 13						
Privacy	1, 3, 8, 9, 12						
Religious Faith	8, 10, 15, 16, 19						
Security	3, 4, 7, 17, 19						
Independence	2, 7, 8, 11, 21						
Recognition	4, 5, 8, 18, 20						

Step 2

In the blank spaces below, list the values, starting with the highest totals, for all 21 values. This list will show the values most important to you.

Values in Order of Importance to You

High-Order Values	Middle-Order Values	Low-Order Values
1. _____	8. _____	15. _____
2. _____	9. _____	16. _____
3. _____	10. _____	17. _____
4. _____	11. _____	18. _____
5. _____	12. _____	19. _____
6. _____	13. _____	20. _____
7. _____	14. _____	21. _____

Step 3

Complete the scoring chart for your partner, Figure 4.7.

FIGURE 4.7

Your Partner's Scoring Chart

Value	Number of groupings listing this value	Your ratings for the value each time it appeared					Total
Aesthetic Values	2, 12, 14, 19, 20						
Power	1, 4, 14, 16, 21						
Physical Pleasure	3, 5, 10, 11, 14						
Order	1, 2, 5, 15, 17						
Achievement	1, 6, 7, 10, 20						
Self-expression	2, 3, 6, 16, 18						
Human Relationships	7, 9, 14, 15, 18						
Material Wealth	9, 11, 16, 17, 20						
Responsibility	10, 12, 17, 18, 21						
Helpfulness	1, 11, 13, 18, 19						
Naturalness	5, 6, 9, 19, 21						
Truth	5, 7, 12, 13, 16						
Leadership	4, 6, 11, 12, 15						
Leisure	6, 8, 13, 14, 17						
Love	3, 13, 15, 20, 21						
Physical Health	2, 4, 9, 10, 13						
Privacy	1, 3, 8, 9, 12						
Religious Faith	8, 10, 15, 16, 19						
Security	3, 4, 7, 17, 19						
Independence	2, 7, 8, 11, 21						
Recognition	4, 5, 8, 18, 20						

Step 4

In the blank spaces below, list the values, starting with the highest totals, for all 21 values. This list will show the values most important to your partner.

Values in Order of Importance to Your Partner

High-Order Values	Middle-Order Values	Low-Order Values
1. _____	8. _____	15. _____
2. _____	9. _____	16. _____
3. _____	10. _____	17. _____
4. _____	11. _____	18. _____
5. _____	12. _____	19. _____
6. _____	13. _____	20. _____
7. _____	14. _____	21. _____

Step 5

Determine the value compatibility between you and your partner according to the following formula.

   a. Count the number of high-order values you share (the exact ranking of the values may differ) and multiply this number by 3.

      Total _____

   b. Count the number of low-order values you share (the exact ranking of the values may differ) and multiply this number by 2.

      Total _____

   c. Count the number of middle-order values you share (the exact ranking of values may differ) and multiply this number by 1.

      Total _____

   d. Add the three totals (a, b, and c), then indicate your compatibility level on the following index, Figure 4.8.

   e. The higher the score on the index (0–42), the greater the level of value compatibility between you and your partner, and the less conflict you would expect to experience.

FIGURE 4.8

Value Compatibility Index

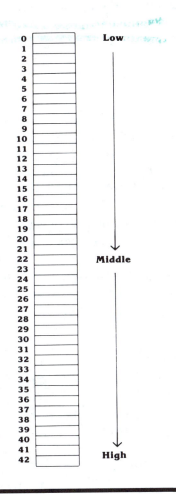

DISCUSSION

After you and your partner have completed the questionnaire, compare the order in which you placed the values and the level of your compatibility index. Discuss how differences and similarities in personal values influence your relationship. Consider whether each person allows the full expression of the values most important to the other person, and consider how points of agreement and difference can be used to improve the relationship. Be tolerant in this discussion. Remember, the questionnaire does not measure many other important factors of compatibility, such as interpersonal sensitivity, interests, and temperament; nor does it measure levels of morality, a critical element in human relationships. Remember also that different people may have different meanings for the words on the questionnaire. One person may define responsibility one way, and another may interpret the word differently. Finally, remember that this questionnaire does not measure negative values, and that complementary values may enrich a relationship. In this spirit, use the following thought as a guide: "Our errors and our controversies in the sphere of human relations often arise from looking on people as though they could be altogether bad, or altogether good."[3]

CONCLUSION

Often, when people hear the word *ethics*, they think, "How dull! How boring! How unimportant to me." They do not realize that ethics touch every aspect of our lives. Far from being dull and boring, ethics stimulate thinking people of all ages, and for many, what is right and wrong and good and bad are life's most fascinating questions.

This book has been written to spark interest in ethics and shed light on basic moral concepts as they apply both on the job and in the home. An important goal, too, has been to personalize the subject. It is hoped that you have a better understanding of your own ethical roots, level of morality, and personal and social values. To the degree these goals have been met, there is "fire in a dark world." When you hear the word *ethics*, may you respond, "How exciting! How interesting! How important to us all."

RECOMMENDED RESOURCES

The following reading, case, and applications are suggested for greater insight into the material in Part Four:

Reading — Rites of Passage

Case — The 19-Year-Old Bride

Applications — The Fallout Shelter
Values Flag
Values Auction

REFERENCE NOTES

1. Norman John Berrill, *Man's Emerging Mind: Man's Progress Through Time* (New York: Dodd, Mead & Company), 1955

2. Alfred Polgar, in Will Forpe and John C. McCollister, *The Sunshine Books: Expressions of Love, Hope and Inspiration* (Middle Village, N.Y.: Jonathan David Publishers, 1979), 57.

3. *The Reflections and Maxims of Vauvenargues*, trans. S. G. Stevens (London: Humphrey Milford, 1940).

STUDY QUIZ

As a test of your understanding and the extent to which you have achieved the objectives in Part Four, complete the following questions. See Appendix E for the answer key.

1. Personal values include all of the following except:

    a. economic
    b. political
    c. aesthetic
    d. religious
    e. psychological

2. Napoleon Bonaparte is an example of a(n) _____ person.

    a. theoretical
    b. aesthetic
    c. political
    d. social

3. Science is an example of a _____ profession.

    a. religious
    b. political
    c. theoretical
    d. social

4. Mother Theresa is an example of a _____ person.

    a. political
    b. religious
    c. theoretical
    d. none of the above

5. In the Pygmy culture, the male with greatest social esteem is usually the

    a. strongest
    b. most artistic
    c. most intelligent
    d. most generous

6. Important elements of interpersonal compatibility include:

    a. personal values
    b. personality temperament
    c. personal interests
    d. all of the above

7. Closed-mindedness, or intolerance of another person's values, usually results in:
   a. business success
   b. communication breakdown
   c. social order
   d. religious freedom

DISCUSSION QUESTIONS AND ACTIVITIES

The following questions and activities help personalize the subject. They are appropriate for classroom exercises and homework assignments.

1. What are your values—theoretical, economic, aesthetic, social, political, religious? What values are high? What values are low? Does your life situation support your value orientation?

2. Can you identify the people and experiences in your life that have helped shape your values? Discuss.

3. Are your values compatible with those of your family and friends? Can you accept and support the values of others? Discuss.

4. Join in small groups to discuss individuals and institutions that represent theoretical, economic, aesthetic, social, political, and religious values. Which of these is most valued in American society? Do you think male and female value orientations are inherently different? Discuss.

5. Consider true-life cases. Has a member of the group experienced value conflict with another person, group, or organization? Discuss.

READINGS

How Could the Jonestown Holocaust Have Occurred? 126

If Hitler Asked You to Electrocute a Stranger, Would You? 133

The Parable of the Sadhu 147

The Myth of Sisyphus 155

Wheels 158

Can an Executive Afford a Conscience? 168

Rites of Passage 179

How Could the Jonestown Holocaust Have Occurred?

The answer to this question necessarily involves tracing the career of the Rev. Jim Jones and the People's Temple movement. From information revealed in the press and in books, a fairly clear picture emerges of the major contributing factors to the final catastrophe. It should be noted at the outset that the term "mass suicide" does not adequately cover the final events in Jonestown. Wooden (1981) states that 276 children—from babies to those near the age of consent—died there. Because under English law, minors cannot legally consent to suicide, their deaths were actually murder. Still, this leaves a very large number of adults who, with only a minor amount of dissent, complied with the urgings of Jones to participate in the final macabre ritual.

James W. Jones was born near Lynn, Indiana, in 1931. After graduating from high school in 1949, he married Marceline Baldwin, who was a nurse and who would support his activities to the last day of their lives. In 1953, Jones opened a small interdenominational church, the Christian Assembly of God, with the laudable intent of eliminating social injustices and improving interracial harmony within the context of a fundamentalist religion. As his church attracted an increasing number of black members, he and his wife created a multiracial family (seven of their eight children were adopted, including a black, a Chinese, and a Korean child), and Jones became outspoken on civil rights issues. After spending 2 years working as a missionary in Brazil, where he established orphanages and a mission, he returned to Indiana. By 1964, Jones had been ordained a minister of the Christian Churches (Disciples of Christ) and had changed the name of his church to People's Temple Full Gospel.

Partly out of fear of the impending nuclear war he had predicted, Mr. Jones and about 100 followers migrated to Ukiah, California. The northern part of the state was thought to be one of the safest havens from the ravages of nuclear war. In Ukiah, Mr. Jones displayed his considerable organizational skills. While the dedication to social programs continued, an increasing amount of energy went into creating the economic and legal

Source: Clifford T. Morgan, Richard A. King, John R. Weisz, and John Shopler, Introduction to Psychology, *7th ed. (New York: McGraw-Hill Book Company, 1986). Reprinted with permission.*

structure that would support future activities. The People's Temple was very successful in raising money. In addition to weekend fund-raising trips to San Francisco and Los Angeles, the membership was increasingly pressured into making contributions. The test of loyalty to the group soon became the willingness of members to assign all of their assets to the People's Temple, which acquired members' houses, wages, and monthly social security checks. The church thus changed from being merely a force in members' lives to being in total control of their life decisions.

The People's Temple movement flourished. Its interracial membership swelled to include the elderly, the well-educated, and the disaffected. Most people were undoubtedly drawn by the avowed social values or the religious fervor of the movement. Financial success also continued. By 1971, the church had bought a building in San Francisco, in the heart of the black community, and a church in Los Angeles. It continued to be a showcase of social programs while also increasing its political clout in the community. Mr. Jones could provide instant crowds for demonstrations or speakers and could supply a cadre of workers for the political candidates he selected. Close races for mayor and district attorney in San Francisco are thought to have been won because of the support of the People's Temple. The American patronage system insured that Mr. Jones could place loyal church members in sensitive, relevant government positions. Tim Stoen, who was at that time Jones's trusted lawyer, was appointed to the district attorney's staff, and Mr. Jones was appointed to the city's housing administration, becoming chairman after a few months. Mr. Jones received many public accolades during this period for the work of the People's Temple.

In the midst of this dazzling success, a darker side to the movement was also surfacing. A variety of serious charges were leveled by people who had managed to leave the movement. These charges—obtaining member obedience by physical brutality, making fraudulent claims in order to obtain legal guardianship over children, sexual abuses, fake "healing" ceremonies, death threats to members considering leaving the group—although later shown to be quite accurate, were not given much currency at the time. Mr. Jones, through his political muscle, had the power to prevent charges from becoming public or to muster potent countercharges to discredit his detractors. Furthermore, a large number of highly respected people came to his defense. During this period, Mr. Jones's self-concept and ideology also appeared to change. Christian religious themes diminished to the vanishing point and were replaced by messianic, revolutionary messages suggesting strong parallels between Jones and Christ. Members were required to address Jones as "Father," and he became the sole arbiter of correct values.

The mass migration to Jonestown in the summer of 1977 was precipitated by the impending publication, in *New West* magazine, of an investigative article which Jones had tried to squelch. What was to have been a gradual shift of members, spanning several years, became a 6-week exodus. While a center remained in San Francisco, the bulk of the membership was transferred to Guyana. Another headquarters was established in the Guyanese capital, Georgetown, staffed by about 40 people. The procedures used so successfully in California were repeated. High-ranking Guyanese officials were courted by members of the People's Temple and willingly cast a protective net around Jonestown. The residents of Jonestown became totally isolated from the rest of the world. Surrounded by an inhospitable jungle, whose dangers were frequently exaggerated by Jones, and linked to their centers in Georgetown and San Francisco only by a radio controlled by Jones, any hope of members receiving accurate information disappeared. Jones portrayed the outside world as filled with CIA- or FBI-inspired conspiracies aimed at destroying their revolutionary movement. Except for an inner circle of advisers and an armed "security" guard, members' lives were harsh, characterized by crowded living conditions, long work hours in the fields, debilitating diets of rice and beans, and frequent, exhausting meetings called by Jones. Despite these factors, however, the settlement made progress. Aside from living quarters, the compound included a medical tent, a playground, an electric generator, and a classroom. Crops were planted and harvested, and some cottage industries were started.

The isolation of Jonestown was occasionally penetrated by outsiders, including some members of the American embassy in Georgetown. These visits typically resulted in positive reports of the encampment's achievements. In response to the pleadings of the Concerned Relatives group, who had submitted a long list of human rights violations committed by Jones, American consular officials made four visits during 1978. According to Krause, (1978): ". . . the last occasion was on November 7, eleven days before the massacre" (p. 10). Their report gave no hint of alarm. Indeed, minutes before his assassination on the dirt airstrip outside of Jonestown, Representative Ryan finished an interview with NBC's Don Harris with the observation, "Can I just add, there are a lot of good people who are there on a positive and supportive and idealistic basis, trying to do something that is different and important to them" (Reston, 1981, p. 320). These positive perceptions were primarily the result of viewing a charade carefully orchestrated by Jones. It was in a comparable web of deceit and lies that members of the People's Temple met their death.

The deaths at Jonestown were clearly not the result of an impulsive decision by a leader and his dedicated band of followers. The final ritual was undoubtedly planned for years by Jones as his mark on history. His mind seems to have become gradually unhinged from reality and obsessed by a vision of glory. According to Wooden (1981), there were as many as 42 suicide rehearsals, dating back to the time they resided in California. These "white nights" would begin with Jones announcing some alarming news and would end with Jones saying that the potion they had collectively drunk actually contained no poison. The concept of a mass death was implanted in the environment of the People's Temple. Though it may still seem incomprehensible to us that so many adults would be obedient to Jones's demented plan, his manipulations of perceptions, of influence, and of interpersonal relationships provide ample bases for the members' conformity.

The people of Jonestown must have harbored many strange perceptions, not only of their leader but also of the outside world. While it will never be known how many of them believed in Jones's messianic self-delusions, it seems clear that they accepted his self-presentation of other characteristics as well as his views and attributions about events. Mass death was termed "revolutionary suicide." "Father" was all-knowing and suffered for the sins of any member. The rainy season was attributed to a CIA plot to destroy their crops, and Jones's varied sexual activities were attributed by him to some vague revolutionary goal that he pursued despite the "pain" the activities caused him. The U.S. government was always portrayed as hostile to the movement. Once Representative Ryan and some members of his group were murdered by Jonestown gunmen, Jones's claim that deadly retaliation was on its way must have seemed credible. But even before this final distortion, the coercive environment prevented people from revealing their own perceptions. Outside visitors were rarely able to penetrate the reality of Jonestown. Jones was certainly no stranger to the staging of fake events. His "ministerial" routines included such tricks as "passing" cancer, an illusion created by the use of chicken organs. He also staged attempts on his own life, events which were then offered as evidence for the existence of hostile plots against the movement. In Jonestown, the days before a visit were always used to rehearse what people would say and do. It is no wonder that the visitors, especially those expecting to see barbed-wire enclosures and imprisoned hostages eager to be freed, were pleasantly surprised. They saw a community busily at work and heard people say they were happy with their lives. They accepted at face value what they heard and saw because it was extremely difficult to detect the psychological pressures producing the manufactured events.

Interviews with former members document that some people were never fooled by the fake healings or staged assassination attempts. They accepted these as necessary means to further noble ends. But such rationalizations were a trap. By suspending their skepticism, Reston (1981) suggests, they were required to increase their faith in Jones. It represented, in Campbell's terms, a lessened weighting of the personal modes of judgment and an increased reliance on the social modes, thereby producing heightened conformity.

Like members of any group, members of the People's Temple were subjected to pressures to conform to group norms, albeit norms primarily defined by Jones. Most people who became members were undoubtedly drawn to the movement because of its professed values and goals. They must have wanted to be "good" members and may have accepted the conformity pressures as guides to proper behavior. The migration to California seemed to coincide with an escalation of these pressures beyond any reasonable bounds. The typical pressures were augmented by such techniques as requiring members, during group meetings, to make "self-confessions" of imperfections and by physical beatings of members whose behavior was deemed deviant (as well as those who objected to the beatings). The movement became extremely intolerant of any behavior that deviated from group norms. Disagreement with Jones was not mere deviation; it was an act of disloyalty. The harshest treatment was reserved for anyone expressing a desire to leave the group. "Defectors" were a threat to the group's survival, and those who left often felt they were risking their lives. While resistance to group pressures is always difficult, resistance was further lowered by having members assign their economic resources to the movement and by systematically cutting them off from their families. The loss of economic independence and of possible family support increased the members' dependence upon the group.

Jones seemed to push to the limit all types of social influence techniques, with one exception—imitation. As the movement prospered, he seemed less and less inclined to serve as a role model for the values and behaviors expected of members. For example, while expecting truthfulness from members, he engaged in trickery and staged events; while decrying homosexuality, he engaged in homosexual relationships; and while the members' Guyana diet was meager, he ate from his own refrigerator. The members' dependence upon their leader's word for what was normative, thus, was increased because they could not use his behavior as a standard for judging what was correct.

Abolishing family relationships was an important goal for the leaders of the movement. Not only were members systematically alienated from their own families, but kinship relationships were intentionally destroyed. For example, the custody of children was legally transferred from natural parents to other members, some husbands and wives were forbidden to live together, and the only relationship that was supported was one with "Father." All members were expected to keep surveillance over each other and to report deviations to Jones. The decision to report information was complicated by the knowledge that events were sometimes staged. Members who overheard someone's desire to leave the movement could never be certain whether the "overhearing" was genuine or a test of their loyalty. In view of the consequences of being disloyal, there must have been a high rate of reporting.

All of the factors noted above were present at the final meeting in Jonestown. Recall that the members were physically and psychologically isolated from their families and the rest of the world; they had a long history of conformity to a leader obsessed by his own martyrdom; they believed in the existence of a hostile world that was probably about to retaliate for the slaying of Representative Ryan; they accepted something termed "revolutionary suicide" as a positive value; they were undernourished and weary; and they had undergone many rehearsals of their own deaths. It is no wonder that Jones's macabre scheme was implemented with so little resistance. During the last meeting, only one member publicly objected to the plan. She was quickly silenced by Jones and the others. Some people, probably from among the armed security guards, did escape into the jungle, but otherwise all of the residents perished in total obedience to Jones. The People's Temple members who were less under the sway of these factors, those in the Georgetown and San Francisco centers, did not comply (with the possible exception of one person) with Jones's command for self-destruction. Their obedience had some limits.

Because the People's Temple movement has much in common with other current cults, it would be reassuring to think that the aftermath of Jonestown produced corrective mechanisms in how society protects individuals, especially children, from suffering similar consequences. Unfortunately, this is not the case. The issues are not simple. In part, they involve the rights of individuals to choose their own style of life. The test of a free choice is typically a person's self-description that he or she is content or happy with the present situation. Yet as we have seen with Jonestown, such self-descriptions can be meaningless in a coercive environment that controls self-descriptions. Our society also has a cherished heritage of protecting all forms of religious worship. This value is embodied in the First Amendment. Government interference with religious cults conflicts with individual and First Amendment rights. Although the government has an obligation to investigate charges of violations of law, even this rudimentary form of protection is apparently of little help. Wooden (1981) asserts that our government has shown a great reluctance ". . . to pursue charges of fraud, misappropriation of property, forgery, and widespread child abuse and neglect, perpetrated within the private confines of churches". It seems abundantly clear that the major protection against involvement in circumstances similar to the People's Temple movement remains in the hands of the individual. It is the individual who must not relinquish his or her own personal mode for weighting information. Whatever massive conformity pressures are brought to bear, it is the individual's ultimate responsibility to judge what is true, moral, and correct in the practices of the group to which he or she belongs.

REFERENCES

Krause, C. A. (1978). *Guyana massacre: The eyewitness account.* New York: Berkley.

Reston, J., Jr. (1981), *Our father who art in hell.* New York: Times Books.

Wooden, K. (1981). *The children of Jonestown.* New York: McGraw-Hill.

QUESTIONS

1. What is your reaction to the Jonestown tragedy? What observations can you make about people, cults, religions? Discuss.

   _____
   _____
   _____

2. Have you ever experienced group pressure? Have you experienced pressure from a charismatic leader? Discuss.

_____
_____
_____

If Hitler Asked You to Electrocute a Stranger, Would You?

In the beginning, Stanley Milgram was worried about the Nazi problem. He doesn't worry much about the Nazis anymore. He worries about you and me, and, perhaps, himself a little bit too.

Stanley Milgram is a social psychologist, and when he began his career at Yale University in 1960 he had a plan to prove, scientifically, that Germans are different. The Germans-are-different hypothesis has been used by historians, such as William L. Shirer, to explain the systematic destruction of the Jews by the Third Reich. One madman could decide to destroy the Jews and even create a master plan for getting it done. But to implement it on the scale that Hitler did meant that thousands of other people had to go along with the scheme and help to do the work. The Shirer thesis, which Milgram set out to test, is that Germans have a basic character flaw which explains the whole thing, and this flaw is a readiness to obey authority without question, no matter what outrageous acts the authority commands.

The appealing thing about this theory is that it makes those of us who are not Germans feel better about the whole business. Obviously, you and I are not Hitler, and it seems equally obvious that we would never do Hitler's dirty work for him. But now, because of Stanley Milgram, we are compelled to wonder. Milgram developed a laboratory experiment which provided a systematic way to measure obedience. His plan was to try it out in New Haven on Americans and then go to Germany and try it out on Germans. He was strongly motivated by scientific curiosity, but there was also some moral content in his decision to pursue this line of research, which was, in turn, colored by his own Jewish background. If he could show that Germans are more obedient than Americans, he could then vary the conditions of the experiment and try to find out just what it is that makes some people more obedient than others. With this understanding, the world might, conceivably, be just a little bit better.

But he never took his experiment to Germany. He never took it any farther than Bridgeport. The first finding, also the most unexpected and disturbing finding, was that we Americans are an obedient people: not

Source: Phillip Meyer, from Esquire *(February, 1970). Reprinted with permission of Esquire. Copyright © 1970 by Esquire Associates.*

blindly obedient, and not blissfully obedient, just obedient. "I found so much obedience," says Milgram softly, a little sadly, "I hardly saw the need for taking the experiment to Germany."

There is something of the theatre director in Milgram, and his technique, which he learned from one of the old masters in experimental psychology, Solomon Asch, is to stage a play with every line rehearsed, every prop carefully selected, and everybody an actor except one person. That one person is the subject of the experiment. The subject, of course, does not know he is in a play. He thinks he is in real life. The value of this technique is that the experimenter, as though he were God, can change a prop here, vary a line there, and see how the subject responds. Milgram eventually had to change a lot of the script just to get people to stop obeying. They were obeying so much, the experiment wasn't working — it was like trying to measure oven temperature with a freezer thermometer.

The experiment worked like this: If you were an innocent subject in Milgram's melodrama, you read an ad in the newspaper or received one in the mail asking for volunteers for an educational experiment. The job would take about an hour and pay $4.50. So you make an appointment and go to an old Romanesque stone structure on High Street with the imposing name of The Yale Interaction Laboratory. It looks something like a broadcasting studio. Inside, you meet a young, crew-cut man in a laboratory coat who says he is Jack Williams, the experimenter. There is another citizen, fiftyish, Irish face, an accountant, a little overweight, and very mild and harmless-looking. This other citizen seems nervous and plays with his hat while the two of you sit in chairs side by side and are told that the $4.50 checks are yours no matter what happens. Then you listen to Jack Williams explain the experiment.

It is about learning, says Jack Williams in a quiet, knowledgeable way. Science does not know much about the conditions under which people learn and this experiment is to find out about negative reinforcement. Negative reinforcement is getting punished when you do something wrong, as opposed to positive reinforcement which is getting rewarded when you do something right. The negative reinforcement in this case is electric shock. You notice a book on the table, titled, *The Teaching-Learning Process*, and you assume that this has something to do with the experiment.

Then Jack Williams takes two pieces of paper, puts them in a hat, and shakes them up. One piece of paper is supposed to say, "Teacher" and the other, "Learner." Draw one and you will see which you will be. The mild-looking accountant draws one, holds it close to his vest like a poker player, looks at it, and says, "Learner." You look at yours. It says "Teacher." You do not know that the drawing is rigged, and both slips say "Teacher." The experimenter beckons to the mild-mannered "learner."

"Want to step right in here and have a seat, please?" he says. "You can leave your coat on the back of that chair . . . roll up your right sleeve, please. Now what I want to do is strap down your arms to avoid excessive movement on your part during the experiment. This electrode is connected to the shock generator in the next room.

"And this electrode paste," he says, squeezing some stuff out of a plastic bottle and putting it on the man's arm, "is to provide a good contact and to avoid a blister or burn. Are there any questions now before we go into the next room?"

You don't have any, but the strapped-in "learner" does.

"I do think I should say this," says the learner. "About two years ago, I was at the veterans' hospital . . . they detected a heart condition. Nothing serious, but as long as I'm having these shocks, how strong are they — how dangerous are they?"

Williams, the experimenter, shakes his head casually. "Oh, no," he says. "Although they may be painful, they're not dangerous. Anything else?"

Nothing else. And so you play the game. The game is for you to read a series of word pairs: for example, blue-girl, nice-day, fat-neck. When you finish the list, you read just the first word in each pair and then a multiple-choice list of four other words, including the second word of the pair. The learner, from his remote, strapped-in position, pushes one of four switches to indicate which of the four answers he thinks is the right one. If he gets it right, nothing happens and you go on to the next one.

If he gets it wrong, you push a switch that buzzes and gives him an electric shock. And then you go to the next word. You start with 15 volts and increase the number of volts by 15 for each wrong answer. The control board goes from 15 volts on one end to 450 volts on the other. So that you know what you are doing, you get a test shock yourself, at 45 volts. It hurts. To further keep you aware of what you are doing to that man in there, the board has verbal descriptions of the shock levels, ranging from "Slight Shock" at the left-hand side, through "Intense Shock" in the middle, to "Danger: Severe Shock" toward the far right. Finally, at the very end, under 435- and 450-volt switches, there are three ambiguous X's. If, at any point, you hesitate, Mr. Williams calmly tells you to go on. If you still hesitate, he tells you again.

Except for some terrifying details, which will be explained in a moment, this is the experiment. The object is to find the shock level at which you disobey the experimenter and refuse to pull the switch.

When Stanley Milgram first wrote this script, he took it to fourteen Yale psychology majors and asked them what they thought would happen. He put it this way: Out of one hundred persons in the teacher's predicament, how would their break-off points be distributed along the 15-to-450-volt scale? They thought a few would break off very early, most would quit someplace in the middle and a few would go all the way to the end. The highest estimate of the number out of one hundred who would go all the way to the end was three. Milgram then informally polled some of his fellow scholars in the psychology department. They agreed that very few would go on to the end. Milgram thought so too.

"I'll tell you quite frankly," he says, "before I began this experiment, before any shock generator was built, I thought that most people would break off at 'Strong Shock' or 'Very Strong Shock.' You would get only a very, very small proportion of people going out to the end of the shock generator, and they would constitute a pathological fringe."

In his pilot experiments, Milgram used Yale students as subjects. Each of them pushed the shock switches, one by one, all the way to the end of the board.

So he rewrote the script to include some protests from the learner. At first, they were mild, gentlemanly, Yalie protests, but "it didn't seem to have as much effect as I thought it would or should," Milgram recalls. "So we had more violent protestation on the part of the person getting the shock. All of the time, of course, what we were trying to do was not to create a macabre situation, but simply to generate disobedience. And that was one of the first findings. This was not only a technical deficiency of the experiment, that we didn't get disobedience. It really was the first finding: that obedience would be much greater than we had assumed it would be and disobedience would be much more difficult than we had assumed."

As it turned out, the situation did become rather macabre. The only meaningful way to generate disobedience was to have the victim protest with great anguish, noise, and vehemence. The protests were tape-recorded so that all the teachers ordinarily would hear the same sounds and nuances, and they started with a grunt at 75 volts, proceeded through a "Hey, that really hurts," at 125 volts, got desperate with, "I can't stand the pain, don't do that," at 180 volts, reached complaints of heart trouble at 195, an agonized scream at 285, a refusal to answer at 315, and only heart-rending, ominous silence after that.

Still, sixty-five percent of the subjects, twenty- to fifty-year-old American males, everyday, ordinary people, like you and me, obediently kept pushing those levers in the belief that they were shocking the mild-mannered learner, whose name was Mr. Wallace, and who was chosen for the role because of his innocent appearance, all the way up to 450 volts.

Milgram was now getting enough disobedience so that he had something he could measure. The next step was to vary the circumstances to see what would encourage or discourage obedience. There seemed very little left in the way of discouragement. The victim was already screaming at the top of his lungs and feigning a heart attack. So whatever new impediment to obedience reached the brain of the subject had to travel by some route other than the ear. Milgram thought of one.

He put the learner in the same room with the teacher. He stopped strapping the learner's hand down. He rewrote the script so that at 150 volts the learner took his hand off the shock plate and declared that he wanted out of the experiment. He rewrote the script some more so that the experimenter then told the teacher to grasp the learner's hand and physically force it down on the plate to give Mr. Wallace his unwanted electric shock.

"I had the feeling that very few people would go on at that point, if any," Milgram says. "I thought that would be the limit of obedience that you would find in the laboratory."

It wasn't.

Although seven years have now gone by, Milgram still remembers the first person to walk into the laboratory in the newly rewritten script. He was a construction worker, a very short man. "He was so small," says Milgram, "that when he sat on the chair in front of the shock generator, his feet didn't reach the floor. When the experimenter told him to push the victim's hand down and give the shock, he turned to the experimenter, and he turned to the victim, his elbow went up, he fell down on the hand of the victim, his feet kind of tugged to one side, and he said, 'Like this, boss?' ZZUMPH!"

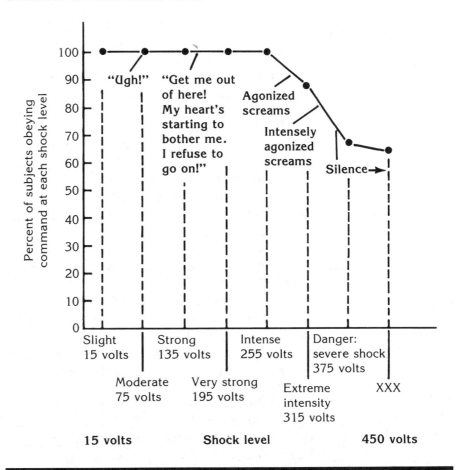

Source: Data from *Obedience to Authority* by Stanley Milgram. Chart from *Psychology: Frontiers of Behavior* by Ronald E. Smith, Irwin G. Sarason, and Barbara R. Sarason. Copyright © 1986 by Harper & Row, Publishers, Inc. Reprinted by permission of Harper & Row, Publishers, Inc.

The experiment was played out to its bitter end. Milgram tried it with forty different subjects. And thirty percent of them obeyed the experimenter and kept on obeying.

"The protests of the victim were strong and vehement, he was screaming his guts out, he refused to participate, and you had to physically struggle with him in order to get his hand down on the shock generator," Milgram remembers. But twelve out of forty did it.

Milgram took his experiment out of New Haven. Not to Germany, just twenty miles down the road to Bridgeport. Maybe, he reasoned, the people obeyed because of the prestigious setting of Yale University. If they couldn't trust a center of learning that had been there for two centuries, whom could they trust? So he moved the experiment to an untrustworthy setting.

The new setting was a suite of three rooms in a run-down office building in Bridgeport. The only identification was a sign with a fictitious name: "Research Associates of Bridgeport." Questions about professional connections got only vague answers about "research for industry."

Obedience was less in Bridgeport. Forty-eight percent of the subjects stayed for the maximum shock, compared to sixty-five percent at Yale. But this was enough to prove that far more than Yale's prestige was behind the obedient behavior.

For more than seven years now, Stanley Milgram has been trying to figure out what makes ordinary American citizens so obedient. The most obvious answer—that people are mean, nasty, brutish and sadistic—won't do. The subjects who gave the shocks to Mr. Wallace to the end of the board did not enjoy it. They groaned, protested, fidgeted, argued, and in some cases, were seized by fits of nervous, agitated giggling.

"They even try to get out of it," says Milgram, "but they are somehow engaged in something from which they cannot liberate themselves. They are locked into a structure, and they do not have the skills or inner resources to disengage themselves."

Milgram, because he mistakenly had assumed that he would have trouble getting people to obey the orders to shock Mr. Wallace, went to a lot of trouble to create a realistic situation.

There was crew-cut Jack Williams and his grey laboratory coat. Not white, which might denote a medical technician, but ambiguously authoritative grey. Then there was the book on the table, and the other appurtenances of the laboratory which emitted the silent message that things were being performed here in the name of science, and were therefore great and good.

But the nicest touch of all was the shock generator. When Milgram started out, he had only a $300 grant from the Higgins Fund of Yale University. Later he got more ample support from the National Science Foundation, but in the beginning he had to create this authentic-looking machine with very scarce resources except for his own imagination. So he went to New York and roamed around the electronic shops until he found some little black switches at Lafayette Radio for a dollar apiece. He bought thirty of them. The generator was a metal box, about the size of a small footlocker, and he drilled the thirty holes for the thirty switches himself in a Yale machine shop. But the fine detail was left to professional industrial engravers. So he ended up with a splendid-looking control panel dominated by the row of switches, each labeled with its voltage, and each having its own red light that flashed on when the switch was pulled. Other things happened when a switch was pushed. Besides the ZZUMPHing noise, a blue light labeled "voltage energizer" went on, and a needle on a dial labeled "voltage" flicked from left to right. Relays inside the box clicked. Finally, in the upper left-hand corner of the control panel was this inscription, engraved in precise block letters:

SHOCK GENERATOR TYPE ZLB
DYSON INSTRUMENT COMPANY
WALTHAM, MASS.
OUTPUT: 15 VOLTS – 450 VOLTS

One day a man from the Lehigh Valley Electronics Company of Pennsylvania was passing through the laboratory, and he stopped to admire the shock generator.

"This is a very fine shock generator," he said. "But who is this Dyson Instrument Company?" Milgram felt proud at that, since Dyson Instrument Company existed only in the recesses of his imagination.

When you consider the seeming authenticity of the situation, you can appreciate the agony some of the subjects went through. It was pure conflict. As Milgram explains to his students, "When a parent says, 'Don't strike old ladies,' you are learning two things: the content, and, also, to obey authority. This experiment creates conflicts between the two elements."

Here is a partial transcription from one of the experiments. The naive "teacher" is a heavy set, worried-looking man with prematurely grey hair. He is wearing a polo shirt. He is very polite. He has just pushed the 180-volt lever. A hidden camera is recording the performance.

LEARNER: *(who, from the teacher's point of view is heard but not seen, an offstage voice)*: Ow, I can't stand the pain. Don't do that. . . .

TEACHER: *(pivoting around in his chair and shaking his head)*: I can't stand it. I'm not going to kill that man in there. You hear him hollering?

EXPERIMENTER: As I told you before, the shocks may be painful, but—

TEACHER: But he's hollering. He can't stand it. What's going to happen to him?

EXPERIMENTER: *(his voice is patient, matter-of-fact)*: The experiment requires that you continue, Teacher.

TEACHER: Aaah, but, unh, I'm not going to get that man sick in there . . . know what I mean?

EXPERIMENTER: Whether the learner likes it or not, we must go on, through all the word pairs.

TEACHER: I refuse to take the responsibility. He's in there hollering!

EXPERIMENTER: It's absolutely essential that you continue, Teacher.

TEACHER: *(indicating the unused questions)*: There's too many left here, I mean, Geez, if he gets them wrong, there's too many of them left. I mean who's going to take the responsibility if anything happens to that gentleman?

EXPERIMENTER: I'm responsible for anything that happens to him. Continue please.

TEACHER: All right. *(Consults list of words.)* The next one's "Slow—walk, truck, dance, music." Answer, please. *(A buzzing sound indicates the learner has signaled his answer.)* Wrong. A hundred and ninety-five volts. "Dance." *(Zzumph!)*

LEARNER: Let me out of here. My heart's bothering me! *(Teacher looks at experimenter.)*

EXPERIMENTER: Continue please.

LEARNER: *(screaming)*: Let me out of here, you have no right to keep me here. Let me out of here, let me out, my heart's bothering me, let me out! *(Teacher shakes head, pats the table nervously.)*

TEACHER: You see, he's hollering. Hear that? Gee, I don't know.

EXPERIMENTER: The experiment requires. . . .

TEACHER: *(interrupting)*: I know it does, sir, but I mean—hunh! He don't know what he's getting in for. He's up to 195 volts! *(Experiment continues, through 210 volts, 225 volts, 240 volts, 255 volts, 270 volts, delivered to the man in the electric chair, at which point the teacher, with evident relief, runs out of word-pair questions.)*

EXPERIMENTER: You'll have to go back to the beginning of that page and go through them again until he's learned them all correctly.

TEACHER: Aw, no. I'm not going to kill that man. You mean I've got to keep going up with the scale. No sir. He's hollering in there. I'm not going to give him 450 volts.

EXPERIMENTER: The experiment requires that you go on.

TEACHER: I know it does, but that man is hollering in there, sir.

EXPERIMENTER: *(same matter-of-fact tone)*: As I said before, although the shocks may be painful. . . .

TEACHER: *(interrupting)*: Awwww. He—he—he's yelling in there.

EXPERIMENTER: Start with "Blue," please, at the top of the page. Continue, please, Teacher. Just go ahead.

TEACHER: *(concentrating intently on list of words in front of him, as if to shut everything else out)*: "Blue—boy, girl, grass, hat." *(Buzz indicates answer.)* Correct. "Night—day, sky, job, chair. *(Buzz)* Wrong. The answer is "day." Two hundred and eighty-five volts. *(Zzumph!)*

LEARNER: Ohhhuhhoohhh!

EXPERIMENTER: Continue please.

TEACHER: "Fat—man, lady, tub, neck." Answer, please. *(Buzz)* Wrong. The answer is "neck." Three hundred volts. *(Zzumph!)*

LEARNER: Ohhh. I absolutely refuse to answer any more. *(Shouting urgently, now)* Let me out of here. You can't hold me here. Get me out. Get—me—out—of—here.

EXPERIMENTER: Continue. The next word is "Green," please.

TEACHER: "Green—grass, hat, ink, apple." (*Nothing happens. No answering buzz. Just gloomy silence.*)

TEACHER: I don't think he is going to answer.

EXPERIMENTER: If the learner doesn't answer in a reasonable time, about four or five seconds, consider the answer wrong. And follow the same procedures you have been doing for wrong answers. Say "Wrong," tell him the number of volts, give him the punishment, read him the correct answer. Continue, please.

TEACHER: "Green—grass, hat, ink, apple." Answer, please. (*More silence. Teacher just sits there.*)

EXPERIMENTER: Go on with the procedure, please, Teacher.

TEACHER: Three hundred and fifteen volts. The answer is "ink." (*Zzumph!*)

LEARNER: Ohh. Ooohh.

TEACHER: (*relieved to hear response*): Next one. . . .

LEARNER: I absolutely refuse to answer.

TEACHER: You got to. You get a shock if you don't answer. (*Experiment continues with learner refusing to answer, and, finally, failing even to grunt or groan. At 375 volts, the teacher stands up. Has he had enough? Will he break off the experiment? Will he disobey?*)

TEACHER: I think something's happened to that fellow in there. I don't get no answer. He was hollering at less voltage. Can't you check in and see if he's all right, please?

EXPERIMENTER: (*same detached calm*): Not once we've started. Please continue, Teacher.

TEACHER: (*sits down, sighs deeply*): "Cool—day, shade, water, paint." Answer, please. Are you all right in there? Are you all right?

EXPERIMENTER: Please continue, Teacher. Continue, please. (*Teacher pushes lever. Zzumph!*)

TEACHER: (*swiveling around in his chair*): Something's happened to that man in there. (*Swiveling back*) Next one. "Low—dollar, necklace, moon, paint." (*Turning around again*) Something's happened to that man in there. You better check in on him, sir. He won't answer or nothing.

EXPERIMENTER: Continue. Go on, please.

TEACHER: You accept all responsibility.

EXPERIMENTER: The responsibility is mine. Correct. Please go on. (*Teacher returns to his list, starts running through words as rapidly as he can read them, works through to 450 volts.*)

TEACHER: That's that.

EXPERIMENTER: Continue using the last switch on the board, please. The four-fifty switch for each wrong answer. Continue, please.

TEACHER: But I don't get no anything!

EXPERIMENTER: Please continue. The next word is "White."

TEACHER: Don't you think you should look in on him, please.

EXPERIMENTER: Not once we've started the experiment.

TEACHER: But what if something has happened to the man?

EXPERIMENTER: The experiment requires that you continue. Go on, please.

TEACHER: Don't the man's health mean anything?

EXPERIMENTER: Whether the learner likes it or not. . . .

TEACHER: What if he's dead in there? *(Gestures toward the room with the electric chair.)* I mean, he told me he can't stand the shock, sir. I don't mean to be rude, but I think you should look in on him. All you have to do is look in the door. I don't get no answer, no noise. Something might have happened to the gentleman in there, sir.

EXPERIMENTER: We must continue. Go on, please.

TEACHER: You mean keep giving him what? Four hundred fifty volts, what he's got now?

EXPERIMENTER: That's correct. Continue. The next word is "White."

TEACHER: *(now at a furious pace):* "White—cloud, horse, rock, house." Answer, please. The answer is "horse." Four hundred and fifty volts. *(Zzumph!)* Next word, "Bag—paint, music, clown, girl." The answer is "paint." Four hundred and fifty volts. *(Zzumph!)* Next word is "Short—sentence, movie. . . ."

EXPERIMENTER: Excuse me, Teacher. We'll have to discontinue the experiment.

(Enter Milgram from camera's left. He has been watching from behind one-way glass.)

MILGRAM: I'd like to ask you a few questions. *(Slowly, patiently, he dehoaxes the teacher, telling him that the shocks and screams were not real.)*

TEACHER: You mean he wasn't getting nothing? Well, I'm glad to hear that. I was getting upset there. I was getting ready to walk out.

(Finally, to make sure there are no hard feelings, friendly, harmless Mr. Wallace comes out in coat and tie. Gives jovial greeting. Friendly reconciliation takes place. Experiment ends.)

Subjects in the experiment were not asked to give the 450-volt shock more than three times. By that time, it seemed evident that they would go on indefinitely. "No one," says Milgram, "who got within five shocks of the end ever broke off. By that point, he had resolved the conflict."

Why do so many people resolve the conflict in favor of obedience?

Milgram's theory assumes that people behave in two different operating modes as different as ice and water. He does not rely on Freud or sex or toilet-training hang-ups for this theory. All he says is that ordinarily we operate in a state of autonomy, which means we pretty much have and assert control over what we do. But in certain circumstances, we operate under what Milgram calls a state of agency (after agent, n . . . one who acts for or in the place of another by authority from him: a substitute; a deputy. — *Webster's Collegiate Dictionary*). A state of agency, to Milgram, is nothing more than a frame of mind.

"There's nothing bad about it, there's nothing good about it," he says. "It's a natural circumstance of living with other people. . . . I think of a state of agency as a real transformation of a person; if a person has different properties when he's in that state, just as water can turn to ice under certain conditions of temperature, a person can move to the state of mind that I call agency . . . the critical thing is that you see yourself as the instrument of the execution of another person's wishes. You do not see yourself as acting on your own. And there's a real transformation, a real change of properties of the person."

To achieve this change, you have to be in a situation where there seems to be a ruling authority whose commands are relevant to some legitimate purpose; the authority's power is not unlimited.

But situations can be and have been structured to make people do unusual things, and not just in Milgram's laboratory. The reason, says Milgram, is that no action, in and of itself, contains meaning.

"The meaning always depends on your definition of the situation. Take an action like killing another person. It sounds bad.

"But then we say the other person was about to destroy a hundred children, and the only way to stop him was to kill him. Well, that sounds good.

"Or, you take destroying your own life. It sounds very bad. Yet, in the Second World War, thousands of persons thought it was a good thing to destroy your own life. It was set in the proper context. You sipped some saki from a whistling cup, recited a few haiku. You said, 'May my death be as clean and as quick as the shattering of crystal.' And it almost seemed like a good, noble thing to do, to crash your kamikaze plane into an aircraft carrier. But the main thing was, the definition of what a kamikaze pilot was doing had been determined by the relevant authority. Now, once you are in a state of agency, you allow the authority to determine, to define what the situation is. The meaning of your action is altered."

So, for most subjects in Milgram's laboratory experiments, the act of giving Mr. Wallace his painful shock was necessary, even though unpleasant, and besides they were doing it on behalf of somebody else and it was for science. There was still strain and conflict, of course. Most people resolved it by grimly sticking to their task and obeying. But some broke out. Milgram tried varying the conditions of the experiment to see what would help break people out of their state of agency.

"The results, as seen and felt in the laboratory," he has written, "are disturbing. They raise the possibility that human nature, or more specifically the kind of character produced in American democratic society, cannot be counted on to insulate its citizens from brutality and inhumane treatment at the direction of malevolent authority. A substantial proportion of people do what they are told to do, irrespective of the content of the act and without limitations of conscience, so long as they perceive that the command comes from a legitimate authority. If, in this study, an anonymous experimenter can successfully command adults to subdue a fifty-year-old man and force on him painful electric shocks against his protest, one can only wonder what government, with its vastly greater authority and prestige, can command of its subjects."

This is a nice statement, but it falls short of summing up the full meaning of Milgram's work. It leaves some questions still unanswered.

The first question is this: Should we really be surprised and alarmed that people obey? Wouldn't it be even more alarming if they all refused to obey? Without obedience to a relevant ruling authority there could not be a civil society. And without a civil society, as Thomas Hobbes pointed out in the seventeenth century, we would live in a condition of war, "of every man against every other man," and life would be "solitary, poor, nasty, brutish and short."

In the middle of one of Stanley Milgram's lectures at C.U.N.Y. recently, some mini-skirted undergraduates started whispering and giggling in the back of the room. He told them to cut it out. Since he was the relevant authority in that time and that place, they obeyed, and most people in the room were glad that they obeyed.

This was not, of course, a conflict situation. Nothing in the coeds' social upbringing made it a matter of conscience for them to whisper and giggle. But a case can be made that in a conflict situation it is all the more important to obey. Take the case of war, for example. Would we really want a situation in which every participant in a war, direct or indirect — from front-line soldiers to the people who sell coffee and cigarettes to employees at the Concertina barbed-wire factory in Kansas — stops and consults his conscience before each action. It is asking for an awful lot of mental strain and anguish from an awful lot of people. The value of having civil order is that one can do his duty, or whatever interests him, or whatever seems to benefit him at the moment, and leave the agonizing to others. When Francis Gary Powers was being tried by a Soviet military tribunal after his U-2 spy plane was shot down, the presiding judge asked if he had thought about the possibility that his flight might have provoked a war. Powers replied with Hobbesian clarity: "The people who sent me should think of these things. My job was to carry out orders. I do not think it was my responsibility to make such decisions."

It was not his responsibility. And it is quite possible that if everyone felt responsible for each of the ultimate consequences of his own tiny contributions to complex chains of events, then society simply would not work. Milgram, fully conscious of the moral and social implications of his research, believes that people should feel responsible for their actions. If someone else had invented the experiment, and if he had been the naive subject, he feels certain that he would have been among the disobedient minority.

"There is no very good solution to this," he admits, thoughtfully. "To simply and categorically say that you won't obey authority may resolve your personal conflict, but it creates more problems for society which may be more serious in the long run. But I have no doubt that to disobey is the proper thing to do in this [the laboratory] situation. It is the only reasonable value judgment to make."

The conflict between the need to obey the relevant ruling authority and the need to follow your conscience becomes sharpest if you insist on living by an ethical system based on a rigid code—a code that seeks to answer all questions in advance of their being raised. Code ethics cannot solve the obedience problem. Stanley Milgram seems to be a situation ethicist and situation ethics does offer a way out: When you feel conflict, you examine the situation and then make a choice among the competing evils. You may act with a presumption in favor of obedience, but reserve the possibility that you will disobey whenever obedience demands a flagrant and outrageous affront to conscience. This, by the way, is the philosophical position of many who resist the draft. In World War II, they would have fought. Vietnam is a different, an outrageously different, situation.

Life can be difficult for the situation ethicist, because he does not see the world in straight lines, while the social system too often assumes such a God-given, squared-off structure. If your moral code includes an injunction against all war, you may be deferred as a conscientious objector. If you merely oppose this particular war, you may not be deferred.

Stanley Milgram has his problems, too. He believes that in the laboratory situation, he would not have shocked Mr. Wallace. His professional critics reply that in his real-life situation he has done the equivalent. He has placed innocent and naive subjects under great emotional strain and pressure in selfish obedience to his quest for knowledge. When you raise this issue with Milgram, he has an answer ready. There is, he explains patiently, a critical difference between his naive subjects and the man in the electric chair. The man in the electric chair (in the mind of the naive subject) is helpless, strapped in. But the naive subject is free to go at any time.

Immediately after he offers this distinction, Milgram anticipates the objection.

"It's quite true," he says, "that this is almost a philosophic position, because we have learned that some people are psychologically incapable of disengaging themselves. But that doesn't relieve them of the moral responsibility."

The parallel is exquisite. "The tension problem was unexpected," says Milgram in his defense. But he went on anyway. The naive subjects didn't expect the screaming protests from the strapped-in learner. But they went on.

"I had to make a judgment," says Milgram. "I had to ask myself, was this harming the person or not? My judgment is that it was not. Even in the extreme cases, I wouldn't say that permanent damage results."

Sound familiar? "The shocks may be painful," the experimenter kept saying, "but they're not dangerous."

After the series of experiments was completed, Milgram sent a report of the results to his subjects and a questionnaire, asking whether they were glad or sorry to have been in the experiment. Eighty-three and seven-tenths percent said they were glad and only 1.3 percent were sorry; 15 percent were neither sorry nor glad. However, Milgram could not be sure at the time of the experiment that only 1.3 percent would be sorry.

QUESTIONS

1. Do you think Hitler could have happened in America? Discuss.

2. How would you respond as a teacher in the obedience experiment: would you obey or disobey the commands of the experimenter?

3. What ethical considerations do you think should be considered when conducting experiments on human subjects?

The Parable of the Sadhu

Last year, as the first participant in the new six-month sabbatical program that Morgan Stanley has adopted, I enjoyed a rare opportunity to collect my thoughts as well as do some traveling. I spent the first three months in Nepal, walking 600 miles through 200 villages in the Himalayas and climbing some 120,000 vertical feet. On the trip my sole Western companion was an anthropologist who shed light on the cultural patterns of the villages we passed through.

During the Nepal hike, something occurred that has had a powerful impact on my thinking about corporate ethics. Although some might argue that the experience has no relevance to business, it was a situation in which a basic ethical dilemma suddenly intruded into the lives of a group of individuals. How the group responded I think holds a lesson for all organizations no matter how defined.

THE SADHU

The Nepal experience was more rugged and adventuresome than I had anticipated. Most commercial treks last two or three weeks and cover a quarter of the distance we traveled.

My friend Stephen, the anthropologist, and I were halfway through the 60-day Himalayan part of the trip when we reached the high point, an 18,000-foot pass over a crest that we'd have to traverse to reach to the village of Muklinath, an ancient holy place for pilgrims.

Six years earlier I had suffered pulmonary edema, an acute form of altitude sickness, at 16,500 feet in the vicinity of Everest base camp, so we were understandably concerned about what would happen at 18,000 feet. Moreover, the Himalayas were having their wettest spring in 20 years; hip-deep powder and ice had already driven us off one ridge. If we failed to cross the pass, I feared that the last half of our "once in a lifetime" trip would be ruined.

The night before we would try the pass, we camped at a hut at 14,500 feet. In the photos taken at that camp, my face appears wan. The last

Source: Reprinted by permission of the Harvard Business Review, *"The Parable of the Sadhu" by Bowen H. McCoy (September/October 1983). Copyright © 1983 by the President and Fellows of Harvard College; all rights reserved.*

village we'd passed through was a sturdy two-day walk below us, and I was tired.

During the late afternoon, four back-packers from New Zealand joined us, and we spent most of the night awake, anticipating the climb. Below we could see the fires of two other parties, which turned out to be two Swiss couples and a Japanese hiking club.

To get over the steep part of the climb before the sun melted the steps cut in the ice, we departed at 3:30 A.M. The New Zealanders left first, followed by Stephen and myself, our porters and Sherpas, and then the Swiss. The Japanese lingered in their camp. The sky was clear, and we were confident that no spring storm would erupt that day to close the pass.

At 15,500 feet, it looked to me as if Stephen were shuffling and staggering a bit, which are symptoms of altitude sickness. (The initial stage of altitude sickness brings a headache and nausea. As the condition worsens, a climber may encounter difficult breathing, disorientation, aphasia, and paralysis.) I felt strong, my adrenaline was flowing, but I was very concerned about my ultimate ability to get across. A couple of our porters were also suffering from the height, and Pasang, our Sherpa sirdar (leader,) was worried.

Just after daybreak, while we rested at 15,500 feet, one of the New Zealanders, who had gone ahead, came staggering down toward us with a body slung across his shoulders. He dumped the almost naked, barefoot body of an Indian holy man — a sadhu — at my feet. He had found the pilgrim lying on the ice, shivering and suffering from hypothermia. I cradled the sadhu's head and laid him out on the rocks. The New Zealander was angry. He wanted to get across the pass before the bright sun melted the snow. He said, "Look, I've done what I can. You have porters and Sherpa guides. You care for him. We're going on!" He turned and went back up the mountain to join his friends.

I took a carotid pulse and found that the sadhu was still alive. We figured he had probably visited the holy shrines at Muklinath and was on his way home. It was fruitless to question why he had chosen this desperately high route instead of the safe, heavily traveled caravan route through the Kali Gandaki gorge. Or why he was almost naked and with no shoes, or how long he had been lying in the pass. The answers weren't going to solve our problem.

Stephen and the four Swiss began stripping off outer clothing and opening their packs. The sadhu was soon clothed from head to foot. He was not able to walk, but he was very much alive. I looked down the mountain and spotted below the Japanese climbers marching up with a horse.

Without a great deal of thought, I told Stephen and Pasang that I was concerned about withstanding the heights to come and wanted to get over the pass. I took off after several of our porters who had gone ahead.

On the steep part of the ascent where, if the ice steps had given way, I would have slid down about 3,000 feet, I felt vertigo. I stopped for a breather, allowing the Swiss to catch up with me. I inquired about the sadhu and Stephen. They said that the sadhu was fine and that Stephen was just behind. I set off again for the summit.

Stephen arrived at the summit an hour after I did. Still exhilarated by victory, I ran down the snow slope to congratulate him. He was suffering from altitude sickness, walking 15 steps, then stopping, walking 15 steps, then stopping. Pasang accompanied him all the way up. When I reached them, Stephen glared at me and said: "How do you feel about contributing to the death of a fellow man?"

I did not fully comprehend what he meant.

"Is the sadhu dead?" I inquired.

"No," replied Stephen, "but he surely will be!"

After I had gone, and the Swiss had departed not long after, Stephen had remained with the sadhu. When the Japanese had arrived, Stephen had asked to use their horse to transport the sadhu down to the hut. They had refused. He had then asked Pasang to have a group of our porters carry the sadhu. Pasang had resisted the idea, saying that the porters would have to exert all their energy to get themselves over the pass. He had thought they could not carry a man down 1,000 feet to the hut, reclimb the slope, and get across safely before the snow melted. Pasang had pressed Stephen not to delay any longer.

The Sherpas had carried the sadhu down to a rock in the sun at about 15,000 feet and had pointed out the hut another 500 feet below. The Japanese had given him food and drink. When they had last seen him he was listlessly throwing rocks at the Japanese party's dog, which had frightened him.

We do not know if the sadhu lived or died.

For many of the following days and evenings Stephen and I discussed and debated our behavior toward the sadhu. Stephen is a committed Quaker with deep moral vision. He said, "I feel that what happened with the sadhu is a good example of the breakdown between the individual ethic and the corporate ethic. No one person was willing to assume ultimate responsibility for the sadhu. Each was willing to do his bit just so long as it was not too inconvenient. When it got to be a bother, everyone just passed the buck to someone else and took off. Jesus was relevant to a more individualistic stage of society, but how do we interpret his teaching today in a world filled with large, impersonal organizations and groups?"

I defended the larger group, saying, "Look, we all cared. We all stopped and gave aid and comfort. Everyone did his bit. The New Zealander carried him down below the snow line. I took his pulse and suggested we treat him for hypothermia. You and the Swiss gave him clothing and got him warmed up. The Japanese gave him food and water. The Sherpas carried him down to the sun and pointed out the easy trail toward the hut. He was well enough to throw rocks at a dog. What more could we do?"

"You have just described the typical affluent Westerner's response to a problem. Throwing money — in this case food and sweaters — at it, but not solving the fundamentals!" Stephen retorted.

"What would satisfy you?" I said. "Here we are, a group of New Zealanders, Swiss, Americans, and Japanese who have never met before and who are at the apex of one of the most powerful experiences of our lives. Some years the pass is so bad no one gets over it. What right does an almost naked pilgrim who chooses the wrong trail have to disrupt our lives? Even the Sherpas had no interest in risking the trip to help him beyond a certain point."

Stephen calmly rebutted, "I wonder what the Sherpas would have done if the sadhu had been a well-dressed Nepali, or what the Japanese would have done if the sadhu had been a well-dressed Asian, or what you would have done, Buzz, if the sadhu had been a well-dressed Western woman?"

"Where, in your opinion," I asked instead, "is the limit of our responsibility in a situation like this? We had our own well-being to worry about. Our Sherpa guides were unwilling to jeopardize us or the porters for the sadhu. No one else on the mountain was willing to commit himself beyond certain self-imposed limits."

Stephen said, "As individual Christians or people with a Western ethical tradition, we can fulfill our obligations in such a situation only if (1) the sadhu dies in our care, (2) the sadhu demonstrates to us that he could undertake the two-day walk down to the village or (3) we carry the sadhu for two days down to the village and convince someone there to care for him."

"Leaving the sadhu in the sun with food and clothing, while he demonstrated hand-eye coordination by throwing a rock at a dog, comes close to fulfilling items one and two," I answered. "And it wouldn't have made sense to take him to the village where the people appeared to be far less caring than the Sherpas, so the third condition is impractical. Are you really saying that, no matter what the implications, we should, at the drop of a hat, have changed our entire plan?"

THE INDIVIDUAL VS. THE GROUP ETHIC

Despite my arguments, I felt and continue to feel guilt about the sadhu. I had literally walked through a classic moral dilemma without fully thinking through the consequences. My excuses for my actions include a high adrenaline flow, a superordinate goal, and a once-in-a-lifetime opportunity—factors in the usual corporate situation, especially when one is under stress.

Real moral dilemmas are ambiguous, and many of us hike right through them, unaware that they exist. When, usually after the fact, someone makes an issue of them, we tend to resent his or her bringing it up. Often, when the full import of what we have done (or not done) falls on us, we dig into a defensive position from which it is very difficult to emerge. In rare circumstances we may contemplate what we have done from inside a prison.

Had we mountaineers been free of physical and mental stress caused by the effort and the high altitude, we might have treated the sadhu differently. Yet, isn't stress the real test of personal and corporate values? The instant decisions executives make under pressure reveal the most about personal and corporate character.

Among the many questions that occur to me when pondering my experience are: What are the practical limits of moral imagination and vision? Is there a collective or institutional ethic beyond the ethics of the individual? At what level of effort or commitment can one discharge one's ethical responsibilities?

Not every ethical dilemma has a right solution. Reasonable people often disagree; otherwise there would be no dilemma. In a business context, however, it is essential that managers agree on a process for dealing with dilemmas.

The sadhu experience offers an interesting parallel to business situations. An immediate response was mandatory. Failure to act was a decision in itself. Up on the mountain we could not resign and submit our résumés to a headhunter. In contrast to philosophy, business involves action and implementation—getting things done. Managers must come up with answers to problems based on what they see and what they allow to influence their decision-making processes. On the mountain, none of us but Stephen realized the true dimensions of the situation we were facing.

One of our problems was that as a group we had no process for developing a consensus. We had no sense of purpose or plan. The difficulties of dealing with the sadhu were so complex that no one person could handle it. Because it did not have a set of preconditions that could guide its action to an acceptable resolution, the group reacted instinctively as individuals. The cross-cultural nature of the group added a further layer of complexity. We had no leader with whom we could all identify and in whose purpose we believed. Only Stephen was willing to take charge, but he could not gain adequate support to care for the sadhu.

Some organizations do have a value system that transcends the personal values of the managers. Such values, which go beyond profitability, are usually revealed when the organization is under stress. People throughout the organization generally accept its values, which, because they are not presented as a rigid list of commandments, may be somewhat ambiguous. The stories people tell, rather than printed materials, transmit these conceptions of what is proper behavior.

For 20 years I have been exposed at senior levels to a variety of corporations and organizations. It is amazing how quickly an outsider can sense the tone and style of an organization and the degree of tolerated openness and freedom to challenge management.

Organizations that do not have a heritage of mutually accepted, shared values tend to become unhinged during stress, with each individual bailing out for himself. In the great takeover battles we have witnessed during past years, companies that had strong cultures drew the wagons around them and fought it out, while other companies saw executives supported by their golden parachutes, bail out of the struggles.

Because corporations and their members are interdependent, for the corporation to be strong the members need to share a preconceived notion of what is correct behavior, a "business ethic," and think of it as a positive force, not a constraint.

As an investment banker I am continually warned by well-meaning lawyers, clients, and associates to be wary of conflicts of interest. Yet if I were to run away from every difficult situation, I wouldn't be an effective investment banker. I have to feel my way through conflicts. An effective manager can't run from risk either; he or she has to confront and deal with risk. To feel "safe" in doing this, managers need the guidelines of an agreed-on process and set of values within the organization.

After my three months in Nepal, I spent three months as an executive-in-residence at both Stanford Business School and the Center for Ethics and Social Policy at the Graduate Theological Union at Berkeley. These six months away from my job gave me time to assimilate 20 years of business experience. My thoughts turned often to the meaning of the leadership role in any large organization. Students at the seminary thought of themselves as antibusiness. But when I questioned them they agreed that they distrusted all large organizations, including the church. They perceived all large organizations as impersonal and opposed to individual values and needs. Yet we all know of organizations where peoples' values and beliefs are respected and their expressions encouraged. What makes the difference? Can we identify the difference and, as a result, manage more effectively?

The word "ethics" turns off many and confuses more. Yet the notions of shared values and an agreed-on process for dealing with adversity and change—what many people mean when they talk about corporate culture—seem to be at the heart of the ethical issue. People who are in touch with their own core beliefs and the beliefs of others and are sustained by them can be more comfortable living on the cutting edge. At times, taking a tough line or a decisive stand in a muddle of ambiguity is the only ethical thing to do. If a manager is indecisive and spends time trying to figure out the "good" thing to do, the enterprise may be lost.

Business ethics, then, has to do with the authenticity and integrity of the enterprise. To be ethical is to follow the business as well as the cultural goals of the corporation, its owners, its employees, and its customers. Those who cannot serve the corporate visions are not authentic business people and, therefore, are not ethical in the business sense.

At this stage of my own business experience I have a strong interest in organizational behavior. Sociologists are keenly studying what they call corporate stories, legends, and heroes as a way organizations have of transmitting the value system. Corporations such as Arco have even hired consultants to perform an audit of their corporate culture. In a company, the leader is the person who understands, interprets, and manages the corporate value system. Effective managers are then action-oriented people who resolve conflict, are tolerant of ambiguity, stress, and change, and have a strong sense of purpose for themselves and their organizations.

If all this is true, I wonder about the role of the professional manager who moves from company to company. How can he or she quickly absorb the values and culture of different organizations? Or is there, indeed, an art of management that is totally transportable? Assuming such fungible managers do exist, is it proper for them to manipulate the values of others?

I see the current interest in corporate culture and corporate value systems as a positive response to Stephen's pessimism about the decline of the role of the individual in large organizations. Individuals who operate from a thoughtful set of personal values provide the foundation for a corporate culture. A corporate tradition that encourages freedom of inquiry, supports personal values, and reinforces a focused sense of direction can fulfill the need for individuality along with the prosperity and success of the group. Without such corporate support, the individual is lost.

That is the lesson of the sadhu. In a complex corporate situation, the individual requires and deserves the support of the group. If people cannot find such support from their organization, they don't know how to act. If such support is forthcoming, a person has a stake in the success of the group, and can add much to the process of establishing and maintaining a corporate culture. It is management's challenge to be sensitive to individual needs, to shape them, and to direct and focus them for the benefit of the group as a whole.

For each of us the sadhu lives. Should we stop what we are doing and comfort him; or should we keep trudging up toward the high pass? Should I pause to help the derelict I pass on the street each night as I walk by the Yale Club en route to Grand Central Station? Am I his brother? What is the nature of our responsibility if we consider ourselves to be ethical persons? Perhaps it is to change the values of the group so that it can, with all its resources, take the other road.

QUESTIONS

1. Discuss the "Parable of the Sadhu" in light of Kohlberg's levels of morality—preconventional, conventional, postconventional.

2. Discuss the "parable" in light of traditional and contemporary definitions of good—sanctity of life, the greatest good for the greatest number, and do unto others as you would have them do unto you.

3. What values do you think an organization should have to provide guidance in moral dilemmas?

___
___
___

The Myth of Sisyphus

The gods had condemned Sisyphus to ceaselessly rolling a rock to the top of a mountain, whence the stone would fall back of its own weight. They had thought with some reason that there is no more dreadful punishment than futile and hopeless labor.

If one believes Homer, Sisyphus was the wisest and most prudent of mortals. According to another tradition, however, he was disposed to practice the profession of highwayman. I see no contradiction in this. Opinions differ as to the reasons why he became the futile laborer of the underworld. To begin with, he is accused of a certain levity in regard to the gods. He stole their secrets. Aegina, the daughter of Aesopus, was carried off by Jupiter. The father was shocked by that disappearance and complained to Sisyphus. He, who knew of the abduction, offered to tell about it on condition that Aesopus would give water to the citadel of Corinth. To the celestial thunderbolts he preferred the benediction of water. He was punished for this in the underworld. Homer tells us also that Sisyphus had put Death in chains. Pluto could not endure the sight of his deserted, silent empire. He dispatched the god of war, who liberated Death from the hands of her conqueror.

It is said also that Sisyphus, being near to death, rashly wanted to test his wife's love. He ordered her to cast his unburied body into the middle of the public square. Sisyphus woke up in the underworld. And there, annoyed by an obedience so contrary to human love, he obtained from Pluto permission to return to earth in order to chastise his wife. But when he had seen again the face of this world, enjoyed water and sun, warm stones and the sea, he no longer wanted to go back to the infernal darkness. Recalls, signs of anger, warnings were of no avail. Many years more he lived facing the curve of the gulf, the sparkling sea, and the smiles of earth. A decree of the gods was necessary. Mercury came and seized the impudent man by the collar and, snatching him from his joys, led him forcibly back to the underworld, where his rock was ready for him.

You have already grasped that Sisyphus is the absurd hero. He *is*, as much through his passions as through his torture. His scorn of the gods, his hatred of death, and his passion for life won him that unspeakable

Source: From The Myth of Sisyphus, *by Albert Camus, translated by Justin O'Brien. Copyright © 1955 by Alfred A. Knopf, Inc. Reprinted by permission of the publisher.*

penalty in which the whole being is exerted toward accomplishing nothing. This is the price that must be paid for the passions of this earth. Nothing is told us about Sisyphus in the underworld. Myths are made for the imagination to breathe life into them. As for this myth, one sees merely the whole effort of a body straining to raise the huge stone, to roll it and push it up a slope a hundred times over; one sees the face screwed up, the cheek tight against the stone, the shoulder bracing the clay-covered mass, the foot wedging it, the fresh start with arms outstretched, the wholly human security of two earth-clotted hands. At the very end of his long effort measured by skyless space and time without depth, the purpose is achieved. Then Sisyphus watches the stone rush down in a few moments toward that lower world whence he will have to push it up again toward the summit. He goes back down to the plain.

It is during that return, that pause, that Sisyphus interests me. A face that toils so close to stones is already stone itself! I see that man going back down with a heavy yet measured step toward the torment of which he will never know the end. That hour like a breathing-space which returns as surely as his suffering, that is the hour of consciousness. At each of those moments when he leaves the heights and gradually sinks toward the lairs of the gods, he is superior to his fate. He is stronger than his rock.

If this myth is tragic, that is because its hero is conscious. Where would his torture be, indeed, if at every step the hope of succeeding upheld him? The workman of today works every day in his life at the same tasks, and this fate is no less absurd. But it is tragic only at the rare moments when it becomes conscious. Sisyphus, proletarian of the gods, powerless and rebellious, knows the whole extent of his wretched condition: it is what he thinks of during his descent. The lucidity that was to constitute his torture at the same time crowns his victory. There is no fate that cannot be surmounted by scorn.

If the descent is thus sometimes performed in sorrow, it can also take place in joy. This word is not too much. Again I fancy Sisyphus returning toward his rock, and the sorrow was in the beginning. When the images of earth cling too tightly to memory, when the call of happiness becomes too insistent, it happens that melancholy rises in man's heart: this is the rock's victory, this is the rock itself. The boundless grief is too heavy to bear. These are our nights of Gethsemane. But crushing truths perish from being acknowledged. Thus, Oedipus at the outset obeys fate without knowing it. But from the moment he knows, his tragedy begins. Yet at the same moment, blind and desperate, he realizes that the only bond linking him to the world is the cool hand of a girl. Then a tremendous remark rings out: "Despite so many ordeals, my advanced age and the nobility of my soul make me conclude that all is well." Sophocles' Oedipus, like Dostoevsky's Kirilov, thus gives the recipe for the absurd victory. Ancient wisdom confirms modern heroism.

One does not discover the absurd without being tempted to write a manual of happiness. "What! by such narrow ways—?" There is but one world, however. Happiness and the absurd are two sons of the same earth. They are inseparable. It would be a mistake to say that happiness necessarily springs from the absurd discovery. It happens as well that the feeling of the absurd springs from happiness. "I conclude that all is well," says Oedipus, and that remark is sacred. It echoes in the wild and limited universe of man. It teaches that all is not, has not been, exhausted. It drives out of this world a god who had come into it with dissatisfaction and a preference for futile sufferings. It makes of fate a human matter, which must be settled among men.

All Sisyphus' silent joy is contained therein. His fate belongs to him. His rock is his thing. Likewise, the absurd man, when he contemplates his torment, silences all the idols. In the universe suddenly restored to its silence, the myriad wondering little voices of the earth rise up. Unconscious, secret calls, invitations from all the faces, they are the necessary reverse and price of victory. There is no sun without shadow, and it is essential to know the night. The absurd man says yes and his effort will henceforth be unceasing. If there is a personal fate, there is no higher destiny, or at least there is but one which he concludes is inevitable and despicable. For the rest, he knows himself to be the master of his days. At that subtle moment when man glances backward over his life, Sisyphus returning toward his rock, in that slight pivoting he contemplates that series of unrelated actions which becomes his fate, created by him, combined under his memory's eye and soon sealed by his death. Thus, convinced of the wholly human origin of all that is human, a blind man eager to see who knows that the night has no end, he is still on the go. The rock is still rolling.

I leave Sisyphus at the foot of the mountain! One always finds one's burden again. But Sisyphus teaches the higher fidelity that negates the gods and raises rocks. He too concludes that all is well. This universe henceforth without a master seems to him neither sterile nor futile. Each atom of that stone, each mineral flake of that night-filled mountain, in itself forms a world. The struggle itself toward the heights is enough to fill a man's heart. One must imagine Sisyphus happy.

QUESTIONS

1. Discuss "The Myth of Sisyphus" as it relates to your life. What is your rock, mountain, and meaning?

   _____
   _____
   _____

2. Discuss "The Myth of Sisyphus" as it relates to the world of work today. Give examples.

   _____
   _____
   _____

Wheels

At a car assembly plant north of the Fisher Freeway, Matt Zaleski, assistant plant manager and a graying veteran of the auto industry, was glad that today was Wednesday.

Not that the day would be free from urgent problems and exercises in survival—no day ever was. Tonight, like any night, he would go homeward wearily, feeling older than his fifty-three years and convinced he had spent another day of his life inside a pressure cooker. Matt Zaleski sometimes wished he could summon back the energy he had had as a young man, either when he was new to auto production or as an Air Force bombardier in World War II. He also thought sometimes, looking back, that the years of war—even though he was in Europe in the thick of things, with an impressive combat record—were less crisis-filled than his civil occupation now.

Already, in the few minutes he had been in his glass-paneled office on a mezzanine above the assembly plant floor, even while removing his coat, he had skimmed through a red-tabbed memo on the desk—a union grievance which he realized immediately could cause a plant-wide walkout if it wasn't dealt with properly and promptly. There was undoubtedly still more to worry about in an adjoining pile of papers—other headaches, including critical material shortages (there were always some, each day), or quality control demands, or machinery failures, or some new conundrum which no one had thought of before, any or all of which could halt the assembly line and stop production.

Zaleski threw his stocky figure into the chair at his gray metal desk, moving in short, jerky movements, as he always had. He heard the chair protest--a reminder of his growing overweight and the big belly he carried around nowadays. He thought ashamedly: he could never squeeze it now into the cramped nose dome of a B-17. He wished that worry would take off pounds; instead, it seemed to put them on, especially since Freda died and loneliness at night drove him to the refrigerator, nibbling, for lack of something else to do.

But at least today was Wednesday.

First things first. He hit the intercom switch for the general office; his secretary wasn't in yet. A timekeeper answered.

Source: Excerpt from Wheels *by Arthur Hailey. Copyright © 1971 by Arthur Hailey. Reprinted by permission of Doubleday & Company, Inc.*

"I want Parkland and the union committeeman," the assistant plant manager commanded. "Get them in here fast."

Parkland was a foreman. And outside they would be well aware which union committeeman he meant because they would know about the red-tabbed memo on his desk. In a plant, bad news traveled like burning gasoline.

The pile of papers—still untouched, though he would have to get to them soon—reminded Zaleski he had been thinking gloomily of the many causes which could halt an assembly line.

Halting the line, stopping production for whatever reason, was like a sword in the side to Matt Zaleski. The function of his job, his personal raison d'etre, was to keep the line moving, with finished cars being driven off the end at the rate of one car a minute, no matter how the trick was done or if, at times, he felt like a juggler with fifteen balls in the air at once. Senior management wasn't interested in the juggling act, or excuses either. Results were what counted: quotas, daily production, manufacturing costs. But if the line stopped he heard about it soon enough. Each single minute of lost time meant that an entire car didn't get produced, and the loss would never be made up. Thus, even a two- or three-minute stoppage cost thousands of dollars because, while an assembly line stood still, wages and other costs went rollicking on.

But at least today was Wednesday.

The intercom clicked. "They're on their way, Mr. Zaleski."

He acknowledged curtly.

The reason Matt Zaleski liked Wednesday was simple. Wednesday was two days removed from Monday, and Friday was two more days away.

Mondays and Fridays in auto plants were management's most harrowing days because of absenteeism. Each Monday, more hourly paid employees failed to report for work than on any other normal weekday; Friday ran a close second. It happened because after paychecks were handed out, usually on Thursday, many workers began a long boozy or drugged weekend, and afterward, Monday was a day for catching up on sleep or nursing hangovers.

Thus, on Mondays and Fridays, other problems were eclipsed by one enormous problem of keeping production going despite a critical shortage of people. Men were moved around like marbles in a game of Chinese checkers. Some were removed from tasks they were accustomed to and given jobs they had never done before. A worker who normally tightened wheel nuts might find himself fitting front fenders, often with the briefest of instruction or sometimes none at all. Others, pulled in hastily from labor pools or less skilled duties—such as loading trucks or sweeping—would be put to work wherever gaps remained. Sometimes they caught on quickly in their temporary roles; at other times they might spend an entire shift installing heater hose clamps, or something similar—upside down.

The result was inevitable. Many of Monday's and Friday's cars were shoddily put together, with built-in legacies of trouble for their owners, and those in the know avoided them like contaminated meat. A few big city dealers, aware of the problem and with influence at factories because of volume sales, insisted that cars for more valued customers be built on Tuesday, Wednesday, or Thursday, and customers who knew the ropes sometimes went to big dealers with this objective. Cars for company executives and their friends were invariably scheduled for one of the midweek days.

The door of the assistant plant manager's office flung open abruptly. The foreman he had sent for, Parkland, strode in, not bothering to knock.

Parkland was a broad-shouldered, big-boned man in his late thirties, about fifteen years younger than Matt Zaleski. He might have been a football fullback if he had gone to college, and, unlike many foremen nowadays, looked as if he could handle authority. He also looked, at the moment, as if he expected trouble and was prepared to meet it. The foreman's face was glowering. There was a darkening bruise, Zaleski noted, beneath his right cheekbone.

Ignoring the mode of entry, Zaleski motioned him to a chair. "Take the weight off your feet, then simmer down."

They faced each other across the desk.

"I'm willing to hear your version of what happened," the assistant plant chief said, "but don't waste time because the way this reads"—he fingered the red-tabbed grievance report—"you've cooked us all a hot potato."

"The hell I cooked it!" Parkland glared at his superior; above the bruise his face flushed red. "I fired a guy because he slugged me. What's more, I'm gonna make it stick, and if you've got any guts or justice you'd better back me up."

Matt Zaleski raised his voice to the bull roar he had learned on a factory floor. "Knock off that . . . nonsense, right now!" He had no intention of letting this get out of hand. More reasonably, he growled, "I said simmer down, and meant it. When the time comes I'll decide who to back and why. And there'll be no more crap from you about guts and justice. Understand?"

Their eyes locked together. Parkland's dropped first.

"All right Frank," Matt said. "Let's start over, and this time give it to me straight, from the beginning."

He had known Frank Parkland a long time. The foreman's record was good and he was usually fair with men who worked under him. It had taken something exceptional to get him as riled as this.

"There was a job out of position," Parkland said. "It was steering column bolts, and there was this kid doing it; he's new, I guess. He was crowding the next guy. I wanted the job put back."

Zaleski nodded. It happened often enough. A worker with a specific assignment took a few seconds longer than he should on each operation. As successive cars moved by on the assembly line, his position gradually changed, so that soon he was intruding on the area of the next operation. When a foreman saw it happen he made it his business to help the worker back to his correct, original place.

Zaleski said impatiently, "Get on with it."

Before they could continue, the office door opened again and the union committeeman came in. He was a small, pink-faced man, with thick-lensed glasses and a fussy manner. His name was Illas and, until a union election a few months ago, had been an assembly line worker himself.

"Good morning," the union man said to Zaleski. He nodded curtly to Parkland, without speaking.

Matt Zaleski waved the newcomer to a chair. "We're just getting to the meat."

"You could save a lot of time," Illas said, "if you read the grievance report."

"I've read it. But sometimes I like to hear the other side." Zaleski motioned Parkland to go on.

"All I did," the foreman said, "was call another guy over and say, 'Help me get this man's job back in position.'"

"And I say you're a liar!" The union man hunched forward accusingly; now he swung toward Zaleski. "What he really said was 'Get this boy's job back.' And it so happened the person he was speaking of, and calling 'boy,' was one of our black brothers to whom that word is a very offensive term."

"Oh, for . . . sake!" Parkland's voice combined anger with disgust. "D'you think I don't know that? D'you think I haven't been around here long enough to know better than to use that word that way?"

"But you did use it, didn't you?"

"Maybe, just maybe, I did. I'm not saying yes, because I don't remember, and that's the truth. But if it happened, there was nothing meant. It was a slip, that's all."

The union man shrugged. "That's your story now."

"It's no story, you son-of-a- . . . !"

Illas stood up. "Mr. Zaleski, I'm here officially, representing the United Auto Workers. If that's the kind of language . . ."

"There'll be no more of it," the assistant plant manager said. "Sit down, please, and while we're on the subject, I suggest you be less free yourself with the word 'liar.'"

Parkland slammed a beefy fist in frustration on the desk top. "I said it was no story, and it isn't. What's more, the guy I was talking about didn't even give a thought to what I said, at least before all the fuss was made."

"That's not the way he tells it," Illas said.

"Maybe not now." Parkland appealed to Zaleski. "Listen, Matt, the guy who was out of position is just a kid. A black kid, maybe seventeen. I've got nothing against him; he's slow, but he was doing his job. I've got a kid brother his age. I go home, I say, 'Where's the boy?' Nobody thinks twice about it. That's the way it was with this thing until this other guy, Newkirk, cut in."

Illas persisted, "But you're admitting you used the word 'boy.'"

Matt Zaleski said wearily, "Okay, okay, he used it. Let's all concede that."

Zaleski was holding himself in, as he always had to do when racial issues erupted in the plant. His own prejudices were deep-rooted and largely antiblack, and he had learned them in the heavily Polish suburb of Wyandotte where he was born. There, the families of Polish origin looked on Negroes with contempt, as shiftless and troublemakers. In return, the black people hated Poles, and even nowadays, throughout Detroit, the ancient enmities persisted. Zaleski, through necessity, had learned to curb his instinct; you couldn't run a plant with as much black labor as this one and let your prejudices show, at least not often. Just now, after the last remark of Illas, Matt Zaleski had been tempted to inject: So what if he did call him "boy?" What the hell difference does it make? When a foreman tells him to, let the bastard get back to work. But Zaleski knew it would be repeated and maybe cause more trouble than before. Instead, he growled, "What matters is what came after."

"Well," Parkland said, "I thought we'd never get to that. We almost had the job back in place, then this heavyweight, Newkirk, showed up."

"He's another black brother," Illas said.

"Newkirk'd been working down the line. He didn't even hear what happened; somebody else told him. He came up, called me a racist pig, and slugged me." The foreman fingered his bruised face which had swollen even more since he came in.

Zaleski asked sharply, "Did you hit him back?"

"No."

"I'm glad you showed a little sense."

"I had sense, all right," Parkland said. "I fired Newkirk. On the spot. Nobody slugs a foreman around here and gets away with it."

"We'll see about that," Illas said. "A lot depends on circumstances and provocation."

Matt Zaleski thrust a hand through his hair; there were days when he marveled that there was any left. This whole stinking situation was something which McKernon, the plant manager, should handle, but McKernon wasn't here. He was ten miles away at staff headquarters, attending a conference about the new Orion, a super-secret car the plant would be producing soon. Sometimes it seemed to Matt Zaleski as if McKernon had already begun his retirement, officially six months away.

Matt Zaleski was holding the baby now, as he had before, and it was a lousy deal. Zaleski wasn't even going to succeed McKernon, and he knew it. He'd already been called in and shown the official assessment of himself, the assessment which appeared in a loose-leaf, leather-bound book which sat permanently on the desk of the Vice President, Manufacturing. The book was there so that the vice president could turn its pages whenever new appointments or promotions were considered. The entry for Matt Zaleski, along with his photo and other details, read: "This individual is well placed at his present level of management."

Everybody in the company who mattered knew that the formal, unctious statement was a "kiss off." What it really meant was: This man has gone as high as he's going. He will probably serve his time out in his present spot, but will receive no more promotions.

The rules said that whoever received the deadly summation on his docket had to be told; he was entitled to that much, and it was the reason Matt Zaleski had known for the past several months that he would never rise beyond his present role of assistant manager. Initially the news had been a bitter disappointment, but now that he had grown used to the idea, he also knew why: He was old shoe, the hind-end of a disappearing breed which management and boards of directors didn't want any more in the top critical posts. Zaleski had risen by a route which few senior plant people followed nowadays—factory worker, inspector, foreman, superintendent, assistant plant manager. He hadn't had an engineering degree to start, having been a high school dropout before World War II. But after the war he had armed himself with a degree, using night school and GI credits, and after that had started climbing, being ambitious, as most of his generation were who had survived *Festung Europa* and other perils. But, as Zaleski recognized later, he had lost too much time; his real start came too late. The strong comers, the top echelon material of the auto companies—then as now—were the bright youngsters who arrived fresh and eager through the direct college-to-front-office route.

But that was no reason why McKernon, who was still plant boss, should sidestep this entire situation, even if unintentionally. The assistant manager hesitated. He would be within his rights to send for McKernon and could do it here and now by picking up a phone.

Two things stopped him. One, he admitted to himself, was pride; Zaleski knew he could handle this as well as McKernon, if not better. The other: His instinct told him there simply wasn't time.

Abruptly, Zaleski asked Illas, "What's the union asking?"

"Well, I've talked with the president of our local . . ."

"Let's save all that," Zaleski said. "We both know we have to start somewhere, so what is it you want?"

"Very well," the committeeman said. "We insist on three things. First, immediate reinstatement of Brother Newkirk, with compensation for time lost. Second, an apology to both men involved. Third, Parkland to be removed from his post as foreman."

Parkland, who had slumped back in his chair, shot upright. "By . . . ! You don't want much." He inquired sarcastically, "As a matter of interest, am I supposed to apologize before I'm fired, or after?"

"The apology would be an official one from the company," Illas answered. "Whether you had the decency to add your own would be up to you."

"I'll say it'd be up to me. Just don't anyone hold their breath waiting."

Matt Zaleski snapped, "If you'd held your own breath a little longer, we wouldn't be in this mess."

"Are you trying to tell me you'll go along with all that?" The foreman motioned angrily to Illas.

"I'm not telling anybody anything yet. I'm trying to think, and I need more information than has come from you two." Zaleski reached behind him for a telephone. Interposing his body between the phone and the other two, he dialed a number and waited.

When the man he wanted answered, Zaleski asked simply, "How are things down there?"

The voice at the other end spoke softly. "Matt?"

"Yeah."

In the background behind the other's guarded response, Zaleski could hear a cacophony of noise from the factory floor. He always marveled how men could live with that noise every day of their working lives. Even in the years he had worked on an assembly line himself, before removal to an office shielded him from most of the din, he had never grown used to it.

His informant said, "The situation's real bad, Matt."

"How bad?"

"The hopheads are in the saddle. Don't quote me."

"I never do," the assistant plant manager said. "You know that."

He had swung partially around and was aware of the other two in the office watching his face. They might guess, but couldn't know, that he was speaking to a black foreman, Stan Lathruppe, one of the half dozen men in the plant whom Matt Zaleski respected most. It was a strange, even paradoxical, relationship because, away from the plant, Lathruppe was an active militant who had once been a follower of Malcolm X. But here he took his responsibility seriously, believing that in the auto world he could achieve more for his race through reason than by anarchy. It was this second attitude which Zaleski — originally hostile to Lathruppe — had eventually come to respect.

Unfortunately for the company, in the present state of race relations, it had comparatively few black foremen or managers. There ought to be more, many more, and everybody knew it, but right now many of the black workers didn't want responsibility, or were afraid of it because of young militants in their ranks, or simply weren't ready. Sometimes Matt Zaleski, in his less prejudiced moments, thought that if the industry's top brass had looked ahead a few years, the way senior executives were supposed to do, and had launched a meaningful training program for black workers in the 1940s and '50s, there would be more Stan Lathruppes now. It was everybody's loss that there were not.

Zaleski asked, "What's being planned?"

"I think, a walkout."

"When?"

"Probably at break time. It could be before, but I don't believe so."

The black foreman's voice was so low Zaleski had to strain to hear. He knew the other man's problem, added to by the fact that the telephone he was using was alongside the assembly line where others were working. Lathruppe was already labeled a "white nigger" by some fellow blacks who resented even their own race when in authority, and it made no difference that the charge was untrue. Except for a couple more questions, Zaleski had no intention of making Stan Lathruppe's life more difficult.

He asked, "Is there any reason for the delay?"

"Yes. The hopheads want to take the whole plant out."

"Is word going around?"

"So fast you'd think we still used jungle drums."

"Has anyone pointed out the whole thing's illegal?"

"You got any more jokes like that?" Lathruppe said.

"No." Zaleski sighed. "But thanks." He hung up.

So his first instinct had been right. There wasn't any time to spare, and hadn't been from the beginning, because a racial labor dispute always burned with a short fuse. Now, if a walkout happened, it could take days to settle and get everybody back at work; and even if only black workers became involved, and maybe not all of them, the effect would still be enough to halt production. Matt Zaleski's job was to keep production going.

As if Parkland had read his thoughts, the foreman urged, "Matt, don't let them push you! So a few may walk off the job, and we'll have trouble. But a principle's worth standing up for, sometimes, isn't it?"

"Sometimes," Zaleski said. "The trick is to know which principle, and when."

"Being fair is a good way to start," Parkland said, "and fairness works two ways—up and down." He leaned forward over the desk, speaking earnestly to Matt Zaleski, glancing now and then to the union committeeman, Illas. "Okay, I've been tough with guys on the line because I've had to be. A foreman's in the middle, catching crap from all directions. From up here, Matt, you and your people are on our necks every day for production, production, more production; and if it isn't you it's Quality Control who say, build 'em better, even though you're building faster. Then there are those who are working, doing the jobs—including some like Newkirk, and others—and a foreman has to cope with them, along with the union as well if he puts a foot wrong, and sometimes when he doesn't. So it's a tough business, and I've been tough; it's the way to survive. But I've been fair, too. I've never treated a guy who worked for me differently because he was black, and I'm no plantation overseer with a whip. As for what we're talking about now, all I did—so I'm told—is call a black man 'boy.' I didn't ask him to pick cotton, or ride Jim Crow, or shine shoes, or any other thing that's supposed to go with that word. What I did was help him with his job. And I'll say another thing: if I did call him 'boy'—so help me, by a slip!—I'll say I'm sorry for that, because I am. But not to Newkirk. Brother Newkirk stays fired. Because if he doesn't, if he gets away with slugging a foreman without reason, you can stuff a surrender flag up your nose and wave goodbye to any discipline around this place from this day on. That's what I mean when I say be fair."

"You've got a point or two there," Zaleski said. Ironically, he thought, Frank Parkland had been fair with black workers, maybe fairer than a good many others around the plant. He asked Illas, "How do you feel about all that?"

The union man looked blandly through his thick-lensed glasses. "I've already stated the union's position, Mr. Zaleski."

"So if I turn you down, if I decide to back up Frank the way he just said I should, what then?"

Illas said stiffly, "We'd be obliged to go through further grievance procedure."

"Okay." The assistant plant manager nodded. "That's your privilege. Except, if we go through a full grievance drill it can mean thirty days or more. In the meantime, does everybody keep working?"

"Naturally. The collective bargaining agreement specifies . . ."

Zaleski flared, "I don't need you to tell me what the agreement says! It says everybody stays on the job while we negotiate. But right now a good many of your men are getting ready to walk off their jobs in violation of the contract."

For the first time, Illas looked uneasy. "The UAW does not condone illegal strikes."

"Well then, stop this one!"

"If what you say is true, I'll talk to some of our people."

"Talking won't do any good. You know it, and I know it." Zaleski eyed the union committeeman whose pink face had paled slightly; obviously Illas didn't relish the thought of arguing with some of the black militants in their present mood.

The union—as Matt Zaleski was shrewdly aware—was in a tight dilemma in situations of this kind. If the union failed to support its black militants at all, the militants would charge union leaders with racial prejudice and being "management lackeys." Yet if the union went too far with its support, it could find itself in an untenable position legally, as party to a wildcat strike. Illegal strikes were anathema to UAW leaders like Woodcock, Fraser, Greathouse, Bannon, and others, who had built reputations for tough negotiating, but also for honoring agreements once made, and settling grievances through due process. Wildcatting debased the union's word and undermined its bargaining strength.

"They're not going to thank you at Solidarity House if we let this thing get away from us," Matt Zaleski persisted. "There's only one thing can stop a walkout, and that's for us to make a decision here, then go down on the floor and announce it."

Illas said, "That depends on the decision." But it was plain that the union man was weighing Zaleski's words.

Matt Zaleski had already decided what the ruling had to be, and he knew that nobody would like it entirely, including himself. He thought sourly: these were lousy times, when a man had to shove his convictions in his pocket along with pride—at least, if he figured to keep an automobile plant running.

He announced brusquely, "Nobody gets fired. Newkirk goes back to his job, but from now on he uses his fists for working, nothing else." The assistant plant manager fixed his eyes on Illas. "I want it clearly understood by you and by Newkirk—one more time, he's out. And before he goes back, I'll talk to him myself."

"He'll be paid for lost time?" The union man had a slight smile of triumph.

"Is he still at the plant?"

"Yes."

Zaleski hesitated, then nodded reluctantly. "Okay, providing he finishes the shift. But there'll be no more talk about anybody replacing Frank." He swung to face Parkland. "And you'll do what you said you would—talk to the young guy. Tell him what was said was a mistake."

"An apology is what it's known as," Illas said.

Frank Parkland glared at them both. "Of all the crummy, sleazy backdowns!"

"Take it easy!" Zaleski warned.

"Like hell I'll take it easy!" The burly foreman was on his feet, towering over the assistant plant manager. He spat words across the desk between them. "You're the one taking it easy—the easy out because you're too much a . . . coward to stand up for what you know is right."

His face flushing deep red, Zaleski roared, "I don't have to take that from you! That'll be enough! You hear?"

"I hear." Contempt filled Parkland's voice and eyes. "But I don't like what I hear, or what I smell."

"In that case, maybe you'd like to be fired!"

"Maybe," the foreman said. "Maybe the air'd be cleaner some place else."

There was a silence between them, then Zaleski growled, "It's no cleaner. Some days it stinks everywhere."

QUESTIONS

1. Have you ever experienced life in a factory? Have you ever been in a leadership position—management or union? Discuss your experiences.

2. Have you ever been involved in a racial conflict? Were you a member of the majority or the minority race? Discuss your experiences.

3. What values should govern life in a work setting? What principles and practices would you support? Discuss.

Can an Executive Afford a Conscience?

Ask a business executive whether his company employs child labor, and he will either think you are joking or be angered by the implied slur on his ethical standards. In the 1970's the employment of children in factories is clearly considered morally wrong as well as illegal.

Yet it was not until comparatively recently (1941) that the U.S. Supreme Court finally sustained the constitutionality of the long-contested Child Labor Act that Congress had passed four years earlier. During most of the previous eight decades, the fact that children 10 years old worked at manual jobs an average of 11 hours a day under conditions of virtual slavery had aroused little indignation in business circles.

To be sure, only a few industries found the practice profitable and the majority of businessmen would doubtless have been glad to see it stopped. But in order to stop it the government had to act, and any interference with business by government was regarded as a crime against God, Nature, and Respectability. If a company sought to hold down production costs by employing children in factories where the work did not demand adult skills or muscle, that was surely a matter to be settled between the employer and the child's parents or the orphanage.

To permit legitimate private enterprise to be balked by unrealistic do-gooders was to open the gate to socialism and anarchy — such was the prevailing sentiment of businessmen, as shown in the business press, from the 1860's to the 1930's.

Every important advance in business ethics has been achieved through a long history of pain and protest. The process of change begins when a previously accepted practice arouses misgivings among sensitive observers. Their efforts at moral suasion are usually ignored, however, until changes in economic conditions or new technology make the practice seem increasingly undesirable.

Businessmen who profit by the practice defend it heatedly, and a long period of public controversy ensues, climaxed at last by the adoption of laws forbidding it. After another 20 or 30 years, the new generation of

Source: Reprinted with permission of the Harvard Business Review. "Can an Executive Afford a Conscience?" by Albert Z. Carr (July/August 1970). Copyright © 1970 by the President and Fellows of Harvard College; all rights reserved.

businessmen regard the practice with retrospective moral indignation and wonder why it was ever tolerated.

A century of increasingly violent debate culminating in civil war had to be lived through before black slavery, long regarded as an excellent business proposition, was declared unlawful in the United States. To achieve laws forbidding racial discrimination in hiring practices required another century. It took 80 years of often bloody labor disputes to win acceptance of the principle of collective bargaining, and the country endured about 110 years of flagrant financial abuses before enactment of effective measures regulating banks and stock exchanges.

In time, all of these forward steps, once bitterly opposed by most businessmen, came to be accepted as part of the ethical foundation of the American private enterprise economy.

JESSE JAMES VS. NERO

In the second half of the twentieth century, with the population, money supply, military power, and industrial technology of the United States expanding rapidly at the same time, serious new ethical issues have arisen for businessmen — notably the pollution of the biosphere, the concentration of economic power in a relatively few vast corporations, increasing military domination of the economy, and the complex interrelationship between business interests and the threat of war. These issues are the more formidable because they demand swift response; they will not wait a century or even a generation for a change in corporate ethics that will stimulate businessmen to act.

The problems they present to business and our society as a whole are immediate, critical, and worsening. If they are not promptly dealt with by farsighted and effective measures, they could even bring down political democracy and the entrepreneurial system together.

In fact, given the close relationship between our domestic economic situation and our military commitments abroad, and the perils implicit in the worldwide armaments buildup, it is not extreme to say that the extent to which businessmen are able to open their minds to new ethical imperatives in the decade ahead may have decisive influence in this century on the future of the human species.

Considering the magnitude of these rapidly developing issues, old standards of ethical judgment seem almost irrelevant. It is of course desirable that a businessman be honest in his accountings and faithful to his contracts — that he should not advertise misleadingly, rig prices, deceive stockholders, deny workers their due, cheat customers, spread false rumors about competitors, or stab associates in the back. Such a person has in the past qualified as "highly ethical," and he could feel morally superior to many of those he saw around him — the chiselers, the connivers, the betrayers of trust.

But standards of personal conduct in themselves are no longer an adequate index of business ethics. Everyone knows that a minority of businessmen commit commercial mayhem on each other and on the public with practices ranging from subtle conflicts of interest to the sale of injurious drugs and unsafe automobiles, but in the moral crisis through which we are living, such tales of executive wrongdoing, like nudity in motion pictures, have lost their power to shock.

The public shrugs at the company president who conspires with his peers to fix prices. It grins at the vice president in charge of sales who provides call girls for a customer. After we have heard a few such stories, they become monotonous.

We cannot shrug or grin, however, at the refusal of powerful corporations to take vigorous action against great dangers threatening the society, and to which they contribute. Compared with such a corporation or with the executive who is willing to jeopardize the health and well-being of an entire people in order to add something to current earnings, the man who merely embezzles company funds is as insignificant in the annals of morality as Jesse James is compared with Nero.

The moral position of the executive who works for a company that fails in the ethics of social responsibility is ambiguous. The fact that he does not control company policy cannot entirely exonerate him from blame. He is guilty, so to speak, by employment.

If he is aware that the company's factories pollute the environment or its products injure the consumer and he does not exert himself to change the related company policies, he becomes morally suspect. If he lends himself to devious evasions of laws against racial discrimination in hiring practices, he adds to the probability of destructive racial confrontations and is in some degree an agent of social disruption. If he knows that his company is involved in the bribery of legislators or government officials, or makes under-the-table deals with labor union officials, or uses the services of companies known to be controlled by criminal syndicates, he contributes through his work to disrespect for law and the spread of crime.

If his company, in its desire for military contracts, lobbies to oppose justifiable cuts in the government's enormous military budget, he bears some share of responsibility for the constriction of the civilian economy; for price inflation; urban decay; shortages for housing, transportation, and schools; and for failure to mitigate the hardships of the poor.

From this standpoint, the carefully correct executive who never violates a law or fails to observe the canons of gentlemanly behavior may be as open to ethical challenge as the crooks and the cheaters.

"TOKENS OF SUPPRESSED GUILT"

The practical question arises: If a man in a responsible corporate position finds that certain policies of his company are socially injurious, what can he do about it without jeopardizing his job?

Contrary to common opinion, he is not necessarily without recourse. The nature of that recourse I shall discuss in the final section of this article. Here, I want to point out that unless the executive's sense of social responsibility is accompanied by a high degree of realism about tactics, then he is likely to end in frustration or cynicism.

One executive of my acquaintance who wrote several memoranda to his chief, detailing instances of serious environmental contamination for which the company was responsible and which called for early remedy, was sharply rebuked for a "negative attitude."

Another, a successful executive of a large corporation, said to me quite seriously in a confidential moment that he did not think a man in a job like his could afford the luxury of a conscience in the office. He was frank to say that he had become unhappy about certain policies of his company. He could no longer deny to himself that the company was not living up to its social responsibilities and was engaged in some political practices that smacked of corruption.

But what were his options? He had only three that he could see, and he told me he disliked them all:

- If he argued for a change in policies that were helping to keep net earnings high, he might be branded by his superiors as "unrealistic" or "idealistic" — adjectives that could check his career and might, if he pushed too hard, compel his resignation.

- Continued silence not only would spoil his enjoyment of his work, but might cause him to lose respect for himself.

- If he moved to one of the other companies in his industry, he would merely be exchanging one set of moral misgivings for another.

He added with a sigh that he envied his associates whose consciences had never developed beyond the Neanderthal stage and who had no difficulty in accepting things as they were. He said he wondered whether he ought not to try to discipline himself to be as indifferent as they to the social implications of policies which, after all, were common in business.

Perhaps he made this effort and succeeded in it, for he remained with the company and forged ahead. He may even have fancied that he had killed his conscience — as the narrator in Mark Twain's symbolic story did when he gradually reached the point where he could blithely murder the tramps who came to his door asking for handouts.

But conscience is never killed. When ignored, it merely goes underground where it manufactures the toxins of suppressed guilt, often with serious psychological and physical consequences. The hard fact is that the executive who has a well-developed contemporary conscience is at an increasing disadvantage in business unless he is able to find some personal policy by which he can maintain his drive for success without serious moral reservations.

DISTRUSTFUL PUBLIC

The problem faced by the ethically motivated man in corporate life is compounded by growing public distrust of business morality.

The corporation executive is popularly envied for his relative affluence and respected for his powers of achievement, but many people deeply suspect his ethics — as not a few successful businessmen have been informed by their children. . . .

This low opinion is by no means confined to youngsters; a poll of 2,000 representative Americans brought to light the belief of nearly half of them that "most businessmen would try anything, honest or not, for a buck." The unfairness of the notion does not make it less significant as a clue to public opinion. (This poll also showed that most Americans are aware of the notable contributions of business to the material satisfactions of their lives; the two opinions are not inconsistent.)

Many businessmen, too, are deeply disturbed by the level of executive morality in their sphere of observation. Although about 90% of executives in another survey stated that they regarded themselves as "ethical," 80% affirmed "the presence of numerous generally accepted practices in their industry which they consider unethical," such as bribery of government officials, rigging of prices, and collusion in contract bidding.

The public is by no means unaware of such practices. In conversations about business ethics with a cross-section sampling of citizens in a New England town, I found that they mentioned kickbacks and industrial espionage as often as embezzlement and fraud. One man pointed out that the kickback is now taken so much for granted in corporations that the Internal Revenue Service provides detailed instructions for businessmen on how to report income from this source on their tax returns.

The indifference of many companies to consumers' health and safety was a major source of criticism. Several of the persons interviewed spoke of conflicts of interest among corporation heads, accounts of which had been featured not long before in the press. Others had learned from television dramas about the ruthlessness of the struggle for survival and the hail-fellow hypocrisy that is common in executive offices.

Housewives drew on their shopping experience to denounce the decline in the quality of necessities for which they had to pay ever-higher prices. Two or three had read in *Consumer Reports* about "planned obsolescence."

<u>I came to the conclusion that if my sample is at all representative — and I think it is — the public has learned more about the ways of men in corporate life than most boards of directors yet realize.</u>

These opinions were voiced by people who for the most part had not yet given much thought to the part played by industrial wastes in the condition of the environment, or to the inroads made on their economic well-being by the influence of corporation lobbyists on military decision makers. It is to be expected that if, as a result of deteriorating social and economic conditions, these and other major concerns take on more meaning for the public, criticism of business ethics will widen and become sharper.

If the threats of widespread water shortage in the 1970's and of regional clean air shortages in the 1980's are allowed to materialize, and military expenditures continue to constrict civilian life, popular resentment may well be translated into active protest directed against many corporations as well as against the government. In that event, the moral pressure on individual executives will become increasingly acute.

Regard for public opinion certainly helped to influence many companies in the 1950's and 1960's to pledge to reduce their waste discharges into the air and water and to hire more people with dark skins. Such declarations were balm for the sore business conscience.

The vogue for "social responsibility" has now grown until, as one commentator put it, "pronouncements about social responsibility issue forth so abundantly from the corporations that it is hard for one to get a decent play in the press. Everybody is in on the act, and nearly all of them actually mean what they say!" More than a few companies have spent considerable sums to advertise their efforts to protect a stream, clean up smokestack emissions, or train "hard-core unemployables."

These are worthy undertakings, as far as they have gone, but for the most part they have not gone very far. In 1970 it has become obvious that the performance of U.S. corporations in the area of social responsibility has generally been trivial, considering the scope of their operations.

BEHIND THE BOARDROOM DOOR

No company that I have ever heard of employs a vice president in charge of ethical standards; and sooner or later the conscientious executive is likely to come up against a stone wall of corporate indifference to private moral values.

When the men who hold the real power in the company come together to decide policy, they may give lip service to the moral element in the issue, but not much more. The decision-making process at top-management levels has little room for social responsibilities not definitely required by law or public opinion.

Proposals that fail to promise an early payoff for the company and that involve substantial expense are accepted only if they represent a means of escaping drastic penalties, such as might be inflicted by a government suit, a labor strike, or a consumer boycott. To invest heavily in antipollution equipment or in programs for hiring and training workers on the fringe of employability, or to accept higher taxation in the interest of better education for the children of a community — for some distant, intangible return in a cloudy future — normally goes against the grain of every profit-minded management.

It could hardly be otherwise. In the prevailing concept of corporate efficiency, a continual lowering of costs relative to sales is cardinal. For low costs are a key not only to higher profits but to corporate maneuverability, to advantage in recruiting the best men, and to the ability to at least hold a share of a competitive market.

Of the savings accruing to a company from lowered costs, the fraction that finds its way into the area of social responsibility is usually miniscule. To expend such savings on nonremunerative activities is regarded as weakening the corporate structure.

The late Chester A. Barnard, one of the more enlightened business leaders of the previous generation and a man deeply concerned with ethics, voiced the position of management in the form of a question: "To what extent is one morally justified in loading a productive undertaking with heavy charges in the attempt to protect against a remote possibility, or even one not so remote?" Speaking of accident prevention in plants, which he favored in principle, he warned that if the outlay for such a purpose weakened the company's finances, "the community might lose a service and the entrepreneur an opportunity."

Corporate managers apply the same line of reasoning to proposals for expenditure in the area of social responsibility. "We can't afford to sink that amount of money in nonproductive uses," they say; and, "We need all our cash for expansion."

The entrepreneur who is willing to accept some reduction of his income — the type is not unknown — may be able to operate his enterprise in a way that satisfies an active conscience; but a company with a competitive team of managers, a board of directors, and a pride of stockholders cannot harbor such an unbusinesslike intention.

Occasionally, statesmen, writers, and even some high-minded executives, such as the late Clarence B. Randall, have made the appeal of conscience to corporations. They have argued that, since the managers and directors of companies are for the most part men of goodwill in their private lives, their corporate decisions also should be guided by conscience.

Even the distinguished economist A. A. Berle, Jr. has expressed the view that the healthy development of our society requires "the growth of conscience" in the corporation of our time. But if by "conscience" he meant a sense of right and wrong transcending the economic, he was asking the impossible.

A business that defined "right" and "wrong" in terms that would satisfy a well-developed contemporary conscience could not survive. No company can be expected to serve the social interest unless its self-interest is also served, either by the expectation of profit or by the avoidance of punishment.

"GRESHAM'S LAW" OF ETHICS

Before responsibility to the public can properly be brought into the framework of a top-management decision, it must have an economic justification. For instance, executives might say:

"We'd better install the new safety feature because, if we don't, we'll have the government on our necks, and the bad publicity will cost us more than we are now saving in production."

"We should spend the money for equipment to take the sulfides out of our smokestacks at the plant. Otherwise we'll have trouble recruiting labor and have a costly PR problem in the community."

It is worth noting that Henry Ford II felt constrained to explain to stockholders of the Ford Motor Company that his earnest and socially-aware effort to recruit workers from Detroit's "hard-core unemployed" was a preventive measure against the recurrence of ghetto riots carrying a threat to the company.

In another situation, when a number of life insurance companies agreed to invest money in slum reconstruction at interest rates somewhat below the market, their executives were quick to forestall possible complaints from stockholders by pointing out that they were opening up future markets for life insurance. Rationally, the successful corporate manager can contemplate expense for the benefit of society only if failure to spend points to an eventual loss of security or opportunity that exceeds the cost.

There can be no conscience without a sense of personal responsibility, and the corporation, as Ambrose Bierce remarked, is "an ingenious device for obtaining individual profit without individual responsibility." When the directors and managers of a corporation enter the boardroom to debate policy, they park their private consciences outside.

If they did not subordinate their inner scruples to considerations of profitability and growth, they would fail in their responsibility to the company that pays them. A kind of Gresham's Law of ethics operates here, the ethic of corporate advantage invariably silences and drives out the ethic of individual self-restraint.

(This, incidentally, is true at every level of the corporate structure. An executive who adheres to ethical standards disregarded by his associates is asking for trouble. No one, for example, is so much hated in a purchasing department where graft is rife as the man who refuses to take kickbacks from suppliers, for he threatens the security of the others. Unless he conforms, they are all too likely to "get him.")

The crucial question in boardroom meetings where social responsibility is discussed is not, "Are we morally obligated to do it?" but rather, "What will happen if we don't do it?" or, perhaps, "How will this affect the rate of return on investment?"

If the house counsel assures management that there will be no serious punishment under the law if the company does not take on the added expense, and the marketing man sees no danger to sales, and the public relations man is confident he can avoid injury to the corporate image, then the money, if it amounts to any considerable sum, will not be spent — social responsibility or no social responsibility.

Even the compulsion of law is often regarded in corporate thinking as an element in a contest between government and the corporation, rather than as a description of "right" and "wrong." The files of the Federal Trade Commission, the Food and Drug Administration, and other government agencies are filled with records of respectable companies that have not hesitated to break or stretch the law when they believed they could get away with it.

It is not unusual for company managements to break a law, even when they expect to be caught, if they calculate that the fine they eventually must pay represents only a fraction of the profits that the violation will enable them to collect in the meantime. More than one corporate merger has been announced to permit insiders to make stock-market killings even though the companies concerned recognized that the antitrust laws would probably compel their eventual separation.

WHAT CAN THE EXECUTIVE DO?

One can dream of a big-business community that considers it sound economics to sacrifice a portion of short-term profits in order to protect the environment and reduce social tensions.

It is theoretically conceivable that top managers as a class may come to perceive the profound dangers for the free-enterprise system and/or themselves in the trend toward the militarization of our society, and will press the government to resist the demand for nonessential military orders and overpermissive contracts from sections of industry and elements in the Armed Services. At the same level of wishfulness we can imagine the federal government making it clear to U.S. companies investing abroad that protection of their investments is not the government's responsibility.

We can even envisage a time when the bonds of a corporation that is responsive to social needs will command a higher rating by Moody's than those of a company that neglects such values, since the latter is more vulnerable to public condemnation; and a time when a powerful Executive League for Social Responsibility will come into being to stimulate and assist top managements in formulating long-range economic policies that embrace social issues. In such a private-enterprise utopia, the executive with a social conscience would be able to work without weakening qualms.

In the real world of today's business, however, he is almost sure to be a troubled man. Perhaps there are some executives who are so strongly positioned that they can afford to urge their managements to accept a reduced rate of returns on investment for the sake of the society of which they are a part. But for the large majority of corporate employees who want to keep their job and win their superiors' approbation, to propose such a thing would be inviting oneself to the corporate guillotine.

HE IS NOT POWERLESS

But this does not necessarily mean that the ethically motivated executive can do nothing. In fact, if he does nothing, he may so bleach his conception of himself as a man of conviction as to reduce his personal force and value to the company. His situation calls for sagacity as well as courage. Whatever ideas he advocates to express his sense of social responsibility must be shaped to the company's interests.

Asking management flatly to place social values ahead of profits would be foolhardy, but if he can demonstrate that, on the basis of long-range profitability, the concept of corporate efficiency needs to be broadened to include social values, he may be able to make his point without injury—

indeed, with benefit — to his status in the company. A man respected for competence in his job, who knows how to justify ethically based programs in economic terms, and to overcome elements of resistance in the psychology of top management, may well be demonstrating his own qualifications for top management.

In essence, any ethically oriented proposal made to a manager is a proposal to take a longer-range view of his problems — to lift his sights. Nonethical practice is shortsighted almost by definition, if for no other reason than that it exposes the company to eventual reprisals.

The longer range a realistic business projection is, the more likely it is to find a sound ethical footing. I would go so far as to say that almost anything an executive does, on whatever level, to extend the range of thinking of his superiors tends to effect an ethical advance.

The hope and the opportunity of the individual executive with a contemporary conscience lies in the constructive connection of the long economic view with the socially aware outlook. He must show convincingly a net advantage for the corporation in accelerating expenditures or accepting other costs in the sphere of social responsibility.

I was recently able to observe an instance in which an executive persuaded his company's management to make a major advance in its antipollution policy. His presentation of the alternatives, on which he had spent weeks of careful preparation, showed in essence that, under his plan, costs which would have to be absorbed over a three-year period would within six years prove to be substantially less than the potential costs of less vigorous action.

When he finished his statement, no man among his listeners, not even his most active rivals, chose to resist him. He had done more than serve his company and satisfy his own ethical urge; he had shown that the gap between the corporate decision and the private conscience is not unbridgeable if a person is strong enough, able enough, and brave enough to do what needs to be done.

It may be that the future of our enterprise system will depend on the emergence of a sufficient number of men of this breed who believe that in order to save itself, business will be impelled to help save the society.

Business ethics can no longer be indexed by standards of personal conduct. Our society accepts as unchangeable business practices that range from conflicts of interest, to price fixing, to the sale of injurious drugs and unsafe automobiles, to providing call girls for customers.

Society must not, however, similarly condone business practices that seriously threaten the very existence of life. The organization that is willing to jeopardize the health and well-being of an entire people in order to increase profit must be confronted and stopped.

This necessary action, however, poses a practical question: If a person in a responsible corporate position finds that certain policies of his company are socially injurious, what can he do without jeopardizing his job?

As the author states, "It may be that the future of our enterprise system will depend on the emergence of men who believe that in order to save itself, business must help save society."

QUESTIONS

1. Do you think business has a moral obligation to society?
   _____
   _____
   _____

2. What is your view: can a modern-day executive afford a conscience?
   _____
   _____
   _____

3. Give an example of how an ethically motivated executive can correct unethical policies of his or her company.
   _____
   _____
   _____

Rites of Passage

It was a bright green day. Big trees on the side streets were raining seeds and the wind stirred in its second sleep. A long flatbed truck came rattling down one of the streets and stopped by the new steel, chrome, and glass building. The building's lines were so "functional" it made Cephas wonder if anyone actually worked in it. Then he saw some women going in. Good.

He checked his appearance by hitching up to the rearview mirror. He was wearing a clean white shirt and a bow tie and his thin gray hair had been slicked down with water. When he was sure he was presentable, he got down out of the cab of the truck, dusted himself off, and began to walk slowly toward the building.

It had been many years . . . perhaps they had moved. No, there was the sign: BOONE COUNTY DEPARTMENT OF PUBLIC WELFARE. The last time he had been here the building had been a temporary shed and people had been lined up outside waiting for the relief trucks to come. That had been in 1934, in the winter. His father had been proud of holding out until '34.

Cephas stopped and looked at the building again. Some secretaries came out, laughing and talking. They didn't look at him, being used to seeing people who came hesitantly to their offices to acknowledge failure in life.

Cephas checked himself again in the big glass door and then went in. There was a large booth with a woman behind it and eight or nine rows of benches facing it. People were sitting quietly, staring at nothing, waiting. To the right there were a series of chutes with numbers over them. Cephas went up to the booth.

"Take a number," the woman said without looking at him.

"Ma'am?"

"You take a number and wait your turn. We'll call you."

He took one of the plastic number cards. It said 15. He sat down and waited.

"Five," the woman called. A heavy woman got up slowly and went to the booth and then to one of the chutes.

Source: Reprinted by permission of the William Morris Agency, Inc. on behalf of Joanne Greenberg. Copyright © 1966 by Joanne Greenberg.

Cephas waited. Minutes were born, ripened, aged, and died without issue.

"Number six." Around him the springtime asthmatics whistled and gasped in their season. He looked at the cracks in his fingers.

"Number seven." An hour went by; another. He was afraid to go out and check his truck lest the line speed up and he lose his place.

"Number thirteen," the woman called . . .

They came to his number at last and he went up to the desk, gave back the plastic card, and was directed to his chute. Another woman was there at another desk. She took his name, Cephas Ribble, and his age, sixty-eight.

Had he been given aid before?

Yes.

Had he been on General Assistance, Aid to the Needy, Disabled or Tuberculosis Aid?

"It was what they called Relief."

"But under what category was it?"

"It was for people that was off their farms or else didn't have nothin' to eat. They called it 'goin' on the county'. It was back in nineteen and thirty-four. We held out 'till thirty-four."

"I see. . . . Now you are applying for the old-age pension?"

He said he wasn't.

"Are you married, Mr. Ribble?" She sighed.

"Never had the pleasure," he said.

"Are you without funds, in emergency status?"

He said he wasn't.

"Then take this card and go to Room Eleven, to your left." She pressed a little light or something and he felt the people shifting their weight behind him, Number 16, he supposed. He made his way to Room Eleven.

The lady there was nice; he could see it right off. She told him about the different requirements for what they called "Aid," and then she had him sign some forms: permission to inquire into his bank account, acceptance of surplus or donated food, release of medical information, and several others. Then she said sympathetically, "In what way are you disabled?"

He thought about all the ways a man might be disabled and checked each one off. It was a proud moment, a man sixty-eight without one thing in the world to complain of in his health.

"I ain't disabled no way. I am pleased you asked me, though. A man don't take time to be grateful for things like his health. If the shoe don't pinch, you don't take notice, do you?" He sat back, contented. Then he realized that the sun was getting hotter, and what with everything in the truck, he'd better get on.

The woman put down her ball-point pen. "Mr. Ribble, if you aren't disabled or without funds, what kind of aid do you want?" A shadow of irritation crossed her face.

"No aid at all," he said. "It's about somethin' different." He tried to hold down his excitement. This was his special day, a day for which he had waited for over a decade, but it was no use bragging and playing the boy, so he said no more.

The woman was very annoyed. "Then why didn't you tell the worker at the desk?"

"She didn't give me no chance, ma'am, an' neither did that other lady. I bet you don't have many repair men comin' in here to fix things—not above once, anyway, except them gets paid by the hour."

"Well, Mr. Ribble, what is it you want?" She heard the noise of co-workers leaving or returning on their coffee breaks. She sighed and began to drum her fingers, but Cephas wasn't aware of her impatience. He was beginning back in 1934. Good God, she thought, he's senile. She knew that she would have to listen to all of it. In his time, in his way.

"Thirty-four cleaned us out—cleaned us bare. You wonder how farmers could go hungry. I don't know, but we did. After the drought hit, there was nothin' to do but come in town an' sign up on the County. Twice a month my pa would come in an' bring back food. Sometimes I came with him. I seen them lines of hungry men just standin' out there like they was pole-axed an' hadn't fallen yet. I tell you, them days was pitiful, pitiful." He glanced at her and then smiled. "I'm glad to see you done good since—a new buildin' an' all. Yes, you come right up." He looked around with approval at the progress they had made.

"Mr. Ribble. . . .?"

He returned. "See, we taken the Relief, but we never got to tell nobody the good it done for us. After that year, things got a little better, and soon we was on toward bein' a payin' farm again. In 'forty-six we built us a new house—every convenience—an' in 'fifty-two we got some of them automated units for cattle care. Two years ago we dug out of debt, an' last year, I knew it was time to think about my plan for real. It was time to thank the Welfare."

"Mr. Ribble, thanks are not necessary———"

"Don't you mind, ma'am, you just get your men an' come with me."

"I beg your pardon. . . ."

"I don't just talk, ma'am; I act. You just bring your men."

Mr. Morrissey had come back from his coffee break and was standing in the hall.

The woman signaled him with her eyes as she followed Cephas Ribble, now walking proud and sure out the door to his truck. Mr. Morrissey sighed and followed, wondering why he was always around when somebody needed to make a madness plan. Why did it never happen to McFarland?

Cephas reached into his pocket and both of the welfare people thought: Gun. He took out a piece of paper and turned to them as they stood transfixed and pale, thinking of death. "I got it all here, all of what's in the truck. Get your men, ma'am, no use wastin' time. It's all in the truck and if it don't get unloaded soon, it's gonna spoil."

"What is this about, Mr. Ribble?"

"My gift, ma'am; my donation. I'm giving the Relief four hundred chickens, thirty barrels of tomatoes, thirty barrels of apricots—I figured, for variety. Don't you think the apricots was a good idea—ten barrels

Eyetalian beans, six firkins of butter. . . . Ma'am, you better get the chickens out—it don't do to keep 'em in the sun. I thought about milk, so I give two cans—that's a hundred gallons of milk in case there's hungry babies."

They were dumbfounded. Cephas could see that. He wanted to tell them that it wasn't a case of trying to be big. He'd figured that everybody gave when they could. He'd even signed a form right there in the office about promising to accept donated food and clothing. Their amazement at his gift embarrassed him. Then he realized that it was probably the only way they could thank him—by making a fuss. People on the State payroll must have to walk a pretty narrow line. They'd have to be on the lookout for people taking advantage. That was it. It was deep work, that Welfare—mighty deep work.

"What are we supposed to do with all that food?" Mr. Morrissey asked.

Cephas knew that the man was just making sure that it wasn't a bribe. "Why, give it to the poor. Call 'em in an let 'em get it. You can have your men unload it right now, an' I'd do it quick if I was you. Like I said, it won't be long 'till it starts to turn in all this heat."

Mr. Morrissey tried to explain that modern welfare methods were different than those in 1934. Even then, the food had been U.S. surplus, not privately donated. It had come from government warehouses.

Cephas spoke of the stupidity and waste of Government in farming, and rained invective on the Soil Bank.

Mr. Morrissey tried again to make his point. "We don't give out any food. There hasn't been any food donated since nineteen sixteen!"

No doubt of it, these Welfare people had to be awful careful. Cephas nodded. "The others do what they can—don't blame 'em if it don't seem like much," he said sympathetically. "I signed that slip in there about the donated food, so there must be a lot of donated food."

"It's an old law," Morrissey argued tiredly. "It's one of the old Poor Laws that never got taken off the books."

"An here you folks are followin' it, right today," Cephas mused. "It must make you mighty proud."

"Mr. Ribble, we have no place to store all this!"

Cephas found his throat tightening with happiness. He had come in humility, waited all morning just so he could show his small gratitude and be gone, and everyone was thunderstruck at the plenty. "Mister," he said, "I pay my taxes without complainin', but I never knowed how hard you people was workin' for your money. You got to guard against every kind of bribes an' invitations to break the law; you got to find ways to get this food to the poor people so fast, you can't even store it! By God, Mister, you make me proud to be an American!"

A policeman had stopped by the truck and was tranquilly writing a ticket. Cephas excused himself modestly and strode off to defend his situation. The two Welfare workers stood staring after him as he engaged the officer.

It was, after all, State law that food could be donated. Were there no loading ramps, no men attending them? Had the department no parking place for donors? The policeman began to look at the two stunned bearers of the State's trust. He had stopped writing.

"Could that truck fit in the workers' parking lot?" Morrissey murmured.

"What are we going to do with it all?" Mrs. Traphagen whimpered. "All those chickens—four hundred chickens!"

Mrs. Traphagen sighed. "The poor will never stand for it."

"First things first," Mr. Morrissey decided, and he went to confront the policeman.

Cephas' truck in the workers' parking lot blocked all their cars. As a consequence, the aid applications of eight families were held pending investigation. Six discharged inmates of the State hospital remained incarcerated for a week longer pending home checkups. Thirty-seven women washed floors and children's faces in the expectation of home visits which did not come about. A Venereal Disease meeting at the Midtown Hotel was one speaker short, and high-school students who had been scheduled to hear a lecture entitled "Social Work, Career of Tomorrow," remained unedified. Applicants who came to apply for aid that afternoon were turned away. There was no trade in little plastic cards and the hive of offices were empty. But the people of the Boone County Department of Public Welfare were not idle. It was only that the action had moved from the desks and files and chutes to the workers' parking lot and into the hands of its glad tyrant, Cephas Ribble.

All afternoon Cephas lifted huge baskets of apricots and tomatoes into the arms of the Welfare workers. All afternoon they went from his truck to their cars, carrying baskets, or with chickens festooned limply over their arms. When they complained to Mr. Unger, the head of the department, he waved them off. Were they to go to every home and deliver the food? He said he didn't care—they were to get rid of it. Were big families to get the same amount as small families? He said that the stuff was political dynamite and that all he wanted was to be rid of it before anybody noticed.

Cephas, from the back of his flat-bed, was a titan. He lifted, smiling, and loaded with a strong hand. He never stopped to rest or take a drink. The truck steamed in the hot spring light, but he was living at height, unbothered by the heat, or the closeness, or the increasing rankness of his chickens. Of course he saw that the Welfare people weren't dressed for loading food. They were dressed for church, looked like. It was deep work, very deep, working for the State. You had to set a good example. You had to dress up and talk very educated so as to give the poor a moral uplift. You had to be honest. A poor man could lie—Cephas had been poor himself, so he knew—but it must be a torment to deal with people free to lie and not be able to do it yourself.

By three-thirty the truck had been unloaded and Cephas was free to go home and take up his daily life again. He shook hands with the director and the case-work supervisor, the head bookkeeper and the statistician. To them he presented his itemized list, with weights carefully noted and items given the market value as of yesterday, in case they needed it for their records. Then he carefully turned the truck out of the parking lot, waved good-bye to the sweating group, nosed into the sluggish mass of afternoon traffic, and began to head home.

A cacophony of high-pitched voices erupted in the lot behind him:

"I've got three mothers of drop-outs to visit!"

"What am I going to do with all this stuff?"

"Who do we give this to? . . . My people won't take the Lady Bountiful bit!"

"Does it count on their food allowance? Do we go down Vandalia and hand out apricots to every kid we see?"

"I don't have the time!"

"Which families get it?"

"Do we take the value off next month's check?"

"It's hopeless to try to distribute this fairly," the supervisor said.

"It will cost us close to a thousand dollars to distribute it at all," the statistician said.

"It will cost us close to two thousand dollars to alter next month's checks," the bookkeeper said, "and the law specifies that we have to take extra income-in-kind off the monthly allowance."

"If I were you," the director said, "I would take all this home and eat it, and not let anyone know about it."

"Mr. Morrissey!" Mrs. Traphagen's face paled away the red of her exertion, "That is fraud! You know as well as I do what would happen if it got out that we diverted Welfare Commodities to our own use! Can you imagine what the Mayor would say? The Governor? The State Department of Health? The HEW, The National Association of Social Workers?!" She had begun to tremble and the two chickens that were hanging limply over her arm nodded to each other with slow decorum, their eyes closed righteously against the thought.

Cars began to clot the exit of the parking lot. The air was redolent.

But many of the workers didn't take the food home. The wolf of hunger was patient in shadowing the poor, even in summer, even on Welfare. As the afternoon wore on, apricots began to appear in the hands of children from Sixteenth and Vandalia Street all the way to the Boulevard. Tomatoes flamed briefly on the windowsills of the Negro ghetto between Fourteenth and Kirk, and on one block, there was a chicken in every pot.

The complaints began early the next day. Sixteen Negroes called the Mayor's Committee on Racial Harmony, claiming that chickens, fruit, and vegetables had been given to the White Disadvantaged, while they had received tomatoes, half of them rotten. A rumor began that the food had been impregnated with contraceptive medicine to test on the poor and that three people had died from it. The Health Department denied this, but its word was not believed.

There were eighteen calls at the Department of Welfare protesting a tomato fight which had taken place on Fourteenth and Vandalia, in which passers-by had been pelted with tomatoes. The callers demanded that the families of those involved be stricken from the Welfare rolls as

Relief cheaters, encouraging waste and damaging the moral fiber of working people.

Eighteen mothers on the Aid to Dependent Children program picketed the Governor's mansion, carrying placards that read: *Hope, Not Handouts; Jobs, Not Charity.*

Sixty-eight welfare clients called to say that they had received no food at all and demanded equal service. When they heard that the Vandalia Street mothers were picketing, a group of them went down as counter-pickets. Words were exchanged between the two groups and a riot ensued in which sixteen people were hospitalized for injuries, including six members of the city's riot squad. Seven of the leaders were arrested and jailed pending investigation. The FBI was called into the case in the evening to ascertain if the riot was Communist-inspired.

At ten o'clock the Mayor appeared on TV with a plea for reason and patience. He stated that the riot was a reflection of the general decline in American morals and a lack of respect for the law. He ordered a six-man commission to be set up to hear testimony and make recommendations. A political opponent demanded a thorough investigation of the county Welfare System, the War on Poverty, and the local university's radicals.

The following day, Mrs. Traphagen was unable to go to work at the Welfare office, having been badly scalded on the hand while canning a bushel of apricots.

Cephas Ribble remembered everyone at the Welfare Office in his prayers. After work, he would think about the day he had spent in the city, and of his various triumphs: the surprise and wonder on the faces of the workers; the open awe of the lady who had said, "You don't need to thank us." How everyone had dropped the work they were doing and run to unload the truck. It had been a wonderful day. He had given his plenty unto the poor, the plenty and nourishment of his own farm. He rose refreshed to do his work, marveling at the meaning and grandeur with which his chores were suddenly invested.

"By God," he said, as he checked the chickens and noted their need for more calcium in the feed, "a man has his good to do. I'm gonna do it every year. I'm gonna have a day for the poor. Yessir, every year." And he smiled genially on the chickens, the outbuildings, and the ripening fields of a generous land.

QUESTIONS

1. What important point(s) are made by author Greenberg in "Rites of Passage"?

2. Have you ever been the recipient of help or aid either from the government or from individuals? Describe.

   _____
   _____
   _____

3. Have you ever been the giver of help or aid, either as a government official or as a private individual? Discuss.

   _____
   _____
   _____

CASES

The Superhonest Politician   188

The Teacher in the Middle   194

A Doctor's Case   196

Locks Versus Lives   200

"We Just Don't Do Things That Way   202
Around Here . . ."

Government Jobs   204

The 19-Year-Old Bride   206

R.V.'s in the Parking Lot   207

The Honor System   209

The Right to Strike   211

The Superhonest Politician

"Alstair M. McIntosh a candidate for United States Senator on the Party ticket?" said a Party worker, "I cannot believe it. He's too much of a cornball. His ideas, his policies are too far from mainstream Party thinking. The Party is a pretty big umbrella, but Alstair is kind of at our lunatic fringe. I mean, I respect what the man has done, but allowing him to run for the senatorial slot is going too far. Are we trying to make jokes, or are we trying to win an election? If we wanted entertainment, we could have hired a comedian to run for Senator."

In contrast to this Party worker's pronouncements, Alstair McIntosh considered himself a very serious candidate for United States Senator. McIntosh looked upon this challenge as the most serious mission of his life, despite his apparent nonchalance. Many times during his life Alstair had been accused of being lethargic, or plain bored, simply because of his casual mannerisms. In actual behavior, he is a fierce competitor, revealed by the highlights of his personal history.

As a law school graduate, young McIntosh went directly into public service. He struggled along in minor jobs for several years until he became a prosecuting attorney for the State. He quickly developed a reputation for objectivity and firmness in his courtroom behavior. Eventually he became a District Attorney at the State level. His penchant for objective investigation led to the conviction of a number of State officials accused of accepting kickbacks from major contractors to the Highway Construction Department.

McIntosh became a controversial figure because of these kickback scandals involving the State. Two of the people he helped get convicted were former superiors who had been helpful in his receiving a promotion to District Attorney. When asked how he could turn in a former boss — one who had helped him in his career — Alstair replied in his just-plain-folks manner, "Heck, when I was a boy working the family store, I caught my brother with his hand in the till and turned him in to my father. My brother proceeded to whup me, but, after he realized that I was really helping him, we became good friends."

McIntosh and his handful of Party workers are launching a modest, rather simple campaign. His opponent is a distinguished Senator, an

Source: Reprinted with permission from Andrew J. DuBrin, Casebook of Organizational Behavior, *copyright 1977, Pergamon Press.*

incumbent who has successfully straddled the middle of the road for six years. The McIntosh campaign headquarters are located in the oldest office building in the State Capitol. Befitting the McIntosh image, the furniture is stark and battered. Ten plain black telephones are constantly ringing and callers are intermittently disconnected. Alstair has refused to install an adequate telephone communication system, despite the pleas of the communication specialists from the telephone company. In his words, "No sense in spending too much time yapping on the phone. Frittering away time on the phone has become a disease in this country."

Contributing to Alstair McIntosh's reputation for uniqueness are several other aspects of his campaign strategy. Originally, Alstair unilaterally decided that he would not accept campaign gifts in excess of $25. As it became apparent that the inflow of money could hardly pay postage and transportation, he upped the figure to $75, and as campaign expenses mounted despite McIntosh's fiscal conservatism, he grudgingly settled for a $100 maximum campaign gift from an individual.

To the glee of Trailways, Greyhound, and other public transporters, McIntosh insists upon taking a non-chartered bus for campaign trips. He reasons, "Why waste money on frills like a chartered bus or airplane? The people I'm trying to impress are more likely to be found on a Greyhound bus than at an airport, anyway." When a bus ride is not feasible, McIntosh packs himself and one or two political aides into his seven-year-old black Checker Cab. "Never was a better car built in the United States," says Alstair, to the chagrin of Big Three automakers. An official of the United Auto Workers claims McIntosh drives a Checker Cab because of his basic dislike for big business and organized labor, the "very heart of our country."

A third campaign strategy (or lack thereof) is Alstair McIntosh's manner of relating to people he meets during his public appearances. He refuses to smile unless somebody says something that he thinks is amusing. Although a minor aspect of total behavior, his deadpan mannerisms do alienate some people. A beauty contest winner proclaimed that "Mr. McIntosh is downright mean. He's the only person I've ever met who did not smile when he saw me." A production worker outside a factory was quoted on television as saying, "I wouldn't vote for a man who looks so unhappy. I figure he has so many problems of his own that he won't be able to help other people with their problems. And that's the reason we elect a person Senator."

To his critics along these lines, McIntosh replies, "I'll smile more when I'm elected and we get some of the country's problems under control."

Even more vexing to conservative members of the Party are some of McIntosh's more radical policies. Although many of his aides and top Party officials agree with some of McIntosh's more controversial policies, they believe that the country is not ready for his innovative suggestions. A strongly held opinion is that McIntosh should wait until (or, if) he is elected, and then work toward incorporating into law some of his more radical ideas.

One policy advocated by Alstair is to reduce the defense budget by $50 billion per year. "My firm conviction is that after we reduce our defense budget about half, we will wonder why we ever spent so much money for defense in the first place. Some of my other policies on improving society will create jobs for the dislocated people, but why are we pouring billions into playing war? It's a great big hoax that is self-perpetuating. My plan is to divert defense funds into urban renewal of a kind that works. If Lockheed can build supersonic jet fighters, they can learn how to refurbish old frame houses. I would like to see the Chairman of Lockheed Aircraft with a paint brush in his hands painting the hallways of a slum building. You can put those thousands of engineers into some crash training for plumbers or electricians.

"After a while we could reduce the defense budget another $25 billion per year. I would put a permanent freeze on hiring on any defense-related business. Every year we could reduce their appropriations another $10 billion until anybody who wanted to be in the defense business would have to work for free."

Another radical, but straightforward suggestion offered by McIntosh for improving life in the United States is to decentralize Health, Education, and Welfare. HEW offices would be moved into areas of the United States plagued by chronic unemployment. For instance, McIntosh has urged that the entire Welfare work force be moved to Buffalo, New York. He says, "This way any bureaucrat who did not want to leave Washington, D.C., would be without a job, and an unemployed auto or steel worker would get a job in his or her place. Think of all the hundreds of inner-city children who could be trained to become clerks for the Welfare Department. We could set up day care centers and give mothers receiving Aid to Dependent Children a chance to earn a living. Creating jobs for people who are currently unemployed might be the best thing the Welfare Department could do for people."

With equal candor, Alstair comments upon the Pentagon: "I would immediately move the Pentagon to the middle of Maine. It would create a number of jobs, at least for a temporary period. All defense business would be operated from the Maine headquarters. If one of the officials wanted to leave town, he would only be given expenses to cover a bus ride. I suspect we will always have some kind of defense operation in the United States, but I would keep it in Maine. When a potato farmer in the area felt that he or she was too old and tired to keep farming, I would give that person a defense job and fire a colonel who had already been riding the gravy train for too many years. When a Russian official wanted to talk about a defense dispute, I would refer him to that old potato farmer."

McIntosh's taxation policies are even more straightforward and iconoclastic: "Our tax system, as everybody recognizes, has become a monstrosity. Something that nobody is really satisfied with, but that is being repaired on a quiltlike basis. You patch up one part, and then you find that another is out of whack. Let's tax everybody and every corporation at a flat 20 percent of their gross income. The rich people who make out a little better on this basis will undoubtedly spend more money that will create more jobs for more people. Instead of the government lopping off a big chunk of successful people's money, little people like maids, tailors, artists, and housepainters will be getting the money. If we stop all these crazy deductions, we'll be able to cut down income tax cheating by 90 percent. Our present tax structure encourages cheating by individuals and tax preparation specialists."

McIntosh also has a plan to help insure that people are reporting their income accurately: "I would immediately convert the Central Intelligence Agency to the Tax Intelligence Agency. Nobody would be out of a job, but they would be doing something worthwhile. I would make sure everybody who used dirty tricks such as electronic bugs would be fired. The remaining honest members of the former C.I.A. would keep the rest of us honest about our taxes."

Alstair's plan for rebuilding our cities goes beyond turning defense workers into city renewal workers: "I would immediately call back every soldier, sailor, or marine located off our shores and give him or her a chance to work for the Corps of Engineers. Their task would be to fix up old buildings and build new ones where reconstruction was not economically feasible. Until the military person learned an appropriate trade, he or she would be simply a construction aide.

"We'd take about one-quarter of these soldiers, sailors, and marines and make rat control specialists out of them. It's going to do a lot more good for the United States to have a soldier killing rats than sitting in an office in South Korea typing out requisitions for supplies we wouldn't need if he wasn't there."

Surprising to his other Party workers, the public, and the media representatives, Alstair McIntosh is as open and candid in his present dealings with people as hinted at by his sweeping proposals. On many occasions, his openness has shocked people. A party official believes that each "shock" is worth 5000 lost votes. Seven of his more shocking comments made directly to people or on talk show appearances are presented next.

Asked how he differs as a person from his opponent, McIntosh replied, "My opponent is a nice guy, which I am not. He is also not as bright as I am. In fact, I believe the man is on the dull side. When he is asked a spontaneous question, even by his chauffeur, he fumbles like a kid in a freshman speech class. If he were brighter, I think he could do a better job."

Asked by the Dean of a College of Criminal Justice what he thought is the most important lesson he learned in his many years of exposure to the criminal justice system, he replied: "I think the jury system is a waste of time. You pull a lot of ordinary people together to decide the fate of a life. If we eliminated the jury system, we would automatically lay the groundwork for revamping our criminal justice system into something more than the farce that presently exists."

In an encounter with a Catholic Cardinal at an airport, McIntosh asked him, "Cardinal, what does the Catholic Church do with all its wealth? If elected, I'm going to sponsor a bill to tax churches on their revenue in excess of expenses."

While visiting a federal prison, McIntosh said on a platform set up for the occasion, "It's hard to tell who the real criminals are around here. I think many of the prison administrators should exchange places with the prisoners."

In chatting with a reporter about internal changes he would make in the Party, McIntosh stated: "I don't like those $100-a-plate fund-raising dinners where we twist the arm of people to attend. We tell them that if they don't attend, or at least pay the $100, their names will be put on a special list. I think that is rotten."

During a Columbus Day rally, he told the Chief of Police that politicians didn't deserve public protection any more than the ordinary citizen deserves protection against muggers. "If I'm damn fool enough to run for office, that's my problem. Besides, my life is no more valuable than that of anybody else in this city."

On a street corner, he saw a woman stepping out of an expensive car with her adolescent daughter. McIntosh approached her and said, "Excuse me, Madame, I'm Alstair McIntosh and I'm running for Senator. May I make a suggestion? Please sell that fancy car of yours and get your daughter's teeth fixed. She needs orthodontia more than you need a $10,000 car."

Toward the middle of his campaign, Alstair was asked to confer with the Party National Chairperson. She begged for an explanation of what he was trying to accomplish by some of his tactics. "Simple," he replied, "I think that both a political party and a politician must be honest. Beyond that, unless we are candid, we never will be honest. Just saying we are an honest Party won't bring about any real change."

QUESTIONS

1. What kind of person would you support for public office? Describe ethical values and practices. Do you know a person who fits this description? Discuss.

2. Critique Alstair McIntosh's views. Which do you support? Which do you oppose? What social and personal values do your choices reflect?

3. Would you ever consider running for office? Discuss.

_____
_____
_____

The Teacher in the Middle

You are a first-year teacher and have joined the National Education Association, more out of ignorance and peer pressure than any sort of formal allegiance. You love the kids and your job and have been complimented by the principal for the fine start you've made. You haven't really gotten to know the other staff yet, but they seem friendly and supportive.

It seems that while you've been busy surviving these first few months and getting ready to be married in June, the teachers and the administration have been at odds concerning pay-scale issues for the upcoming year. The salary of beginning teachers is one of the lowest in the state, and the teachers feel they are losing quality beginning teachers because of it. After numerous Association meetings the teachers finally vote to strike. They feel their concerns have been ignored by the administration.

Suddenly, you are put in the middle! Your colleagues have appealed to you to illustrate the plight of the first-year teacher. On the other hand, the principal is not bound to rehire you while you're under a probationary contract, and he does not support the teachers.

Do you strike or do you report to school to teach on Monday?

QUESTIONS

1. What are the rights of a teacher? What are the responsibilities?

   _____
   _____
   _____

2. What are the rights of a school employer? What are the responsibilities?

   _____
   _____
   _____

Source: Kevin Ryan and James M. Cooper, Those Who Can, Teach *(Instructor's Manual)(Boston: Houghton Mifflin, 1975). Reprinted with permission.*

3. Should teachers, police personnel, doctors, and other public service employees be allowed to strike? Discuss.

_____
_____
_____

A Doctor's Case

Let me give you a case. At least, I think this is a case.

In my first year in medical school I had an experience which has always stuck with me. One afternoon during an examination, I became aware that two of my classmates were passing pieces of paper back and forth between themselves. I noticed that one would read it, write something on his examination paper, then write something on a piece of paper and pass it back to his friend. During the examination, this happened several times. I was positive that they were cheating.

I was torn by inner conflict in wondering what, if anything, I should do about the situation. It seemed to me that such conduct could not be tolerated in any student. It seemed to me that anyone who would cheat in an examination was not worthy or fit to assume the responsibilities of the medical profession. Also, it seemed to me that it was unfair to the rest of the class that these people should have the advantage of two minds while taking the examination. Of course, I thought, the advantage they would have over the rest of the class wouldn't be much. At most, it probably wouldn't do much more than move them up on the rank list from, say 38th place to 36th, or from 10th to 9th, or something of the sort. But in the awarding of scholarships and prizes, even one place could make a difference. And anyway, it just struck me as unfair to the rest of us. Moreover, cheating seemed to me to be something of a "sin" against the traditions of our school for which I had already developed great loyalty and respect.

I felt something ought to be done. But I couldn't think what. I knew that I simply could not bring myself to report them. I told myself again and again that I *could* be wrong, even though, actually, it was really crystal clear in my mind that they had been exchanging information and that that was *cheating* in anybody's book. But even so, I could not—would not—be a "squealer."

Over the weekend I was home, and I told my father about it. I told him that I felt that something ought to be done but that I didn't know what to do. I told him I couldn't bring myself to "squeal." He agreed

Source: Copyright © 1956, 1984 by the President and Fellows of Harvard College. This case was prepared by John D. Glover and Ralph M. Hower as the basis for class discussion rather than to illustrate either effective or ineffective handling of an administrative situation. Reprinted by permission of the Harvard Business School.

with me, both that something ought to be done and that I couldn't, or shouldn't, be a "squealer." He also said he thought the school shouldn't give the kind of examinations where it would be possible for anyone to gain an advantage over the rest by being able to confer surreptitiously with another. He said they were giving the wrong kind of examination. He argued that in real life doctors can and do consult one another. He said they should give examinations in which the students were perfectly free to consult with each other, any medical books, and anything else they thought might be useful before writing their answers. He said he thought that the real measure of a person's ability was how good a judgment that person could come up with after putting his or her own ideas together with any other ideas—some of which might well be conflicting—from available sources.

I said I thought there was a lot in that, but that it really was beside the point, circumstances being what they were. He agreed, but repeated that the school shouldn't give examinations wherein any question of cheating could be involved. He said it wasn't "worthy" of the school to give examinations like that. I said perhaps he was right, but repeated that it didn't help me in this particular situation. We left it at that.

On Monday I was still very much disturbed about this matter, perhaps even more so than at first because I had been "stewing" over it for several days. It seemed to me I was like Hamlet when he couldn't figure out whether "to be or not to be." At lunch I told a couple of my friends about what had been on my mind and asked them what *they* could do. Both seemed to feel strongly that something ought to be done about it but that, "certainly," I couldn't "snitch." One of them asked who the people involved were. I said I felt that I couldn't say. He replied, "Yeah, that's right. I guess you really shouldn't." We talked about it for an hour without getting anywhere.

That afternoon I went to Dr. Griswold, one of my professors in another course, and told him the situation. I didn't mention any names. I asked him if he had any ideas as to what he would do in a similar circumstance. I also told him what my father had said. He was very disturbed that there were students at the school who would cheat. He said they should be "thrown out," and that if he had to vote on it in a faculty meeting he would vote to expel them immediately. But he said that, "of course," I, as their fellow student, couldn't report them. He didn't ask me their names. He agreed with my father about the examinations. He also went on to say that this kind of situation had come up at least once before. He had formed the opinion that if they were going to give examinations of that sort, they ought to either monitor the examination so thoroughly that it would be impossible to cheat undetected, or else have an honor system whereby it would be thoroughly accepted that each student would be honor-bound to report any cheating that came to his or her attention. He said that if they were going to give examinations like that, the school should decide whether it was "going to be fish or fowl," and adopt one system or another and not leave it up in the air. I pointed out that that didn't help me in my problem. He agreed and said it was a "tough one."

That night, the situation seemed to go round and round in my head. And it did all the next morning, too. I happened to run into Dr. Griswold in the hall at noon. He said that he and his wife had had another doctor and his wife in for dinner the night before and that he had told them about the situation I had described to him "without mentioning any names." He said that the four of them had talked about the case for almost two hours, and that the discussion had gotten "pretty warm" at moments. He said that his wife and the other doctor had argued that I should report the cheaters immediately and that I had made a serious mistake in delaying the matter. In fact, the other doctor said he doubted I had the "right attitude" since I had even hesitated about reporting the incident. The other doctor's wife had argued that a person in my position really shouldn't pass judgment on others or "feel any holier than anyone else." Dr. Griswold laughed, and said, "So there you are." The idea that *I* might be showing the wrong attitude by *not* reporting these people bothered me deeply. But so did the comment of the other doctor's wife about being "holier" than someone else. I wondered if I was being "stuffy," "self-righteous," or quixotic.

That afternoon, I went to Dean Parker and told him about this situation without mentioning any names — not even which examination had been involved. I told him that I felt kind of foolish bringing such a problem to him, but I felt that an important issue was involved. I also told him about my conversations with my father, my friends, and "one of the professors," whom I did not name. He listened very quietly and attentively. When I got through he said that he thought it was serious, all right. He said that if the matter was brought to him officially, he would call the people in and tell them he thought such conduct was outrageous and completely unworthy, and that they had better think things over and "search their hearts" to decide whether they were up to the responsibilities they would assume as doctors. He said that, as far as he was concerned, he would probably hesitate to expel them, since he felt that everyone deserves a second chance, but that this breach of ethics should, at least, be brought to the attention of and profoundly impressed upon these men. He went on to say that he was quite sure that most of the faculty, especially the younger members, would vote to expel these people forthwith. I asked him if he thought I should report the two to him officially. He said, "No — I don't think so. I don't really see how you could. I don't think I could." He asked me if I had considered just going to these people myself and telling them that I had seen what they had done and ask them if they thought it was right. I said I hadn't.

My talk with Dean Parker wound up with his suggesting that, if I wanted to, I might talk it over with Dr. Sorrel, one of the members of the faculty who had come to be sort of an informal personal counselor to students. I know Dr. Sorrel slightly. I thanked him for talking it over with me and said that I'd think about it some more.

QUESTIONS

1. Critique the pros and cons of a student "honor system."

   _____
   _____
   _____

2. Discuss moral dilemmas faced by doctors, nurses, and hospital personnel.

   _____
   _____
   _____

Locks Versus Lives

The administrator of the State Mental Hospital learned that keys to security wards for dangerous criminals had been lost or stolen when he received an early morning telephone call the first of May from the night administrator of the hospital. Since duplicate keys were available in the hospital safe, the administrator, Mr. Jackson, knew that loss of the keys would not interfere with the routine functioning of the hospital. But he decided to call a general staff meeting the next morning to consider the problem.

At the meeting, Mr. Jackson explained the problem of the missing keys and asked for suggestions on what to do. The assistant administrator suggested that the matter be kept confidential among the staff since public knowledge could lead to damaging publicity and possibly to an investigation by higher officials in the Department of Health and Rehabilitative Services.

The head of security for the hospital reported that only two keys were missing and that, although he could not yet determine if the keys had been stolen or lost, he thought they probably had been stolen. He emphasized that the missing keys were "master keys" that could open the doors to all the security wards where the most dangerous criminals were housed. In his opinion, immediate replacement of the locks on those doors was required.

The director of accounting estimated the cost of replacing the locks at over $5,000. He reminded the meeting that the operating costs of the hospital already exceeded its operating budget by about 10 percent due to unexpected inflation and other unforeseen expenses, and that an emergency request for a supplemental budget appropriation to cover the deficit had been sent to the Department of Health and Rehabilitative Services the previous week. In sum, he concluded, no funds were available in the budget for replacing the locks, and an additional request for $5,000 might jeopardize the request for supplementary operating funds that had already been submitted. Besides, since it was early May, the hospital would begin operating under the budget for the next fiscal year in approximately sixty days. The locks could then be replaced and the costs charged against the new budget. Another staff member reasoned aloud that if the keys had

Source: John M. Champion and John H. James, Critical Incidents in Management, *3rd ed. (Homewood, Ill.: Richard D. Irwin, Inc., 1975), 130–31. Reprinted with permission.*

been lost, any person finding them would not likely know of their purpose, and that if the keys had been stolen they probably would never be used in any unauthorized way.

Mr. Jackson thanked the staff members for their contributions, ended the meeting, and faced the decision. He reflected upon the fact that behind the doors to the security wards were convicted first-degree murderers and sexual psychopaths, among others. He also remembered his impeccable thirteen-year record as an efficient and effective hospital administrator.

As Mr. Jackson continued his deliberations, the thought occurred to him that perhaps the most important action would be to find and place the blame on the person who was responsible for the disappearance of the two keys. Moreover, security procedures might need reviewing. Mr. Jackson could not clearly see how best to proceed.

QUESTIONS

1. Have you ever experienced a moral dilemma when doing your job? Describe. What level of morality did your actions reflect — personal satisfaction, avoiding punishment, social acceptance, respect for authority, majority view, personal conviction? Discuss.

2. How should leaders of organizations be judged? What values should they reflect in moral dilemmas? What standards should they meet?

"We Just Don't Do Things That Way Around Here . . ."

Bud Johnson is waiting to see Paul Selman, director of his sales region, and he's really excited. Bud has just returned from his third trip as a field representative for Bartlett Systems, Inc., a young but rapidly growing producer of computer software, and he's almost overflowing with good news. Against all odds, he has just landed two — count 'em! — two major orders for the company. He can hardly wait to share the good news, and literally jumps to his feet when Paul opens the door and beckons him inside.

Motioning him to a seat, Paul begins: "Well, how'd it go? Did you make out all right with all your travel arrangements?"

"Oh yeah, sure, fine. But let me tell you my news: I got a big order from Dunwood Co."

Paul looks pleased. "No kidding! Good work. They're a tough nut to crack. Which system did they take?"

"The 600 series. It turned out to be just what they need. All I had to do was point out the pluses of our package, and they were sold."

"Nice going, nice going," Paul comments with a smile. "You're really off to a good start. Anything else?"

Bud smiles; here's his big moment. "Oh nothing much . . . just an order from an outfit called IPC."

"IPC!" Paul exclaims, almost falling off his chair. "You got an order from IPC! Why, they're practically married to Unicomp. What a breakthrough! How'd you do it?"

"Well, I have to admit it wasn't easy," Bud says, hoping to make this moment of triumph last. "That Unicomp rep, Jennifer O'Reilly, is pretty sharp. She's had them all sewed up for a long time. But when I mentioned that I'd heard some rumors about Unicomp being acquired, they started to listen."

Paul looks surprised. "Unicomp's being bought out? Where did you hear that? I don't know anything about it."

"Oh, I didn't really hear it, I just kind of made it up. See, the way I figure it, they're really concerned about getting stuck with systems they can't use. So I played that card for all it was worth — and it worked."

Source: From Robert A. Baron, Behavior in Organizations: Understanding and Managing the Human Side of Work, *Second Edition.* Copyright © 1986 by Allyn and Bacon, Inc. Reprinted with permission.

Now Paul is looking angry rather than surprised. "You mean you just made it up? You told them a deliberate lie just to get the order?"

Bud is taken aback; this isn't the reaction he expected. But he forges bravely ahead. "Yeah, that's what I did. You know what they say, all's fair in love, war, and sales . . ."

Paul leans forward in his chair, and the look in his eyes, plus the way he is gripping the edges of his desk, warn Bud that the storm is about to break: "Look, we just don't do things that way around here. We've got a reputation for integrity and honesty, and we're not going to have idiots like you blowing it for us. You'd better learn the ropes, my boy, or you're not long for this job!"

QUESTIONS

1. Have you ever had a sales position or known someone well who has? What were the norms of behavior regarding honesty to customers? Discuss.

2. If you were the president of a company, what policy would you have regarding honesty — employee to employee, employee to employer, employee to customer? Discuss.

Government Jobs

Otto Schneider was 48 years old and was probably one of the best glass blowers to be found in the city of Pittsburgh. There were many people who might be considered hacks in the field of making glass figurines and art objects, but Otto was not one of them. In fact, he easily would rank among the best with the skills and capabilities that he had.

Otto had been fortunate in finding a job at one of the major industrial plants in the Pittsburgh area several years ago and had spent much of his time at work making specialized glass objects for use in the R & D laboratory of his employer.

Once in a while, of course, because of Otto's unique skills and abilities, some of the scientists and chemists working in the R & D laboratory would ask Otto to make a special item of glassware. Otto knew, of course, that some of these special gadgets were not necessarily going to be used by the R & D people to do research projects for the company, but rather would probably end up at the scientist's or chemist's workbench at home — or possibly even somewhere on display in their homes if it was a particularly nice piece. Otto had never minded cooperating with the scientists and engineers to do rush jobs, and for the most part they had pretty well given him ample lead time to get out the work that they wanted him to do. Because of this he was more than willing to do these special little jobs that they wanted done.

Unfortunately, the other day Otto's boss caught him making a distinctive piece of glassware which pretty obviously didn't have a lot to do with anything that was going on in the company. When his boss had asked Otto what he was making, Otto had been deliberately vague about it. But for some reason the boss had demanded to see the job ticket for the item Otto was making. Of course there was none, because this was a special request put in by one of Otto's personal friends in the chemistry department. When Otto was unable to substantiate that what he was making was the result of a legitimate work order submitted through the proper channels, his boss had gotten very mad and had sent him home for the day, without pay, in order to get him to either tell what he was doing or think about getting a job somewhere else.

Source: Pp. 249–250 from Human Relations: People and Work *by Lawrence L. Steinmetz. Reprinted by permission of Harper & Row, Publishers, Inc.*

Otto had talked to the union shop steward about being sent home without pay. The shop steward said that the supervisor couldn't do that on such a flimsy case and that he would file a grievance on Otto's behalf.

QUESTIONS

1. What is your opinion about employees doing personal work on company time? Discuss.

   _____

   _____

   _____

2. What is your stance on employees using company property, such as tools and supplies, for personal use? Explain.

   _____

   _____

   _____

The 19-Year-Old Bride

A young engineer acquired his degree, a 19-year-old bride, a new job in June, and moved to the town where the company is located. His job calls for him to test company equipment being used in nearby installations. The company is young and small, and the people in it are friendly to the young couple, including them in all the social affairs. The young man and his bride don't drink and are uncomfortable around people who are drinking, so they decide not to attend any more of the parties and not to become obligated to invite people to their house for drinks. The wife enrolled for some college courses so she could claim heavy assignments as an excuse for refusing invitations.

The young man's boss keeps urging him to bring his wife to the parties and become one of the group. The young man isn't sure if this is an invitation or an order, so he decided that if he put in an appearance himself at the parties, and left early, he would be taking care of his obligation.

QUESTIONS

1. How should the young couple handle the problem?

2. How much should advancement depend on party going and party giving?

Source: William J. McLarney and William M. Berliner, Management Training: Cases and Principles, 5th ed. (Homewood, Ill.: Richard D. Irwin, Inc., 1970), 181–182. Reprinted with permission.

R.V.'s in the Parking Lot

In forty years, I had never seen anything like it. I had been a labor representative since 1930, but what we faced in 1970 was a brand new problem.

First of all, we had never had all those women out there in the plant before. Oh, we had women working during the war, but it was a different time and the women were different acting. Secondly, we had never had R.V.'s before. And I can tell you, women and R.V.'s were causing us a problem.

It all came to a head when a committee of concerned wives showed up demanding to see the plant manager. They said our company had become a den of iniquity and was causing the breakdown of families in our community. It seems a habit had developed where men and women during their lunch breaks, particularly during the afternoon and midnight shifts, would go to the parking lot where they would have get-togethers in their R.V.'s. According to the wives, this was a widespread practice involving more than an isolated few of our 5,000 employees.

As I look back on it, I have to admit our solution to the R.V. problem was masterful. One of our security guards said the R.V.'s were difficult to police because there were so many of them, and they were parked throughout our large parking lot area. His suggestion, which we adopted, was to fence in a certain section of the lot and to require all R.V.'s to park in this area. The clear visibility and constant inspection by security officers soon resulted in an end to R.V. get-togethers.

Now, looking back at the R.V. incident, I think serious questions were raised during the women's liberation movement and the sexual revolution. I think these social movements vastly changed our country. I know they changed our company. I am still trying to decide if the changes have been good.

QUESTIONS

1. Do you think the women's liberation movement and sexual revolution of the 1960s and 1970s helped or hurt our country?

2. Do you think these social movements helped or hurt the business world?
___
___
___

3. What effect has women's liberation had on family life in the United States?
___
___
___

4. What effect has the sexual revolution had on you?
___
___
___

The Honor System

When I was in college, they had an honor system. If you saw a fellow student cheating, you were supposed to report this to the authorities. In actual fact, some students did cheat, but only rarely did other students report the transgressions. There seemed to be three reasons for this: (1) it was a hassle to get involved (entailing meetings, forms, and other time-consuming procedures); (2) nobody wanted to be considered a rat or tattletale; and (3) even if you were sure the person cheated, hard evidence was required to support the charge.

Now I am out of college and law school, and I am a lawyer in group practice. Here, too, there is an honor system of sorts. And here, too, there are obstacles for bringing a complaint against another professional: (1) it takes time and energy to get involved; (2) no one trusts or likes a person who turns in a fellow professional; and (3) evidence to support a complaint is often poor or unavailable.

QUESTIONS

1. What are the moral dilemmas students face while going to college?

2. Discuss moral dilemmas faced by lawyers while performing their jobs.

3. Discuss moral issues faced by other professional groups, such as accountants, engineers, and psychologists.

4. Critique the pros and cons of the "honor system."
_____
_____
_____

The Right to Strike

I have to admit, I can see an argument for both sides of the question. On the one hand, I don't think it's good for public employees — myself included — to go on strike. I keep thinking of firefighters, police officers, teachers, and, yes, air traffic controllers like me. People need and depend on us.

But on the other hand, it isn't right for an employee to go along with conditions that are unsafe and unfair over the long haul. I think this is what happens if you don't pay people fairly and if you don't provide reasonable working conditions. I don't refer to conditions that are unavoidably dangerous; I am talking about things that can be fixed.

Well, that was my view when I joined my fellow employees in a strike to try to correct the situation.

You know the story; we were unsuccessful on all counts. We didn't make the skies any safer, and we lost our jobs. To me, it was a tragedy. I ask you, what would you do?

QUESTIONS

1. Should public employees have the right to strike over safety and working conditions? How about wages?

2. What would you have done if you were president during the air traffic controllers' strike?

3. What would you have done if you were an air traffic controller?

APPLICATIONS

Beliefs and Values Questionnaire (BVQ)   215

The Kidney Machine   219

The Fallout Shelter   223

Values Flag   225

Values Auction   229

Beliefs and Values Questionnaire (BVQ)

This questionnaire surveys beliefs and values about life and people. You will agree with some of the statements and disagree with others. In some cases, you may find it difficult to make a decision, but you should force a choice. Record your answers next to each statement according to the following scale:

>   strongly agree = 5
>
>   somewhat agree = 4
>
>   somewhat disagree = 2
>
>   strongly disagree = 1

____ 1. People should be concerned with God and life after death.

____ 2. Great accomplishments make life worth living.

____ 3. The best way to live is to keep emotions and behaviors under control. People should follow the adage, "less is more."

____ 4. Because people have different needs, values, and personalities, we should follow the sayings, "live and let live" and "different strokes for different folks."

____ 5. Understanding why people do what they do is more science than art.

____ 6. Despite what we read and see in the news, life is getting better for people. Conditions are better in modern times than ancient times.

____ 7. There is a divine purpose in everything that happens, even if it is hard to understand at the time.

____ 8. Idle hands are the devil's workshop.

Source: *George Jana Foltz and Naomi Miller, Northern Kentucky University, 1979.*

____ 9. It is good to keep ideas and feelings to yourself; you should follow the principle, "trust not, suffer not."

____ 10. People should remember truth is relative and what is right for one person may be wrong for another.

____ 11. If you could completely control a person's environment, you could completely control the person's behavior.

____ 12. People should accentuate the positive in life; they should look for a silver lining in every cloud and good in every person.

____ 13. God is an idea created by human beings.

____ 14. You only pass this way once, so live life to its fullest.

____ 15. People should have the attitude, "nothing ventured, nothing gained."

____ 16. What the world needs is more people with principles and the strength to stand up for them.

____ 17. You can never fully control people because each person has free will.

____ 18. The way the world is going, civilization will probably be destroyed by disease or some other calamity.

____ 19. Belief in God is based on superstition and is not supported by fact.

____ 20. Good advice is, "If it feels good, do it."

____ 21. People should learn from the turtle, who never makes progress until it sticks its neck out.

____ 22. Obedience and respect for authority are two important values a society must develop in its people.

____ 23. A scientific understanding of human behavior is limited because each person is a unique individual with immeasurable and unpredictable qualities.

____ 24. The world is full of poverty, sickness, prejudice, and cruelty, and there is little reason to believe things will change.

Scoring

To score the questionnaire, obtain each of the following subscores:

A: total scores for 1 and 7   = _____
B: total scores for 13 and 19   = _____
C: total scores for 2 and 8   = _____
D: total scores for 14 and 20   = _____

E: total scores for 3 and 9 = ____
F: total scores for 15 and 21 = ____
G: total scores for 4 and 10 = ____
H: total scores for 16 and 22 = ____
I: total scores for 5 and 11 = ____
J: total scores for 17 and 23 = ____
K: total scores for 6 and 12 = ____
L: total scores for 18 and 24 = ____

The Beliefs and Values Questionnaire (BVQ) contains six scales. The formula for each scale is as follows:

Scale I: $10 + A - B =$ ____
Scale II: $10 + C - D =$ ____
Scale III: $10 + E - F =$ ____
Scale IV: $10 + G - H =$ ____
Scale V: $10 + I - J =$ ____
Scale VI: $10 + K - L =$ ____

Interpretation

There are six important dimensions of life measured by the Beliefs and Values Questionnaire (BVQ). The dimensions are represented by the following scales:

- Scale I measures a theistic versus nontheistic orientation. High scores indicate a conventional religious outlook and low scores reflect a secular outlook. The average score for college students on this scale is 10.

- Scale II measures an achievement versus experience orientation. High scorers value the constructive use of time and accomplishing goals. Low scorers believe in living for the moment. They tend to be spontaneous and are less inclined to make long-term plans. The average score on this scale is 11.

- Scale III shows detachment versus involvement. The high scorer avoids emotional risk. This person values control and predictability. The low scorer considers it important to make commitments and get involved with life and people, even if this includes personal risks. The average score is 6.

- Scale IV is tolerance versus intolerance. The low scorer believes there is one true system of beliefs and standards in matters of personal and social conduct. The high scorer has a liberal or tolerant outlook and rejects the idea of absolute truths. The average score is 10.

- Scale V is called behaviorism versus humanism. The high scorer tends to have a deterministic viewpoint with a strong faith in science as a means of understanding and dealing with people. The low scorer places emphasis on the uniqueness of each person and places high value on individualism and free will. The average score is 7.
- Scale VI is a measure of positive versus negative orientation. The high scorer is optimistic about life and people and believes times are becoming progressively better. The low scorer finds life to be sad and is pessimistic about the future. The average score is 10.

These six dimensions help explain why people differ in their outlook on the world. They influence our views and relationships and tend to color our whole style of living. There is no simple "right" view on any one of the dimensions.

The Kidney Machine

The following exercise forces you to make moral decisions with life-and-death consequences. Your level of morality and personal and social values will influence you as you deal with difficult ethical questions.

Directions

In a group of three to seven people, read the following problem and attempt to solve it. Respond to the Questions for Discussion only after the group has completed discussion and reached agreement (approximate time: 30 minutes).

Located at a Swedish hospital in Seattle, Washington, is the famous Kidney Machine. It is a marvel of technological ingenuity, and it is the only hope of life for people with rare kidney diseases. In actuality, the machine functions as a kidney for people who have lost the use of their own. By connecting themselves to the machine for 24 hours each week, their lives can be preserved.

There are several problems associated with using the kidney machine, because there are many more people who need it than there is time available on the machine. In fact, only about five people can be placed on it at any one time. Doctors examine all potential patients and determine those who could profit most from connection to the machine. They screen out those with other diseases for whom the machine would be only a temporary expedient, and they turn their list of recommended patients over to the hospital administration.

At present, the doctors have submitted the names of five persons for two places on the machine. Read the biographical data and psychological reports on each of the candidates presented below. You and your colleagues constitute the committee that has been assembled to make the decision which two of these candidates may have access to the machine. It is assumed that each person has an equal chance of remaining alive if allowed to use the machine.

Remember, there are only two vacancies, and they must be filled with two of these five people. Further, you must agree unanimously on the individuals who are to be permitted to remain alive, although you may decide your own criteria for making this choice. The only medical information you have is that people over 40 tend to do poorer on the machine than those under 40 (although they do not necessarily find it useless). The decision is up to you.

Source: Contributed by Gerald M. Phillips, in T. William Pfeiffer and John E. Jones, eds., *The 1974 Annual Handbook for Group Facilitators* (San Diego: University Associates, 1974), 78–83. Reprinted with permission.

Background Information

Biographical data for each patient are as follows:

Alfred: White, male, American, age 62. Married for 31 years. Two children (boy 28, girl 25), both married. Research physicist at University medical school, working on cancer immunization project. Current publications indicate that he is on the verge of a significant medical discovery.

On the health service staff of local university, member of county medical society, member of Rotary International, and Boy Scout Leader for 20 years.

Bill: Black, male, American, age 27. Married for five years. One child (girl 3). Wife six months pregnant. Currently employed as an auto mechanic in local car dealership.

Attending night school and taking courses in transmission repair and rebuilding. No community service activities listed. Plans to open auto-transmission repair shop upon completion of trade school course.

Cora: White, female, American, age 30. Married for eleven years. Five children (boy 10, boy 8, girl 7, girl 5, girl 7 months). Husband self-employed (owns and operates tavern and short-order restaurant). High school graduate. Never employed.

Couple has recently purchased home in local suburbs, and Cora is planning the interior to determine whether she has the talent to return to school for courses in interior decoration. Member of several religious organizations.

David: White, male, American, age 19. Single, but recently announced engagement, and plans to marry this summer. Presently a sophomore at large eastern university, majoring in philosophy and literature. Eventually hopes to earn Ph.D. and become a college professor.

Member of several campus political organizations, an outspoken critic of the college "administration," was once suspended briefly for "agitation." Has had poetry published in various literary magazines around the New York area. Father is self-employed (owns men's haberdashery store), mother is deceased. Has two younger sisters (15, 11).

Edna: White, female, American, age 34. Single, presently employed as an executive secretary in a large manufacturing company, where she has worked since graduation from business college. Member of local choral society; was alto soloist in Christmas production of Handel's *Messiah*. Has been very active in several church and charitable groups.

Psychological reports on each patient are as follows:

Alfred: He is presently distraught about his physical condition and reports that it interferes with his work. He seems committed to his work, but it was hard for the staff to get him to talk about his work in terms that they could understand.

Family relations seem strained and have been for some time. The staff feels that he is a first-rate scientist and scholar who has contributed much and could contribute more to medical research. But they also believe him to be a mentally disturbed individual who, in time, will probably need psychiatric help.

Bill: He is a well-balanced person, who does not appear to be swayed by the blandishments of black extremist groups. He is strongly devoted to his family and appears to be an excellent husband and father.

Bill's capacity for growth in his chosen occupation seems limited. His high school record was poor, although he was always regarded by his teachers as a student who tried hard. He will probably not succeed with his business plans and will remain employed at his present level permanently.

His wife is trained as a legal secretary. Her prognosis for employment is good, although Bill has discouraged her from seeking work because of the mutual agreement to have her be a full-time mother. Bill seems unaware of the serious implications of his illness.

Cora: One of the staff members evaluating Cora described her as a professional Jew. She is president of the local Hadassah organization and seems able to talk about nothing but her religion and her children. Although her recently-found interest in interior decorating may be a sign of change, it was not clear to the staff whether this interest was real or only generated artificially when she heard of the interview requirement.

She seems resigned to her illness and likely death. Her husband works long hours, is in good health, and enjoys the respect and love of his children. Cora's mother, who also lives with the family, handles most of the child care.

David: Typical of young student activists, David is a bright, almost straight "A" student, who enjoys the respect of most of his teachers and friends. But he appears confused about his future and demonstrates a penchant for jeopardizing it by involving himself in various student "causes." Indeed, his college's Dean of Student Affairs regards him as an individual who will "demonstrate for anything."

He is bitter, almost paranoid, about his illness. His father has invested a good deal of money, time, and emotion in him and has always hoped that David would become a lawyer. His relations with his father are presently strained, however, and he seems only mildly concerned about his two sisters, although they still think highly of him. His future father-in-law, who is a highly successful businessman, expects him to enter the family enterprise upon college graduation.

Edna: She is a self-reliant, inner-directed person and a model of the "career woman." It was clear to the staff that her natural aggressiveness and combative tendencies militated against any sort of marital attachment, and it is not impossible that she has lesbian tendencies.

Her employers regard her as indispensable. Her work record is superb, and her activities in church and charitable groups have been very effective. She is well regarded by all who know her, although she seems to have few, if any, close friends. She has indicated that she would prefer to have someone other than herself go on the machine. Her offer did not seem in the least insincere.

Questions for Discussion

1. From which ethical tradition did you address this problem — religious or secular? How did this influence your decision?

2. Who played a leadership role in solving this ethical problem? What concept of good did the leader reflect — greatest good for greatest number, will of God, allegiance to duty, love of fellowman, etc?

3. At what level and stage of morality did you approach this problem? For example, were you primarily influenced by the opinions of others or by your own sense of right and wrong?

4. How was your ethical behavior in this problem-solving exercise influenced by your personal values — theoretical, economic, aesthetic, social, political, and religious — and by your social values — self-interest versus interest in others?

The Fallout Shelter

This problem-solving exercise raises many ethical questions. It can be a dramatic example of how our values differ, how difficult it is to determine the "best" values, and how we often have trouble listening to people whose beliefs are different from our own.

Directions

Complete the steps in order.

Step 1 Gather in a small group (approximately three to seven people).

Step 2 Read the following situation:

> Your group is an important department in Washington, D.C., in charge of civil disaster fallout shelters. Suddenly, World War III breaks out and bombs begin dropping. Locations all across the globe are being destroyed. People are heading for whatever fallout shelters are available. You receive a desperate call from one of your shelters at the far reaches of civilization. They are asking for help.
>
> It seems there are ten people who want to use the fallout shelter, but there is only enough space, air, food, and water available for six people for a period of three years — which is how long it is estimated people can safely stay in the shelter. They say that if they have to decide among themselves which six should use the shelter, they are likely to become irrational and begin fighting. So they have decided to call your department and leave the decision up to you. They will abide by your decision. You now have a half-hour to decide which four of the ten people will have to be eliminated from the shelter.

Before you begin, you should remember several important considerations: (1) You have only one-half hour to solve the problem; then you will have to go to your own shelter. (2) It is entirely possible that the six people you choose to stay in the shelter might be the only six people left to start the human race over again; therefore, this choice is very important. (3) If you do not make a decision in a half hour, then the ten people will be left to fight it out among themselves with the possibility that more than four might perish. (4) Here is all you know about the ten people:

Source: Joe Levin, in Sidney B. Simon, Leland W. Howe, and Howard Kirshbaum, *Values Clarification* (New York: Hart Publishing Co., 1972), 281–286.

1. Businessman; 31 years old
2. His 16 year old daughter; six months pregnant
3. Black militant; third-year medical student
4. Famous historian-author-humanitarian; 62 years old
5. Hollywood starlette; questionable I.Q.
6. Former prostitute; 30 years old, "retired"
7. Female social worker; 40 years old
8. Olympic athlete; all sports, alcoholic
9. College coed; emotional problems
10. Policeman with gun (they cannot be separated)

Step 3 Begin the exercise and decide on the six who should use the fallout shelter. Do not refer to the questions in Step 4 until the group has completed discussion and reached agreement.

Step 4 After you have made your decision, discuss the following questions:

a. How well did you listen to the other people in your group?
b. Did you go along with something you did not agree with?
c. Did you feel personal conviction toward the group decision?
d. What did your own behavior say about your level of morality and personal and social values?
e. Do you live your life in line with the morality you expressed in this exercise?

Values Flag

The following is a values clarification exercise. The purpose is to increase self-understanding and examine current behaviors in light of personal values. Use the questions below to construct your own Values Flag. (See page 226.) Answer each question in the appropriate space on the flag. Use words, short statements, and symbols as directed.

1, 2, 3, 4. Draw four symbols or pictures that represent your most cherished values in life.

5. Use a sentence or two to answer the question, Who am I?

6. State three peak experiences in your life (most exhilarating).

7. State your three best skills or aptitudes.

8. State your two best physical characteristics or attributes.

9. When most people think of you, what do they say?

10. What three things about yourself would you like to improve?

11. Use a sentence or two to describe your occupational goals.

12. Who have been the three same-sex individuals who have had the most influence on your life?

13. Who have been the three opposite-sex individuals who have had the most influence on your life?

14. What are your three biggest fears?

15. What are your three greatest accomplishments to this point in your life?

16. What are your three highest priority life goals?

17. What is the personal motto by which you try to live?

Discussion

Consider your answers on the Values Flag. Are you satisfied with your experiences, values, and goals to this point in your life? Are you satisfied with the direction your life seems to be going? Consider alone or discuss with others. A valuable exercise is to use the Values Flag to develop short- and long-term action plans. Concentrate on points 1, 2, 3, 4, 10, 11, and 16 as you fill out the short- and long-term action plans.

VALUES FLAG

1.
2.
3.
4.
5.
6. (a)
7. (a)
8. (a)
9.
10. (a)
11.
12. (a)
13. (a)
14. (a)
15. (a)
16. (a)
17.

6. (b)
7. (b)
8. (b)
10. (b)
12. (b)
13. (b)
14. (b)
15. (b)
16. (b)

6. (c)
7. (c)
8. (c)
10. (c)
12. (c)
13. (c)
14. (c)
15. (c)
16. (c)

Short- and Long-Term Action Plans

Short-term action plan: _____

_____

_____

_____

_____

_____

_____

_____

_____

_____

Long-term action plan: _____

_____

_____

_____

_____

_____

_____

_____

_____

_____

_____

_____

Signed _____

Date _____

Values Auction

Introduction

> We are not born with values, but we are born into cultures and societies that promote, teach, and impart their values to us. The process of acquiring values begins at birth. But it is not a static process. Our values change continually throughout our lives. For example, as children, our highest value might have been play; as adolescents, perhaps it was peer relationships; as young adults, our highest value may be the work we do. For many older people, service to others is the highest value. . . . We are formed largely by the experiences we have, and our values form, grow, and change accordingly.
>
> — Maury Smith

Because values are significant in an individual's personal, social, marital, and occupational adjustment, it is important to understand basic value patterns. In the following exercise, you will:

1. determine those life values that are of greatest importance to you
2. explore the degree of trust you have in the group
3. examine how well you compete and cooperate
4. invite consideration of how your values affect your decisions concerning personal and professional life goals

Values Auction Rule Sheet

During this Value Auction, you will have the opportunity to use your ten tokens to buy, and thus own, any of the values listed—if your bid is highest. Owning a value means you have full rights and privileges to do with the value whatever you choose at the conclusion of the exercise. Keep in mind the following rules:

1. Each person will receive ten tokens valued at $100 each to be used for bidding. Only these tokens will be accepted as payment for any value purchased.

Source: Mary Gray, Northern Kentucky University, and Jerry Jewler and Mary Stuart Hunter, University of South Carolina, 1986.

2. You may elect to pool your resources with other people in order to purchase a particularly high-priced value. This means that two, three, four, or more people may extend a bid for any one value. You are allowed to participate (and win) in such a pool one time only.

3. The auctioneer's task is to collect the highest number of tokens possible in the course of the auction. After the auction has begun, no further questions will be answered by the auctioneer.

VALUES AUCTION SHEET

	Amount I Budgeted	Highest Amount I Bid	Top Bid
1. All the food and drink you want without getting fat			
2. Freedom to be and do what you want in life			
3. A chance to direct the destiny of a nation			
4. The love and admiration of good friends			
5. Travel and tickets to any cultural or athletic event as often as you wish			
6. Complete self-confidence with a positive outlook on life			
7. A happy healthy family			
8. Recognition as the most desirable person in the world			
9. A long life free of illness			
10. A complete library with all the time you need to enjoy it			
11. A deep and satisfying religious faith			
12. A lifetime of financial security and material wealth			
13. A lovely home in a beautiful setting			

14. A world without prejudice and cruelty   _____   _____   _____

15. A world without sickness and poverty   _____   _____   _____

16. International fame and renown for your achievements   _____   _____   _____

17. An understanding of the meaning of life   _____   _____   _____

18. As much sexual pleasure as you want with anyone, anytime   _____   _____   _____

19. The highest success in your chosen profession or vocation   _____   _____   _____

20. A deep and satisfying love with someone   _____   _____   _____

APPENDIX A

Background Information, Teaching Suggestions, and Testing and Grading

The Human Side of Work is a series of desk books for managers, handbooks for practitioners, and workbooks for students. These are applied books that combine behavior theory with business practice. Each book teaches central concepts and skills in an important area of the world of work. The set of eight books includes stress management, communication skills, employee motivation, leadership principles, quality of work life, managing for excellence, employee participation, and the role of ethics.

Each book combines theory with practice, gives commonsense answers to real-life problems, and is easy to read and fun to use. The series may be used as a set or as stand-alone books. The subject areas are made more forceful and the impact greater by the self-evaluation questionnaires and practical exercises that are used for personal development.

AUDIENCE

The Human Side of Work is written for two audiences. One audience includes managers and professionals interested in personal and professional development on their own or within the context of a management development program. Another audience includes students in human relations, organization behavior, and other management-related courses.

The material is appropriate for use at the four-year college and university level as well as in community colleges, proprietary schools, extension programs, and management training seminars.

CONTENT AND STYLE

The difference between most organization behavior texts and *The Human Side of Work* can be compared to the difference between a lecture and a seminar. Although both are good educational vehicles, the lecture is better for conveying large amounts of information, while the seminar is better for developing skills. The good lecture is interesting and builds knowledge; the good seminar is stimulating and builds competency. *The Human Side of Work* emphasizes the interactive, seminar approach to learning.

The writing style is personal and conversational, with minimal professional jargon. True-life examples clarify points under consideration. Concepts are supported by stories and anecdotes, which are more meaningful and easy to remember than facts, figures, and lists. Each book includes learning activities to bridge the gap between classroom theory and on-the-job practice.

The Human Side of Work is more than a series of textbooks. These are "learning" books that actively involve the reader in the learning process. Our goal has been to include material that is interesting to read, relates to the reader's own concerns, and is practical to use. The following captures the spirit of our effort:

I Taught Them All

I have taught in high school for ten years. During that time, I have given assignments, among others, to a murderer, an evangelist, a pugilist, a thief, and an imbecile.

The murderer was a quiet little boy who sat on the front seat and regarded me with pale blue eyes; the evangelist, easily the most popular boy in school, had the lead in the junior class play; the pugilist lounged by the window and let loose at intervals with a raucous laugh that startled even the geraniums; the thief was a gay-hearted Lothario with a song on his lips; and the imbecile, a soft-eyed little animal seeking the shadows.

The murderer awaits death in the state penitentiary; the evangelist has lain a year in the village churchyard; the pugilist lost an eye in a brawl in Hong Kong; the thief, by standing on tiptoe, can see the windows of my room from the county jail; and the once gentle-eyed little moron beats his head against a padded wall in the state asylum.

All of these young men once sat in my room, sat and looked at me gravely across worn brown desks. I must have been a great help to those pupils—I taught them the rhyming scheme of the Elizabethan sonnet and how to diagram a complex sentence.

Naomi John White

The focus of *The Human Side of Work* is self-discovery and personal development as the reader "learns by doing." The material covered is authoritative and up to date, reflecting current theory and practices. The level of material is appropriate for all levels of expertise (new and experienced managers) and all levels of education (undergraduate and graduate).

TESTING AND REVIEW PROCESS

The Human Side of Work has been tested and refined in our classes at Northern Kentucky University. The information and activities have been used with hundreds of organizations and thousands of employees in business, industry, and government. Users include American Telephone and Telegraph Co., International Business Machines Corp., John Hancock, Marriott Corporation, Sun Oil, and Ford Motor Co. in the private sector and the Department of Transportation, the Environmental Protection Agency, the Internal Revenue Service, the National Institutes of

Health, and state governments in the public sector.
The following are sample evaluations:

Good for student participation. My students like the exercises and learning instruments, and the fact each is a stand-alone book that is bite-size. Their reaction: "Everyone should read them!"

Joseph F. Ohren, Eastern Michigan University

A comprehensive series dealing with employee development and job performance. Information is presented in an interesting and easy-to-use style. Case studies and readings help teach the topics, and applications make the material more meaningful. It is an excellent guide for the practicing manager. Ideal as desk books.

David Duncan, IBM

I am a non-traditional student. As one who has worked for over twenty years, I thoroughly enjoyed the material. An understanding of the world of work is presented in a way that is usable at any level of an organization. The books present a common sense approach to management.

Naomi Miller, Northern Kentucky University

Best I've seen on the people side of work. Helps the person. Helps the company. Good for personal and management development. Popular with participants from all backgrounds.

Charles Apple, University of Michigan

This is an easy-to-read, comprehensive series in organization behavior. It puts theory into relevant, usable terminology. Methods for identifying and solving human relations problems are pinpointed. It sets the stage for understanding how people, environment and situations interact in an organization.

David Sprouse, AT&T

TEACHING FORMATS

The Human Side of Work is versatile and can be used in many formats:

- for seminars and training programs
- as classroom texts
- as supplemental information and activities

The following is a discussion of each option.

Seminars and Training Programs

Books used for seminars and training programs should be selected to meet the objectives and needs of the participants—communication, stress, leadership, etc. Material can be mixed and matched for training programs in personal development, professional development, management development, and team building. Material in each book is appropriate for a variety of time periods: one-half day (3 to 4 hours), one full day (6 to 8 hours), and two full days (12 to 16 hours).

The books provide excellent learning activities and questionnaires to encourage participation and personalize the subject. Books then serve as "take-home" material for further reading and personal development. In this format, study quizzes are rarely used for grading, and homework assignments are seldom given. See the following table for appropriate audiences, program focus, and recommended books when using *The Human Side of Work* for seminars and training programs.

Classroom Texts

The series is appropriate for use as texts in college courses in human relations, organization behavior, and organizational psychology. The following is a sample lesson plan using the set for a one-semester course:

Week	Focus on the Person	
1	Stress	Part One, Part Two
2	Stress	Part Three, Part Four
3	Communication	Part One, Part Two
4	Communication	Part Three, Part Four
5	Human Behavior	Part One, Part Two
6	Human Behavior	Part Three
7	Ethics	Part One, Part Two
8	Ethics	Part Three, Part Four

	Focus on the Organization	
9	Morale	Part One, Part Two
10	Morale	Part Three
11	Leadership	Part One, Part Two
12	Leadership	Part Three, Part Four

Appendix A • Background, Teaching Suggestions, Testing and Grading

USING THE HUMAN SIDE OF WORK FOR SEMINARS AND TRAINING PROGRAMS

Appropriate Audiences	Program Focus	Recommended Books
Personal and professional development	Focus on the individual	* Stress Without Distress: Rx for Burnout * Communication: The Miracle of Dialogue * Human Behavior: Why People Do What They Do * Ethics at Work: Fire in a Dark World * Morale: Quality of Work Life (optional) * Performance: Managing for Excellence (optional)
New and experienced managers	Focus on management	* Morale: Quality of Work Life * Leadership: Nine Keys to Success * Performance: Managing for Excellence * Groupstrength: Quality Circles at Work * Stress Without Distress: Rx for Burnout (optional) * Communication: The Miracle of Dialogue (optional) * Human Behavior: Why People Do What They Do (optional) * Ethics at Work: Fire in a Dark World (optional)
Employee development and team building	Focus on the organization	* Communication: The Miracle of Dialogue * Morale: Quality of Work Life * Groupstrength: Quality Circles at Work * Stress Without Distress: Rx for Burnout (optional) * Human Behavior: Why People Do What They Do (optional) * Performance: Managing for Excellence (optional)

Popular seminar and program titles with corresponding books are as follows:

Managing Change: Personal and Professional Coping Skills
Communication: One to One; One to Many
Human Relations and the Nature of Man
Business Ethics and Corporate Culture
Quality of Work Life
The Human Side of Management
Managing for Productivity: People Building Skills
Employee Involvement: If Japan Can Do It, Why Can't We?

* Stress Without Distress: Rx for Burnout
* Communication: The Miracle of Dialogue
* Human Behavior: Why People Do What They Do
* Ethics at Work: Fire in a Dark World
* Morale: Quality of Work Life
* Leadership: Nine Keys to Success
* Performance: Managing for Excellence
* Groupstrength: Quality Circles at Work

13	Performance	Part One, Part Two
14	Performance	Part Three
15	Groupstrength	Part One, Part Two
16	Groupstrength	Part Three

Related Activities and Homework Assignments

Week	Suggested Readings, Cases and Applications
1	*Anatomy of an Illness as Perceived by the Patient* (reading) *The Price of Success* (case)
2	*Death of a Salesman* (reading) *Scientific Relaxation* (application)
3	*Barriers and Gateways to Communications* (reading) *The Power of Vocabulary* (application)
4	*The Dyadic Encounter* (application) *Attitudes toward Women Working* (application)
5	*The Human Side of Enterprise* (reading) *Significant People and Critical Events* (application)
6	*Values Auction* (application) *Personal and Interpersonal Growth* (application)
7	*If Hitler Asked You to Electrocute a Stranger, Would You?* (reading) *How Could the Jonestown Holocaust Have Occurred?* (reading)
8	*Values Flag* (application) *The Kidney Machine* (application)
9	*Work* (reading) *The Joe Bailey Problem* (application)
10	*The Coffee Break* (case) *In Search of Excellence* (application)
11	*What Happened When I Gave Up the Good Life and Became President* (case) *Black, Blue, and White* (case)
12	*The Forklift Fiasco* (case) *Train the Trainers* (application)
13	*Games Mother Never Taught You* (reading) *How Will You Spend Your Life?* (application)

14 *How to Manage Your Time: Everybody's No. 1 Problem* (reading)
    Chrysler's Turnaround Strategy (case)

15 *Groupthink* (reading)
    The Dean Practices Participative Management (case)

16 *Decisions, Decisions, Decisions* (reading)
    The Bottleneck (application)

This format for a one-semester course uses selected readings, cases, and applications from all eight books. For a two-semester course, additional readings, cases, and applications are provided.

Another popular format is to use fewer books in a one-semester course, and to use these more thoroughly. The books can be selected by the instructor or the class. For example, stress, communication, morale, and leadership may be best suited for a given group.

Testing and Grading

When using *The Human Side of Work* as classroom texts, study quizzes in each book can be used to evaluate content knowledge. Although quiz scores can be used to assign formal grades, students learn best when they are also asked to apply the concepts in some personal way. Examples include a term journal, a related research paper, a small-group project, a field assignment, and/or a self-improvement project.

Grades can be assigned on the basis of test scores and term project(s). Projects can be evaluated according to the three C's: clarity, comprehensiveness, and correctness. Half the course grade could be based on study quiz scores, and the other half on the term project(s).

Supplemental Information and Activities

The books in *The Human Side of Work* can provide supplemental information and activities for various college courses. State-of-the-art questionnaires and user-friendly exercises add variety and increase student involvement. Books matched with appropriate college courses are as follows:

Recommended Books	College Courses
Stress Without Distress: Rx for Burnout	Personal Development
	Personal Health
	Human Relations
	Organization Behavior
	Organizational Psychology
	Supervisory Development

Communication: The Miracle of Dialogue	Personal Development Communications Human Relations Organization Behavior Organizational Psychology Supervisory Development
Human Behavior: Why People Do What They Do	Personal Development Human Relations Organization Behavior Organizational Psychology Supervisory Development
Ethics at Work: Fire in a Dark World	Personal Development Business Ethics Human Relations Organization Behavior Organizational Psychology Supervisory Development
Morale: Quality of Work Life	Personnel/Human Resources Human Relations Organization Behavior Organizational Psychology Supervisory Development
Leadership: Nine Keys to Success	Management Principles Human Relations Organization Behavior Organizational Psychology Supervisory Development
Performance: Managing for Excellence	Management Principles Human Relations Organization Behavior Organizational Psychology Supervisory Development
Groupstrength: Quality Circles at Work	Personnel/Human Resources Human Relations Organization Behavior Organizational Psychology Supervisory Development

When used as supplemental material, books are rarely tested for grades. The emphasis is on using the questionnaires, exercises, cases, and applications to increase interest and participation and to personalize the subject.

APPENDIX B

Additional References

ADDITIONAL REFERENCES

The following books are recommended for further reading in the area of ethics. Each is included because of its significance in the field, support to this text, and value for further personal development.

Barry, Vincent. *Moral Issues in Business.* 3d ed. Belmont, Calif.: Wadsworth, Inc., 1986.

Bayles, Michael D. *Professional Ethics.* Belmont, Calif.: Wadsworth, Inc., 1981.

Beauchamp, Tom L. *Case Studies in Business, Society, and Ethics.* Englewood Cliffs, N.J.: Prentice-Hall, Inc., 1983.

Beauchamp, Tom L., and Norman E. Bowie, *Ethical Theory in Business.* Englewood Cliffs, N.J.: Prentice-Hall, Inc., 1979.

Belasques, Manuel. *Business Ethics: Concepts and Cases.* Englewood Cliffs, N.J.: Prentice-Hall, Inc., 1982.

Bible, American Revised. New York: T. Nelson & Sons, 1929.

Bible, Authorized King James version. Clover, S.C.: Riverhills Plantation, 1979.

Braybrooke, David. *Ethics in the World of Business.* Totowa, N.J.: Rowman & Allanheld, 1983.

Camus, Albert. *The Stranger.* New York: Vintage Books, 1954.

Cavanaugh, Gerald V. *American Business Values.* 2d ed. Englewood Cliffs, N.J.: Prentice-Hall, Inc., 1984.

Cressey, Donald R., and Charles A. Moore. *Corporation Codes of Ethical Conduct.* Santa Barbara, Calif.: University of California Press, 1980.

Deal, Terrence E., and Allen A. Kennedy, *Corporate Cultures: The Rites and Rituals of Corporate Life.* Reading, Mass.: Addison-Wesley Publishing Co., Inc., 1985.

Donaldson, Thomas. *Case Studies in Business Ethics.* Englewood Cliffs, N.J.: Prentice-Hall, Inc., 1984.

Donaldson, Thomas, and Patricia H. Werhane, eds. *Ethical Issues in Business—A Philosophical Approach.* 2d ed. Englewood Cliffs. N.J.: Prentice-Hall, Inc., 1983.

Frankena, William K. *Ethics.* Englewood Cliffs, N.J.: Prentice-Hall, Inc., 1963.

Frankl, Viktor E. *Man's Search for Meaning*. Boston: Beacon Press, 1975.

Galbraith, John Kenneth. *The Affluent Society*. Boston, Mass.: Houghton Mifflin Company, 1976.

Galbraith, John Kenneth. *The New Industrial State*. New York: New American Library, Inc., 1969.

Gibran, Kahlil. *The Prophet*. New York: Alfred A. Knopf, Inc., 1923.

Grassian, Victor. *Moral Reasoning*. Englewood Cliffs, N.J.: Prentice-Hall, Inc., 1981.

Hare, R. M. *Moral Thinking: Its Levels, Method, and Point*. New York: Oxford University Press, 1981.

Harvard Business Review. *Ethics for Executives: Part II*. Cambridge, Mass.: President and Fellows of Harvard, 1968.

Harvard Business Review. *Ethics for Executives Series*. Cambridge, Mass.: President and Fellows of Harvard, 1968.

Hay Associates. *Linking Employee Attitudes and Corporate Culture to Corporate Growth and Profitability*. Philadelphia: Hay, 1984.

Heilbroner, Robert L. *The Worldly Philosophers*. New York: Simon & Schuster, Inc., 1972.

Heilbroner, Robert L., and Paul London. *Corporate Social Policy*. Reading, Mass.: Addison-Wesley Publishing Co., Inc., 1975.

Hesse, Hermann. *Siddhartha*. New York: Macmillan, Inc., 1962.

Hospers, John. *Human Conduct: Problem of Ethics*. New York: Harcourt, Brace & World, 1972.

Jones, William T., et al. *Approaches to Ethics*. New York: McGraw-Hill, Inc., 1973.

Keeton, Morris T. *Ethics for Today*. 5th ed. Florence, Ky.: D. Van Nostrand Company, 1973.

Kopp, Sheldon B. *If You Meet the Buddha on the Road, Kill Him*. Des Plaines, Ill.: Bantam Books, Inc., 1972.

McCoy, Charles S. *Management of Values: The Ethical Difference in Corporate Policy*. Marshfield, Mass.: Pitman Publishing, Inc., 1985.

Nader, Ralph. *The Big Business Reader: Essays on Corporate America*. Edited by Mark Green and Robert Massie, Jr. New York: Pilgrim Press, 1980.

Nader, Ralph, Mark Green, and Joel Seligman. *Taming the Giant Corporation*. New York: W. W. Norton & Co., Inc., 1976.

O'Toole, James. *Work and the Quality of Life*. Cambridge, Mass.: The MIT Press, 1974.

Pirsig, Robert M. *Zen and the Art of Motorcycle Maintenance*. New York: William Morrow & Co., Inc., 1979.

Richardson, Elliot. *Work in America.* Cambridge, Mass.: The MIT Press, 1980.

Russell, Bertrand. *Bertrand Russell's Philosophy.* New York: Barnes & Noble Books, 1974.

Saint-Exupery, Antoine de. *The Little Prince.* San Diego, Calif.: Harcourt Brace Jovanovich, Inc., 1943.

Schumacher, E. F. *Small is Beautiful.* New York: Harper & Row, Publishers, Inc., 1973.

Schumacher, E. F., and Peter N. Gilligham. *Good Work.* New York: Harper & Row, Publishers, Inc., 1979.

Schuster, M. Lincoln. *Treasury of the World's Great Letters: From Ancient Days to Our Own Time.* New York: Simon & Schuster, Inc., 1960.

Solomon, Robert C., and Kristine R. Hanson. *Above the Bottom Line: An Introduction to Business Ethics.* New York: Harcourt Brace Jovanovich, Inc., 1983.

Watson, Thomas J., Jr. *A Business and Its Beliefs: The Ideas That Helped Build IBM.* New York: McGraw-Hill, 1963.

Wellman, Carl. *Morals and Ethics.* Glenview, Ill.: Scott, Foresman & Company, 1975.

Westin, Alan. *Whistle Blowing: Loyalty and Dissent in the Corporation.* New York: McGraw-Hill, Inc., 1981.

Williams, Oliver, and John Houch. *The Judeo-Christian Vision and the Modern Corporation.* Notre Dame, Ind.: University of Notre Dame Press, 1982.

APPENDIX C

Suggested Films

The following films are excellent learning aids. These are supplementary media that can enrich a class or training program. They are ideal for small-group discussion, panel debates, and question-and-answer periods. Topics are listed in the order in which they appear in the text.

YOUNG GOODMAN BROWN
(Pyramid, 30 min.)

The classic short story by Nathaniel Hawthorne deals with the human propensity for evil and the Puritan way of opposing it. As the film opens, the pious minister, Goody Clyse, Young Goodman Brown, and his wife, Faith, watch a woman who was found "deep" in a clearing in the forest tied to a stake, where she will be burned the next morning. Young Goodman takes leave of his wife, despite her misgivings, then journeys into the forest to assure himself that he can resist the evil he believes exists there.

Pyramid Films
P. O. Box 1048
Santa Monica, CA 90406

MORAL DEVELOPMENT
(CRM, 28 min.)

An experiment is re-created in which one of two participants is required to administer painful electric shocks to the other participant. The individual administering the shock must make a moral decision about an action that is required, but hurtful. Award winner; highest rating.

CRM Educational Films
Del Mar, CA 92014

CONFORMITY AND INDEPENDENCE
(Harper & Row, 26 min.)

This film reenacts the classic conformity studies in social psychology (Sheriff's autokinetic studies, Asch's standard line studies, and Milgram's obedience research).

Harper & Row
Order Fulfillment/Customer Service
2350 Virginia Avenue
Hagerstown, MD 21740

THE ABILENE PARADOX
(CRM, 28 min.)

These group members go along with each other because they think they have to, not because they think it's right. Sound familiar? Learn how to recognize the dangerous Abilene Paradox and how to counter it. Winner of two film awards.

CRM Education Films
Del Mar, CA 92014

COPING WITH TECHNOLOGY: BEYOND BUREAUCRACY, TOWARD A NEW DEMOCRACY
(Document Associates, 26 min.)

Technology has changed our lives and organizations and will bring even greater change in the future. How will we fit into the new world of technology? How will our organizations adapt to change? In this film, Warren Bennis provides a provocative analysis of the impact of technology on human life. He discusses the inability of rigid, bureaucratic organizations to cope with rapid technological growth, and suggests that new, more open and democratic forms must develop to keep pace with change.

The program makes clear that technology is a two-edged sword, which offers a universe of potential achievement but at the same time threatens the individual with loss of control. Robert Heilbroner, economist, and Buckminster Fuller, futurist, comment on the prospects of man and his organizations in the face of rapid technological progress.

Document Associates, Inc.
211 East 43rd Street
New York, NY 15017

SOCIAL NEEDS AS BUSINESS OPPORTUNITIES
(BNA, 30 min.)

Robert Hansberger and Peter Drucker discuss the social responsibilities of business and touch on other areas, such as education, vocational training, employing the disadvantaged, community rebuilding, and the relocating of obsolete plants. They agree that good intentions are no substitute for competence and that businessmen should resist being pushed into projects merely because there is nobody else to do them.

BNA Films
5615 Fishers Lane
Rockville, MD 20852

POLLUTION CONTROL — THE HARD DECISIONS
(BNA, 30 min.)

This film points up the responsibilities of business in relation to problems of the environment. These environmental issues are all trade-offs, says Peter Drucker, of risks against costs, against benefits, and against jobs. The film gives the manager a general, sophisticated introduction to the subject. As the film evolves, viewers are encouraged to think in terms of how they, as managers and citizens, can strive for environmental betterment.

BNA Films
5615 Fishers Lane
Rockville, MD 20852

THE POWER PINCH
(MTI, 28 min.)

This film deals with sexual harassment in the workplace and the responsibility of controlling it. It also discusses methods to resolve sexual harassment situations.

MTI Teleprograms, Inc.
3710 Commercial Avenue
Northbrook, IL 60062

APPENDIX D

Inventory of Philosophical Beliefs

INVENTORY OF PHILOSOPHICAL BELIEFS

This questionnaire uses the three categories of the philosopher's pie to help clarify your personal philosophy of life. Questions 1 to 15 deal with the question What is Real?; questions 16 to 25 deal with the question What is True?; and questions 26 to 38 deal with the question What is Valuable? Read each question, consider responses, then circle your answer. Note that these are philosophical questions with no right or wrong answers.

WHAT IS REAL?

1. How did human beings originate?

    a. Don't know.
    b. They evolved slowly from lower forms of life without divine intervention.
    c. They were made by God in a special act of creation and did not evolve gradually.
    d. They evolved gradually, but God made humans different from other animals, so humans evolved and were created.
    e. Other: _____

2. Of what does a human being consist?

    a. Don't know.
    b. Matter or bodily substance only. (Mind is merely a name for material impulses in the brain.)
    c. Body (material substance) and soul or spirit (spiritual substance).
    d. Spirit or mind only. (Matter is merely a name for mind which exists habitually and regularly.)
    e. Other: _____

3. Is human nature the same for all people at all times and in all cultures?

    a. Don't know.
    b. Yes, human nature is the same for all people everywhere at any time.
    c. No, each person creates a personal nature that changes with time and place.
    d. Other: _____

4. What is death?

    a. Don't know.
    b. The end of any type of bodily function (primarily brain function, but also heartbeat, pulse, and respiration).

Source: Joseph Petrick, University of Cincinnati, 1986.

c. The separation of the soul from the body.
d. The loss of any sense of meaning or purpose in life.
e. Other: _____

5. Do you have a center or core identity that can be referred to as "self"?

   a. Don't know.
   b. No, there is no such thing as a core identity or self. I am different at different times and places. I can become any kind of person I want to or am conditioned to be.
   c. Yes, I have a core identity or self, which protects my individuality from change brought on by my own desires or the expectations of others.
   d. No, I have many selves that loosely resemble each other. This loose set of selves prevents me both from becoming anyone I'd not want to be and from claiming that I have only one self or core identity.
   e. Other: _____

6. What happens to a person after death?

   a. Don't know.
   b. The body decays and that is the end of the person.
   c. The soul separates from the body. The body decays, but the soul enters into an eternal life either of reward in heaven or punishment in hell.
   d. The soul and body enter into an eternal life either of reward in heaven or punishment in hell.
   e. The body decays. The soul separates from the body and is reincarnated in the form of some other body, either human or nonhuman.
   f. Other: _____

7. Do normal healthy people have enough freedom to be morally responsible for their actions?

   a. Don't know.
   b. People are totally free to be morally responsible for their actions.
   c. People are partly determined and partly free, so that most of the time they can make moral choices and be responsible for their actions.
   d. People are partly determined and partly free, so that they can make moral choices and be held responsible for their actions only some of the time.
   e. People are completely determined by heredity and environment, so they are never morally responsible for their actions.
   f. Other: _____

8. How do you explain the origin of the universe?

   a. Don't know.
   b. It is composed of matter and energy and some matter and energy have always existed. Therefore, the universe has always existed but has slowly evolved to its present form.
   c. The universe was created by God out of nothing; the universe has not always existed.
   d. Other: _____

9. What is the nature of the universe?

   a. Don't know.
   b. It is a purely physical realm composed of matter and energy (materialism).
   c. It is a purely mental or spiritual realm (idealism).
   d. It is a realm consisting of both matter and spirit or mind (dualism).
   e. Other: _____

10. Do we live in an orderly universe?

    a. Don't know.
    b. The universe has always been a place of complete natural order. There are no chance occurrences or miracles.
    c. The universe is completely chaotic. We live in a chance world.
    d. A combination of natural order plus chance happenings describes the universe.
    e. The universe has a natural order given by its divine creator. This order persists due only to God's will and can be changed, suspended, or interrupted at any moment if God so wills.
    f. Other: _____

11. Is there any pattern in history?

    a. Don't know.
    b. No, there is no real pattern in history.
    c. Yes, it is the history of salvation. Humankind fell from a heavenly paradise and is trying to return to God but needs divine help.
    d. Yes, all history is cyclical. Every event eternally returns. There is no progress; we are going in circles.
    e. Yes, all history is linear. History reveals a steady, straight line of progress.
    f. Yes, all history has a spiral pattern. We both progress and go in circles, so that the overall pattern of history is spiraling upward.
    f. Other: _____

12. Does God exist?

    a. Don't know (agnostic).
    b. No, there is no such thing as God (atheist).
    c. Yes, there is one God (monotheist).
    d. There are many gods (polytheist).
    e. Other: _____

13. Does God have to be good?

    a. Don't know.
    b. Yes, God is by nature good. God is incapable of evil.
    c. No, God does not have to be good. To limit God by goodness would restrict God's freedom or power.
    d. Other: _____

14. What is the relationship between God and the world?

    a. Don't know.

b. There is no relationship between God and the world because there is no God.
   c. God created the world and gave it a natural order, then left it on its own. God does not interact with creation (complete transcendence, deist position).
   d. God created the world and gave it a natural order, and God continues to exert a providential concern for creation (transcendence and immanence position).
   e. God and the natural world are one and the same. Nature is divine (complete immanence, pantheist position).
   f. Other: _____

15. What is the real relationship between humankind and God?
    a. Don't know.
    b. God created human beings. God cares for people, who in turn should worship God.
    c. People created God. God is a human security myth that has developed a certain independent power in emotionally immature people.
    d. People created the myth of God out of fear, but with the advent of science the myth has lost its power. Now, there is no longer any relationship because people have overcome the need for the God myth.
    e. Other: _____

WHAT IS TRUE?

16. How do you explain the existence of evil and suffering in the world?
    a. Don't know.
    b. Evil and suffering are only human illusions.
    c. Evil and suffering exist because we are imperfect beings living in an imperfect world that simply evolved by chance. It would be strange to expect such a world to be perfect. People must do what they can to achieve progress and relieve human suffering.
    d. The existence of evil and suffering is a mystery, given that God is perfect.
    e. The existence of evil and suffering is not a mystery but can be fully explained as the result of original sin, which serves as a test of human faith in God.
    f. Evil and suffering exist because, although God is perfectly good, God is limited in power to overcome evil.
    g. All evil and suffering exist because they were deserved either in this life or in a previous life (karma and reincarnation).
    h. Other: _____

17. Can we know anything for sure?
    a. Don't know.
    b. Yes, there are many things of which we can be absolutely certain.
    c. No, we can never have certain knowledge, only individual opinions that are better or worse in their justification and strength.
    d. There is no such thing as absolute certainty for a human being because people lack perfect knowledge; still, there are some opinions we have that no sane person

would doubt, such as one's personal existence.
   e. Other: _____

18. What is the most certain or dependable source of knowledge?
    a. Don't know.
    b. Personal experience and reasoning.
    c. Scientific verification.
    d. Divine revelation in Scripture.
    e. Common sense—the belief of the majority of people in a culture.
    f. Other: _____

19. What basis (or bases) is (are) there for a belief in the existence of God?
    a. No experiential or rational basis; belief in God is a sign of emotional weakness and lack of intellectual strength.
    b. No rational basis, but a direct, positive, loving experience of God.
    c. No rational basis, but fear of hell or some punishment for disbelief.
    d. No rational basis, but a total trust in the scriptures.
    e. Experiential and rational bases; lack of belief in God is a sign of poor intelligence.
    f. Other: _____

20. When do we know a belief or opinion is true?
    a. Don't know.
    b. When it corresponds with external reality (correspondence theory).
    c. When it agrees with other beliefs of which we are convinced (coherence theory).
    d. When it works or provides good practical results (pragmatic theory).
    e. Other: _____

21. Can science eventually explain everything in the world?
    a. Don't know.
    b. Yes, at least in principle.
    c. No, the world contains chance, values, and mysteries that science will never explain.
    d. Other: _____

22. Can everything people desire to express eventually be expressed in language, signs, or symbols?
    a. Don't know.
    b. Yes, all meaning can ultimately be captured in language, signs, or symbols.
    c. No, there are some things that will always be inexpressible for people.
    d. Other: _____

23. What is the best way to know yourself?
    a. Don't know.
    b. Undertake psychoanalysis or behavioral or other therapies.
    c. Take mind-altering drugs.

    d. Engage in consciousness-expanding techniques such as Arica, TM, Rolfing, est, Silva Mind Control, Psychosynthesis, or Bioenergetics.
    e. Personal introspection and rational reflection.
    f. Intimate conversations with friends and loved ones.
    g. Other: _____

24. What should be the goal(s) of education?

    a. To prepare the individual for a job.
    b. To develop all the abilities of an individual.
    c. To prepare an individual for citizenship.
    d. To help an individual become wise and lead a happy life.
    e. Other: _____

25. What is the meaning of life?

    a. Don't know.
    b. The meaning of life is to be found in maximum self-realization, being the best person one can in this life.
    c. The meaning of life is not fully realized on earth, but rather in the next life.
    d. The meaning of human life is found in liberation from the cycle of birth and death through experiencing nirvana.
    e. Human life has no meaning.
    f. Other: _____

WHAT IS VALUABLE?

26. What is most worthwhile for a human being?

    a. Don't know.
    b. Happiness.
    c. Doing one's duty.
    d. Pleasure (short and long term).
    e. Eternal salvation.
    f. Rational understanding.
    g. Other: _____

27. Are ethics relative?

    a. Don't know.
    b. Yes, what is good and right varies with person, place, and time.
    c. No, there are certain actions that are right or wrong for everyone anywhere, anytime.
    d. Other: _____

28. Are humans born good?

    a. Don't know.
    b. Yes, human beings are born good and will lead good lives naturally without structure or discipline.

c. No, human beings are born evil; they are born with original sin and need divine help to live properly.
d. No, human beings are born neither good or evil, but unfulfilled, and need structured, disciplined, but humane civilization.
e. Other: _____

29. Are people basically selfish (egoistic) or basically generous (altruistic)?
    a. People are always selfish.
    b. People are usually selfish, but sometimes they will be generous.
    c. People are usually generous, but sometimes they will be selfish.
    d. People are always generous.
    e. Other: _____

30. Is it ever morally right to take a human life?
    a. Yes, one's own life in suicide in some cases.
    b. Yes, others' lives in a just war.
    c. Yes, others' lives in capital punishment.
    d. All of the above.
    e. No one ever has a moral right to take a human life.
    f. Other: _____

31. Is the individual or society more important?
    a. Don't know.
    b. Society exists for the sake of individuals and individual fulfillment. Society should encroach as little as possible on the freedom of the individual.
    c. The individual exists for the sake of society, the collective. It may be necessary to sacrifice the freedom or even the lives of some individuals for the welfare of society.
    d. Other: _____

32. On what basis should the authority of government rest?
    a. Don't know.
    b. The consent of the governed.
    c. Divine authority.
    d. Power (might makes right).
    e. The wisdom of leaders.
    f. Other: _____

33. What is the best form of government?
    a. Don't know.
    b. Democracy (rule by majority).
    c. Aristocracy (rule by the few).
    d. Monarchy (rule by one).
    e. Whatever produces political order in a society.
    f. Other: _____

34. Where does beauty reside?

   a. Don't know.
   b. Beauty is subjective; it is in the eye of the beholder.
   c. Beauty is objective; things are or are not beautiful to anyone.
   d. Beauty is objective to the extent that trained observers, or aesthetically cultivated persons, will substantively agree on what is beautiful.
   e. Other: _____

35. When does sexual activity promote human happiness?

   a. Seldom.
   b. Often, but only within the confines of marriage.
   c. Always, because it relieves human tension within and outside of marriage.
   d. Often, but only when the sexual activity is accompanied by love for the other party.
   e. Other: _____

36. What is the source of moral values?

   a. Ultimately, moral values are given by God.
   b. Ultimately, moral values are the result of cultural pressures.
   c. Ultimately, each person chooses moral values as an individual.
   d. Other: _____

37. Who should have children?

   a. Only those who are physically and economically able.
   b. Only those who are physically, economically, emotionally, and intellectually able.
   c. Only those who want children.
   d. Only those who are married.
   e. All; and those who are married have a duty to have children.
   f. Other: _____

38. Which of the following attributes best promote a happy life?

   a. Being wealthy, attractive, and famous.
   b. Being healthy, intelligent, and having friends.
   c. Being attractive, in love, and wealthy.
   d. Being healthy, wealthy, and intelligent.
   e. Being intelligent, in love, and having friends.
   f. Being healthy, in love, and having friends.
   g. Other: _____

DISCUSSION

There are no right or wrong answers on this questionnaire. Questions are asked and responses offered to help clarify personal beliefs on the three central questions of philosophy: What is real? What is true? What is valuable?

APPENDIX E

Study Quiz Answers

STUDY QUIZ ANSWERS

Part One	Part Two	Part Three	Part Four
1. d	1. b	1. c	1. e
2. c	2. c	2. a	2. c
3. b	3. b	3. a	3. c
4. a	4. c	4. c	4. b
5. d	5. b	5. a	5. d
6. a	6. c	6. b	6. d
7. b	7. c	7. a	7. b
8. a	8. c	8. c	
9. d	9. c	9. b	
10. d		10. b	
11. b		11. c	
12. c			

APPENDIX F

The Relationship of the Quiz Questions and the Discussion and Activities to the Part Objectives

The following chart shows the relationship of the quiz questions and the discussion and activities to the part objectives:

PART ONE

Objective Number	Quiz (Q), Discussion and Activities (D&A)
1	Q: 1, 2 D&A: 1
2	Q: 13 D&A: 1, 2
3	Q: 7, 8 D&A: 1, 4
4	Q: 3, 4, 5, 6 D&A: 1, 3
5	Q: 9, 11 D&A: 1
6	Q: 10 D&A: 1
7	Q: 12 D&A: 2, 4

PART TWO

Objective Number	Quiz (Q), Discussion and Activities (D&A)
1	Q: 1, 2, 3 D&A: 1, 4
2	Q: 4, 5, 6, 7 D&A: 2
3	Q: 8, 9 D&A: 3, 5

PART THREE

Objective Number	Quiz (Q), Discussion and Activities (D&A)
1	Q: 1, 2, 3, 4, 5, 6, 7 D&A: 1, 2
2	Q: 8, 9 D&A: 3, 6, 7
3	Q: 10 D&A: 1, 6
4	Q: 11 D&A: 4, 5, 9

PART FOUR

Objective Number	Quiz (Q), Discussion and Activities (D&A)
1	Q: 1, 2, 3, 4, 5 D&A: 1, 4
2	Q: 5, 6 D&A: 2, 3, 4
3	Q: 6 D&A: 3, 5
4	Q: 7 D&A: 3, 5